DEMOICRATIC AUTHORITY

What is the nature of the EU's authority? This fascinating book explores this question, and is much needed given the increased scrutiny of the EU's actions in the face of growing nationalism and various other internal and external challenges.

By setting out an original account of the preferred moral standard to evaluate such authority, ie demoicratic authority, it illustrates how that standard affects the practical reasoning of those subject to the EU's authority. Theoretically significant, the book also has important practical value as legitimacy challenges in the EU increase. Constitutional lawyers and theorists, as well as political scientists, will welcome this innovative new work.

Volume 31: Studies of the Oxford Institute of European and Comparative Law

Recent titles in this Series

Volume 21: The Images of the Consumer in EU Law: Legislation, Free Movement and Competition Law
Edited by Dorota Leczykiewicz and Stephen Weatherill

Volume 22: Passing Wealth on Death: Will-Substitutes in Comparative Perspective
Edited by Alexandra Braun and Anne Röthel

Volume 23: General Principles of Law: European and Comparative Perspectives
Edited by Stefan Vogenauer and Stephen Weatherill

Volume 24: The Future of Contract Law in Latin America: The Principles of Latin American Contract Law
Edited by Rodrigo Momberg and Stefan Vogenauer

Volume 25: The Code Napoléon Rewritten: French Contract Law after the 2016 Reforms
Edited by John Cartwright and Simon Whittaker

Volume 26: Discretion in EU Public Procurement Law
Edited by Sanja Bogojevic, Xavier Groussot and Jörgen Hettne

Volume 27: New Economic Constitutionalism in Europe
George Gerapetritis

Volume 28: French Civil Liability in Comparative Perspective
Edited by Jean-Sébastien Borghetti and Simon Whittaker

Volume 29: Better Regulation in EU Contract Law: The Fitness Check and the New Deal for Consumers
Edited by Esther van Schagen and Stephen Weatherill

Volume 30: Property and Contract: Comparative Reflections on English Law and Spanish Law
Edited by John Cartwright and Ángel M López y López

Volume 31: Democratic Authority: On the Nature and Grounds of the EU's Right to Rule
Josef Weinzierl

Demoicratic Authority

On the Nature and Grounds of the EU's Right to Rule

Josef Weinzierl

• HART •
OXFORD • LONDON • NEW YORK • NEW DELHI • SYDNEY

HART PUBLISHING
Bloomsbury Publishing Plc
Kemp House, Chawley Park, Cumnor Hill, Oxford, OX2 9PH, UK
1385 Broadway, New York, NY 10018, USA
29 Earlsfort Terrace, Dublin 2, Ireland

HART PUBLISHING, the Hart/Stag logo, BLOOMSBURY and the Diana logo are trademarks of Bloomsbury Publishing Plc

First published in Great Britain 2024

A catalogue record for this book is available from the British Library.

A catalogue record for this book is available from the Library of Congress.

Library of Congress Control Number: 2023943911

ISBN: HB: 978-1-50996-504-5
ePDF: 978-1-50996-506-9
ePub: 978-1-50996-505-2

Typeset by Compuscript Ltd, Shannon

ACKNOWLEDGEMENTS

This book is a result of my doctoral research at the Faculty of Law of the University of Oxford. I am immensely grateful to my supervisor Pavlos Eleftheriadis, who kindled my enthusiasm for the Philosophical Foundations of the EU and who helped me to pursue my own ideas while preventing me from straying from the right course. Thank you, Pavlos, for your kindness, generosity and support.

During my academic journey, I was very fortunate to meet mentors who not only opened doors for me, but encouraged me to go through them. I am deeply grateful to Professor Christoph Herrmann for invaluable mentorship and for guiding a naïve second-year law student towards a passion for EU law. I thank Hans-Georg Kamann and Advocate General Juliane Kokott for invaluable work experience and for their counsel. Finally, I will forever be indebted to the late John Gardner, who opened the world of legal and political philosophy to me and whose teaching and encouragement gave me the confidence to pursue this project.

The Oxford Law Faculty has provided the most stimulating research environment I could have hoped for. I greatly appreciate the valuable input of my thesis examiners Nick Barber, Stephen Weatherill and Joseph Weiler at various stages of the project. I am very grateful to Birke Häcker for her role in turning my doctoral thesis into this book. I am moreover much obliged to Julian Nowag and the Faculty of Law of Lund University for hosting me as guest researcher and for allowing me to present my ideas.

I would like to express my sincere gratitude to those who showed their faith in my doctoral project by deciding to fund it. In that regard, I thank the *Cusanuswerk* not only for financial support, but for the wonderful community I found there. I thank the Arts and Humanities Research Council Open-Oxford-Cambridge Doctoral Training Partnership for their support and for enriching my understanding of humanities more broadly. And I thank the *Studienstiftung* for allowing me to access their training opportunities and seminars.

It is hard work to support someone if you know what they are doing. I can't imagine how hard it is if you don't. The only reason a farmer's boy from Bavaria can end up submitting this manuscript is with the unwavering support and love of family. I am thus grateful beyond measure to my parents Bernhard and Heidi, to my siblings Kathrin and Max, to my siblings-in-law Corinna and Tobias, and – most importantly – to my four nephews for grounding and supporting me despite the very different way in which I lead my life.

Josef Weinzierl,
May 2023

CONTENTS

LIST OF ABBREVIATIONS

AFSJ	Area of Freedom, Security and Justice
AG	Advocate General
BIS	Bank for International Settlements
BVerfG	Bundesverfassungsgericht (German Constitutional Court)
Council	Council of the European Union
COVID 19	Coronavirus Disease 2019
EAW	European Arrest Warrant
EC	European Community
ECB	European Central Bank
ECJ	European Court of Justice
ECtHR	European Court of Human Rights
EEC	European Economic Community
EFSF	European Financial Stability Facility
EP	European Parliament
ESM	European Stability Mechanism
EU	European Union
ICC	International Criminal Court
ICJ	International Court of Justice
IMF	International Monetary Fund
IO	International Organisation
IT	Information Technology
MEP	Member of the European Parliament
OECD	Organisation for Economic Cooperation and Development
PSPP	Public Sector Purchase Programme

TEU	Treaty on European Union
TFEU	Treaty on the Functioning of the European Union
UK	United Kingdom of Great Britain and Northern Ireland
UN	United Nations
US	United States of America
VCLT	Vienna Convention on the Law of Treaties
WHO	World Health Organisation
WTO	World Trade Organisation

TABLE OF CASES

European Court of Justice

General Court

Canada

Czech Republic

Denmark

Germany

Italy

Poland

Spain

TABLE OF STATUTES

TABLE OF OTHER PRIMARY (LEGAL) SOURCES

Introduction

> Freedom is not possible without authority – otherwise it would turn into chaos and authority is not possible without freedom – otherwise it would turn into tyranny.
>
> —Stefan Zweig

It is not hard to illustrate the importance of reflecting on the authority of European Union (EU) law. For one, various national constitutional court judgments have recently questioned the authority of EU law and sent shockwaves well beyond the narrow community of EU constitutional lawyers.[1] For another, controversial statements of national politicians show how the seemingly too intrusive authority claim of EU law enters the political arena. Already in 1988, former United Kingdom (UK) Prime Minister Margaret Thatcher opined that: '(w)e have not successfully rolled back the frontiers of the state in Britain, only to see them re-imposed at a European level with a European super-state exercising a new dominance from Brussels'.[2]

It is undeniable that this sentiment contributed to the outcome of the Brexit referendum. David Cameron, then Prime Minister of the UK, remarked in 2014 that 'Brussels has got too big, too bossy, too interfering'.[3] In addition, the Polish Prime Minister Mateusz Morawiecki petitioned the Polish Constitutional Tribunal in 2021, asking for a 'comprehensive settlement' of the conflict between the supremacy of EU law and national law in favour of the latter. But these remarks only concern the relationship between the realms of authority of the EU and the Member States and are thus only part of the story. Russia's barbaric war against Ukraine and China's growing influence on the world stage have recently put the question of the reach and basis of the EU's authority in relation to the rest of the world into the spotlight.

While this evidence seems anecdotal, it highlights a practical salience that seems at odds with the fact that many aspects of the EU's authority remain under-theorised. I am, of course, not referring to the library-filling literature on the apex courts' conflicting claims to ultimate authority and on how best to conceptualise them. Instead, I want to draw attention to writing on the nature of the EU's authority claim and on the ground for its moral legitimacy, which is relatively scarce. These two distinct questions merit particular attention considering the

[1] One stands out: BVerfG, Judgment of 05 May 2020–2 BvR 859/15 (*Weiss*).

[2] Margaret Thatcher, 'Bruges Speech' (*The Bruges Group*, 1988), www.brugesgroup.com/component/content/article/8-papers/808-bruges-revisited?Itemid=101.

[3] 'Brussels Too Big and Too Bossy, Cameron Tells EU Leaders' (*BBC News*, 27 May 2014), www.bbc.com/news/uk-politics-27583545.

general observation that political theory increasingly considers emerging forms of governance and *loci* of authority above and beyond the state.[4] The growing realisation of the breadth and intrusiveness of EU law only raises the moral profile of these questions. Finally, the very issue of political authority – independent of the regulatory level under scrutiny – underscores the theoretical relevance of the present topic. As Raz rightly put it, authority is 'one of the most controversial concepts'[5] of political theory and thus merits our continuous attention.

The relevance of an inquiry into the nature and moral grounds of the EU's authority for legal practitioners shouldn't be understated either. We will see at various stages of this book how the European Court of Justice (ECJ) often labours in a theoretical vacuum when interpreting fundamental as well as novel instruments of EU law. An account of the ground and, importantly, limits of EU law's authority can help to guide and constrain the legitimate realm of interpretation. Beyond the political statements quoted above, there is a queasy feeling in parts of the theoretical literature on the EU that the EU's 'authority is under stress'.[6] The reasons are familiar: the rise of populism and nationalism, ever more widespread scepticism about institutional cooperation beyond the state, or simply the growing realisation of the tremendous impact of the EU and its laws on our lives. It helps, so I argue, to take a step back and ask this deceptively simple question: what gives the EU the right to rule in the first place?

I. Objectives

This book has one overarching objective. It seeks to direct the attention of academics and legal officials alike away from the sovereignty-related issues of ultimate decision-making and '*Kompetenz-Kompetenz*'. Let's instead focus on the moral ground for the EU's authority, ie how it legitimately binds whom and what, if anything, underpins the EU's right to rule. In what follows, I show how both institutions and academics often argue based on theoretical preconceptions they either don't spell out or don't appear to be aware of. This awareness is the first step to a systematic understanding of ground and limits of the EU's authority. In addition, I hope to contribute to analytical clarity in relation to two issues that only rarely get the attention they deserve:

- The first issue is the nature, scope and addressees of the EU's authority claim in relation to state and international authority (chapter two). Many avoid this crucial step in the argument. They either rely on neologisms that piggyback on

[4] See only Joseph Raz, 'Why the State?' in Nicole Roughan and Andrew Halpin (eds), *In Pursuit of Pluralist Jurisprudence* (Cambridge, CUP, 2017) 160 et seq.

[5] Joseph Raz, *The Authority of Law: Essays on Law and Morality*, 2nd edn (Oxford, OUP, 2009) 3.

[6] Joseph Weiler, 'The Authority of European Law: Do We Still Believe in It?' in Wolfgang Heusel and Jean-Philippe Rageade (eds), *The Authority of EU Law: Do We Still Believe in It?* (Berlin, Springer, 2019) 3.

the most well-known authority claim of sovereignty (European sovereignty, etc) or limit themselves to individual doctrines of the ECJ as object of inquiry (especially primacy).

- The second issue is who is the main entity/agent on which we should place our focus? Everyone agrees that states bind their citizens qua individual humans, and it is still almost unanimously accepted that international law binds states and their (executive) officials. In the EU, both in theory and in practice, there are three distinctly identifiable entities that play a noticeable role as addressees and source of the EU's authority: Member States and their officials, EU citizens, and the EU peoples (*demoi*). My book does not study them in isolation. Instead, it provides an account of how they relate to each other in the EU's normative architecture.

II. Previous Work

Most of the writing on the EU's authority claim has so far focused exclusively on a distinct set of institutions: the ECJ and the national constitutional courts, the conflict between their claims to ultimate authority, and how best to conceptualise a system with such conflicting jurisprudential authority claims (monism, dualism and pluralism). This is not the focus of this book, which is about the moral ground of the EU's authority, ie why EU law has authority in the first place. Although there is substantial literature on the broader legitimacy of the EU, normative accounts on the authority of EU law have so far been rare and mostly implicit.

The growing scholarship on the authority of international law helped me identify the relevant questions. Many scholars in that field discuss the EU either as an example of international authority or ask whether the EU needs to be distinguished from instances of international authority.[7] It is not surprising to find that theories of authority inherit the difficulties from more traditional EU scholarship that has tended to grapple with the extent (if any) of the EU's emancipation of its international origins. This book takes up this challenge at various stages.

Many issues at the heart of this book are discussed in a collection of essays on the authority of EU law which I take as evidence that there is a need for further

[7] See only Başak Cali, *The Authority of International Law: Obedience, Respect, and Rebuttal* (Oxford, OUP, 2015); Armin Von Bogdandy, Matthias Goldmann and Ingo Venzke, 'From Public International to International Public Law: Translating World Public Opinion into International Public Authority' (2017) 28 *European Journal of International Law* 115; Mattias Kumm, 'The Rule of Law, Legitimate Authority and Constitutionalism' in Christoph Bezemek, Michael Portacs and Alexander Somek (eds), *Legal Positivism, Institutionalism and Globalisation: Vienna Lectures on Legal Philosophy* (London, Hart Publishing, 2018) Vol 1.

discussion of the nature and grounds of the EU's authority.[8] More specifically, the argument developed in this book has benefitted greatly from the work of Pavlos Eleftheriadis on authority and political obligation beyond the state;[9] from Richard Bellamy's thought-provoking reflections on the EU as a demoicracy;[10] and from the work of Martijn van den Brink on demoicratic authority.[11]

III. Scope and Limits

The scope of this book seems broad. It tries to advance political theory beyond the state in the field of political authority, and touches on various areas of EU constitutional law. I thus wish to manage expectations and to explain the limits of this work.

First, I won't provide an empirical account of the de facto authority of the EU, ie to what extent citizens and state officials actually believe that EU law as a whole or certain aspects of it are morally binding. I actively distinguish my normative inquiry from such a project in chapter one.

While I advance an argument on how best to evaluate the EU's authority, I neither spell out the practical nor the institutional implications of this account in detail. That not only relates to issues of institutional balance (Art 13 (2) Treaty on European Union (TEU)). More broadly, an important issue for future research lies in the role of non-majoritarian institutions (first and foremost the ECJ and the Commission, but also the European Central Bank (ECB) or agencies) in an account of the legitimate authority of EU law. That is, what is the authority of individual EU institutions in relation to each other? While I engage with the authority of EU law as such, ie the product, and reflect on what the EU institutions think about EU law's authority basis (chapter three), I leave to one side the authority basis of the individual institutions themselves.

Finally, the present project in an important sense restricts itself to the 'internal' authority of the EU, ie how the EU's authority claim can be reconciled with the individual and collective autonomy of its subjects. I only mentioned this external dimension above to highlight the practical salience of the topic at hand. This book contains no in-depth analysis of how the EU's authority relates to international law and third states – an issue that will gain only more relevance in the future

[8] Wolfgang Heusel and Jean-Philippe Rageade (n 6).

[9] Pavlos Eleftheriadis, 'Citizenship and Obligation' in Julie Dickson and Pavlos Eleftheriadis (eds), *Philosophical Foundations of European Union Law* (Oxford, OUP, 2012); Pavlos Eleftheriadis, *A Union of Peoples* (Oxford, OUP, 2020) ch 7.

[10] Richard Bellamy, *A Republican Europe of States: Cosmopolitanism, Intergovernmentalism and Democracy in the EU* (Cambridge, CUP, 2019).

[11] Martijn van den Brink, 'Justice, Legitimacy and the Authority of Legislation within the European Union' (2019) 82 *MLR* 293; Martijn van den Brink, 'The European Union's Demoicratic Legislature' (2021) 19 *International Journal of Constitutional Law* 914.

in light of the EU's ever growing contractual and factual relationships to global actors and third states in the EU's neighbourhood and beyond.[12]

IV. A Brief Note on Structure

This book revolves around a distinction essential to theories of authority, namely between the conceptual nature of an authority claim on the one hand and the moral legitimacy of authority on the other. In short, '(u)nderstanding authority involves answers to two questions: what is authority and when is it legitimate?'[13]

Chapter one reflects this distinction internally. It discusses both the nature of authority and what legitimate authority entails and how it relates to political obligation. I am convinced that this theoretical groundwork is necessary. In a sense, chapter one is the basement of my argumentative house. You might not notice it when observing the end-product, but without it the house would lack foundation.

The rest of the book mirrors this core distinction. Chapter two seeks to identify the nature, scope and addressees of the EU's authority claim. In other words, it asks what kind of authority the EU actually claims in order to gain analytical clarity on the claims in need of evaluation. The rest of the book (chapters three to six) engage with different attempts on how to evaluate legitimate authority. Chapters three and four evaluate what institutions and academics think about the grounds for the EU's authority. Finally, chapters five and six flesh out my own proposal on how best to understand the grounds and limits of the EU's right to rule.

V. Conclusion

It can feel daunting to embark on such a project without having exhaustively considered all the big philosophical concepts necessarily connected to studying legitimate political authority (legitimacy, rights, democracy, justice, etc). However, this should allow me to avoid getting lost in the maze of conceptual disagreements and important debates that are relevant, but not essential, to the study of the EU's authority. In other words, I intend to provide a fresh account of an issue that comprises important questions of political theory, and that, in relation to the EU, hasn't yet received the attention it so justly deserves.

[12] For recent work in this area see Aravind Ganesh, *Rightful Relations with Distant Strangers: Kant, the EU, and the Wider World* (London, Hart Publishing, 2021).

[13] Nicole Roughan, *Authorities: Conflicts, Cooperation, and Transnational Legal Theory* (Oxford, Oxford University Press, 2014) 19. See also Cali (n 7) 5.

1

Authority Claims in Europe

I. Introduction

Evaluating the legitimate authority of the EU and its laws presupposes a firm grasp of the nature and scope of the EU's authority claim. That, in turn, requires an understanding of the nature of political authority. This chapter seeks to provide this understanding. It zooms in from general observations about claims in the political arena and leads to an overview of the labels the EU's authority claim has attracted in the literature at the beginning of the next chapter. On the way, this chapter sheds light on the nature of practical and political authority, introduces a taxonomy to compare authority claims on different regulatory levels, and discusses what it means to have legitimate authority. Many issues will perhaps not get the attention they justly deserve, but the remainder of the book requires such theoretical grounding, lest the argumentative house built on it can be knocked down all too easily.

II. Understanding the Importance of Claims

Many writers take it for granted that states, the EU, and various international organisations *claim* (sometimes conflicting) authority. But what does it mean to claim something in the political realm? According to Feinberg, 'it is claiming that gives rights their special moral significance'.[1] Rights manifest the position of an individual in relationship to political communities as well as to fellow citizens. Claims provide the overarching framework for understanding and communicating about relationships in a polity. In essence, the political community is constituted as a platform for dealing with competing valid claims.[2] Darwall develops this idea, namely that citizens constitute a moral community and have valid claims on each other, into a fully-fledged account of political authority. For Darwall, authority necessarily relies on an accountability relationship between

[1] Joel Feinberg, *Rights, Justice, and the Bounds of Liberty: Essays in Social Philosophy* (Princeton, Princeton University Press, 2014) 151. On the relation between claims and rights, see Pavlos Eleftheriadis, *Legal Rights* (Oxford, OUP, 2008) 72 et seq.

[2] James Sheehan, 'The Problem of Sovereignty in European History' (2006) 111 *The American Historical Review* 1, 3.

two agents based on second-personal-reasons, ie reasons stemming from the moral relationship between the two agents.[3] Instead of defending or endorsing his account, I simply take it to exemplify the importance of claims for framing morally important questions in a political community.

The importance of claims has three crucial implications for political authority. First, political communities necessarily claim moral authority through their laws. The nature of legal systems entails that they claim to morally obligate the subjects of the community in question. In other words, 'while not all governments have legitimate authority, all of them claim to have legitimate authority – this is one of the defining marks of governments'.[4] The idea that law (and thereby the political community producing it) necessarily claims moral authority is not undisputed, however.

Since the bulk of the objections seem to pertain to the agency of law, this brings me to the second implication. Legal officials make these claims on behalf of the law. Gardner makes a convincing case for understanding the personification of law and the relevance of legal officials' private opinions. He argues that voicing the authority claim of the law is constitutive of being a legal official, independent of their private belief about the truth of law's claims. Legal officials give agency to the law by making claims on law's behalf.[5] Put differently, legal officials become mouthpieces of law's moral claims. While legal officials utter claims on behalf of the law, the law ultimately expresses the claims the citizens have as members of a people. In essence, legal officials administer claims citizens have in relation to each other.

The third implication of the idea of authority *claims* is that authority claim can be false so that the law in question lacks moral authority. The claim-structure necessarily entails a 'logical space'[6] for the claim's falsity. That is one of the recurring themes of this book. In other words, it is vital to distinguish between the claimed self-assertion that something constitutes a legitimate exercise of authority, and the separate inquiry whether it is indeed objectively legitimate. Theories of authority evaluate the exercise of authority, they don't rubber-stamp it. Authority claims thus only show the 'self-image' of the respective states/polities/organisations.[7]

Understanding the importance of claims ultimately provides the relevant background for analysing the EU's authority claim and its moral significance in chapter two. Whereas individuals claim rights to secure their autonomy in a political space, political authority claims purport to manifest and ensure the authority

[3] Stephen Darwall, *Morality, Authority, and Law: Essays in Second-Personal Ethics I* (Oxford, OUP, 2013) ch 10; Stephen Darwall, 'Authority, Accountability, and Preemption' (2011) 2 Jurisprudence 103.

[4] Joseph Raz, 'Why the State?' in Nicole Roughan and Andrew Halpin (eds), *In Pursuit of Pluralist Jurisprudence* (Cambridge, CUP, 2017) 157; Joseph Raz, *Ethics in the Public Domain: Essays in the Morality of Law and Politics*, Rev edn (Oxford, Clarendon, 1995) ch 10.

[5] John Gardner, 'How Law Claims, What Law Claims' in Matthias Klatt (ed), *Institutionalized Reason: The Jurisprudence of Robert Alexy* (Oxford, OUP, 2012) 29–33.

[6] ibid 34.

[7] Leslie Green, *The Authority of the State* (Oxford, Clarendon, 1988) ch 3.

of the polity in question, both internally and externally. I don't intend to equate political communities and their institutions with individual citizens. I only point out that their respective claims serve similar functions. The fundamental split between an individual's claim and a polity's claim kicks in at the stage of their moral justification. The authority of individual persons to claim rights is ultimately grounded in personhood itself, ie the moral standing as an autonomous agent.[8] No one seriously questions a person's entitlement to claim rights. 'Who are you to claim a right?' sounds odd as a defence against another person's claim not to be harmed, for example. By contrast, no artificial social entity – like the state or the EU – is based on natural moral authority that would entitle them to claim a certain standing towards others. Quite the opposite. The interference of any political authority claim with the individual or collective autonomy of another agent is the moral puzzle theories of authority are trying to solve.

After this brief discussion of the relevance of claims for discussions of political authority, let us look at the nature of political authority itself.

III. Political Authority as Manifestation of Practical Authority

Political authority is practical authority. What characterises practical authorities is a normative power, exercised through offering *pro tanto* binding reasons for acting as the authoritative directive requires (subsection A). As such, practical authority is different from both counsel and coercion, and is necessarily relational, ie a normative power addressed to another agent in order to change their normative position (subsection B).

A. The Essence of Practical Authority: Binding Reasons to Act

It is vital to distinguish between understanding what authority is (analytical) on the one hand, and the conditions under which the exercise of authority is justified on the other (normative).[9] The present chapter and chapter two tackle the first question, while the second is reserved for the remainder of the book. In a sense, explaining the nature of political authority must always be a hopeless exercise, since 'authority is a notion bound up with most, if not all, of the central questions of political philosophy'.[10] Such humbling observations nonetheless make the

[8] Feinberg (n 1) 151.

[9] See only Jeremy Waldron, *Law and Disagreement* (Oxford, Clarendon, 1999) 99.

[10] Richard B Friedman, 'On the Concept of Authority in Political Philosophy' in Richard E Flathman (ed), *Concepts in Social and Political Philosophy* (New York, Macmillan, 1973) 121. On the

case for analytical clarity in its use. Logically, the first question must be: what is authority?

My first point is that political authority is practical authority. Whereas theoretical authorities give reasons for belief (such as experts), viz. they tell you what you ought to do, practical authorities give reasons for action.[11] That is, they tell you what to do. Political authorities are a kind of practical authority. They tell you what to do.

I have no stake in the debate about the precise nature of the practical reasons involved in practical authority. The debate is about whether they are content-independent or not, ie whether the binding force of the authoritative directive is at least partly influenced by its content, or exclusively by the fact that the authority says so.[12] I will thus avoid the term content-independence altogether. What I take from this discussion is that the binding force of a practical authority's reasons cannot depend on the approval of every individual subjected to it. Otherwise, it would be unable to fulfil its many functions. Crucially, due to fundamental and reasonable disagreements among citizens on the 'right' way to govern a society, any obligation to obey political authorities cannot be grounded in the merits of the law. For if political authority were contingent on the subject's assessment of the merits – of whether they think this is a 'good law' – the very anarchy it is supposed to remedy would re-enter via the back door.[13]

Similarly, my argument doesn't hinge on choosing between the two models concerning how exactly authoritative reasons bind (as second-order or weighty first-order reasons), neither does the choice make a practical difference.[14] In essence, authoritative reasons offer *pro tanto* binding reasons for acting as the authoritative directive requires. I will thus simply refer to authoritative reasons as binding, instead of the *Razian* terminology, exclusionary reasons.

Summing up, practical (and thus also political) authority purports to establish binding reasons to act. Practical authority offers binding, particularly forceful reasons to do as the authority says on the ground that the authority says so – that is, independently of one's own approval of the merits in the individual case. The next step distinguishes practical authority from related phenomena.

relationship between authority and analytical jurisprudence see Liam Murphy, 'The Normative Force of Law: Individuals and States' in Leslie Green, John Gardner and Brian Leiter (eds), *Oxford Studies in Philosophy of Law* (Oxford, OUP, 2018) vol 3.

[11] Darwall, 'Authority, Accountability, and Preemption' (n 3) 104 adds that practical authority also tells you to do it, ie to follow the binding directives in question. Andrei Marmor, 'The Dilemma of Authority' (2011) 2 *Jurisprudence* 121, 121.

[12] For a recent overview see only Laura Valentini, 'The Content-Independence of Political Obligation: What It Is and How to Test It' (2018) 24 *Legal Theory* 135.

[13] Friedman (n 10) 141.

[14] See on the one hand Joseph Raz, *The Authority of Law: Essays on Law and Morality*, 2nd edn (Oxford, OUP, 2009) 23; Joseph Raz, *The Morality of Freedom* (Oxford, Clarendon, 1986) 38. On the other DS Clarke, 'Exclusionary Reasons' (1977) 86 *Mind* 252; Richard E Flathman, *The Practice of Political Authority: Authority and the Authoritative* (Chicago, University of Chicago Press, 1980) 110 et seq.

B. Practical Authority as Normative Power between Counsel and Coercion

Authority is a means of social control. It is necessarily relational since authority claims are addressed to someone. Such claims intend to change the normative position of the addressee.

For one, practical authority is different from counsel and advice, both of which are not uttered as binding, but as persuasive reasons.[15] Authoritative reasons contain a distinct 'surrender of judgment' element in the sense that an agent subject to an authoritative command must not act on the balance of their reasoning, even if it would lead to a different action.[16] The difference is that persuading someone requires convincing them of my reasons for or against a certain action, whereas authoritative directives prescribe to act as directed solely by virtue of having been prescribed by that practical authority. Law is the best example.

For another, the reason-giving element of authority distinguishes it from coercion, which does not appeal to reasons at all. Whereas social scientists have always emphasised coercion as means of a state to control or influence a large population and territory,[17] coercion is conceptually alien to political authority. Indeed, the monopoly to use legitimate force represents but one tool in the toolbox of the state to uphold public order in practice. In other words, the state's claim to legitimate political authority distinguishes it from a 'band of robbers', since the whole point of the threat to use force is to reduce its actual application.[18] As Arendt reminded us, 'authority precludes the use of external means of coercion; where force is used, authority itself has failed'.[19] The threat of coercion in that sense is anti-authoritarian. It does not seek to bind in the same way as authorities to, that is, by way of *giving reasons* to act.

The social scientists' preoccupation with coercion thus underpins the de facto authority of the state, viz. the ability to effectively secure widespread obedience by the subjects, to have one's authority acknowledged by the bulk of people.[20] Further, since states claim the authority to uphold public order by the monopoly of the legitimate use of force, coercion plays a role in securing said authority. The nexus between coercion and authority results from the state's specific 'job profile', rather than from the nature of authority. In Estlund's no-nonsense words: 'Even without authority or legitimacy, of course, the state might yet have enormous

[15] Hannah Arendt, 'What Is Authority?' in Hannah Arendt (ed), *Between Past and Future* (New York, The Viking Press, 1961) 93; Thomas Hobbes, *Elementa philosophica de cive* (Apud Ludovicum Elzevirium 1647) ch 14.

[16] Flathman (n 14) 107. Friedman (n 10) 129.

[17] For a classic take, see Max Weber, 'Politics as a Vocation', *From Max Weber: Essays in Sociology* (Abingdon, Routledge, 2009) 78. On that element see Green (n 7) 71–75.

[18] Saint Augustine, *City of God: De Civitate Dei Contra Paganos* (Limovianet, 2013) bk 4.

[19] Arendt (n 15) 92 et seq. Similarly Richard S Peters, 'Authority' in Richard E Flathman (ed), *Concepts in Social & Political Philosophy* (New York, Macmillan, 1973) 154.

[20] Joseph Raz, *Authority* (New York, New York University Press 1990) 3; Peters (n 19) 151–53.

power. But we are not investigating brute power as such, since brute power is not a moral thing'.[21] We gain a lot if both are kept distinct.

This leaves us with the following picture. Practical authority purports to give binding reasons to act for the addressees of its directives. The normative force of the reasons, unlike counsel, is not open to debate based on its merit. Authority excludes coercion as an anti-reason mode of social control, to which the state, however, has recourse once its authority is flouted.

IV. The Specific Characteristics of Political Authority Claims

In what follows, I propose a three-fold taxonomy for analysing political authority claims, namely *law and institutions, territoriality* and *membership/addressees*. This framework enables both an external distinction from other manifestations of practical authority (such as parents and employers), as well as an internal differentiation among manifestations of authority on different regulatory levels. My hope is to provide analytical clarity about the nature, scope and force of authority claims on individual regulatory levels. The criteria law and institutions, territoriality and membership/addressees simply spell out the idea of an authority claim according to the question: *How* and *where* does the political community in question seek to bind *whom*? While I briefly introduce each element here, chapter two will engage with them in greater detail.

A. Law and its Institutions

Political authority is inseparable from law and the institutional system administering it. Law is the instrument to exercise political authority, the channel through which a political community orders, shapes, and – in a sense – constitutes the society under its jurisdiction. It seems like a trivial point. But law and law-administering institutions provide the primary means for distinguishing political authority from other practical authorities.[22] It shares the structural feature of practical authority to issue binding directives for addressees. While parents or teachers use direct communication with their children, however, political authorities use law.

The institutional aspect of political authority means that authority is necessarily bound to holding a public office rather than to a natural person. As we have already seen, legal officials are 'mouthpieces' of the law who claim authority on

[21] David Estlund, *Democratic Authority: A Philosophical Framework* (Princeton, Princeton University Press, 2008) 2.

[22] Green (n 7) 42 plausibly argues that institutions as such are unique to political authority.

law's behalf. In short, political authority is 'institutionalized practical authority'.[23] According to Raz, '(l)egitimacy relates primarily to the normative force of institutional action'.[24] That applies to law-administering institutions beyond the state as well. One main characteristic of political authority hence results from its way of structuring, monitoring and policing compliance in a polity by recourse to an institutionalised legal system.

The degree of institutional sophistication and the breadth of jurisdiction moreover allows one to compare the scope of different authority claims internally, ie on individual regulatory levels (the state and beyond). For example, states claim a comprehensive social ordering power intending to bind millions of subjects (comprehensiveness). States exclude other authorities in their substantive realm of action (exclusiveness). And states claim to be the supreme authority of the land (supremacy). By contrast, this kind of comprehensiveness, exclusivity and supremacy/hierarchy is rather uncommon in international law, where numerous organisations usually operate in the same, functionally circumscribed area.[25] For example, the International Monetary Fund (IMF), the World Bank, the Bank for International Settlements (BIS), and others all regulate international finance in one way or the other. Chapter two will show that the EU sits uneasily between the two, in terms of exclusiveness (autonomy of EU law), comprehensiveness (difficult policing of principle of conferral) and supremacy (primacy of EU law).

B. Territoriality

Territoriality expresses a normative relationship between humans, a distinct patch of the earth, and how political institutions administer it. Territorial rule is about administering a bordered space by linking geographic place, the people who live there, and the exercise of normative power. In short, territoriality is a function of the relationship between people, place and power. And there is room for territoriality in governing supra-state polities. The emerging field of EU legal geography will have a lot to say about that.[26] And as I have shown elsewhere and will illustrate in chapter two, both historically and conceptually, the notion of territoriality permits a non-state polity, such as the EU, to develop its own notion of territorial rule.[27]

The idea of territoriality is fundamental to political authority and intrinsically connected to membership: Whom to govern necessarily triggers the question of

[23] Daniel Voelsen and Leon Valentin Schettler, 'International Political Authority: On the Meaning and Scope of Justified Hierarchy in International Relations' (2019) 33 *International Relations* 540, 545.

[24] Joseph Raz, 'The Democratic Deficit' (King's College London Dickson Poon School of Law, Legal Studies Research Paper Series) 2018–07 6.

[25] Allen Buchanan, 'The Legitimacy of International Law' in Samantha Besson and John Tasioulas (eds), *The Philosophy of International Law* (Oxford, OUP, 2010) 84.

[26] Floris De Witte, 'Here Be Dragons: Legal Geography and EU Law' (2022) I *European Law Open* 113.

[27] Josef Weinzierl, 'Territoriality beyond the State: The EU's Territorial Claims and the Search for Their Legitimacy' (2021) 22 *German Law Journal* 650.

where to govern. It presupposes that everyone is born into a politically bounded society, which defines its normative borders quite literally in membership and spatial terms. Relatedly, territoriality often regulates the question of jurisdiction. That is, the enforcement of the (paradigmatically) state's law through the mentioned institutions stops at the spatial and coincidentally normative borders of the respective polity. This compartmentalisation enables the coexistence of a plethora of non-overlapping political authorities in our world. At the same time, it creates the need for justification. Simmons, for example, explains how many attempts to justify the authority of states find it incredibly difficult to address the particularity problem, ie why precisely this territory falls under the legitimate reach of a state and why citizens have a duty to obey just the law of their particular state.[28]

The *territorial* demarcation of the boundaries of jurisdiction as the daily bread of states can be juxtaposed with the overtly *functional* jurisdiction of many international organisations. There, a functional mandate to achieve a goal (for example promoting policies of high economic growth in the case of the Organisation for Economic Co-operation and Development (OECD)) or regulate a certain sector (such as energy cooperation in the case of the International Energy Charter) defines the reach of jurisdiction and of any ensuing legal obligations.

Territorial rule or its absence thus constitutes a useful criterion to categorise authority claims in Europe and – as we will see in chapter two – the EU's authority claim in particular.

C. Membership

Membership allows one to distinguish externally between political authority and other practical authorities with far-reaching normative systems, such as churches, trade unions or even sports federations. While the latter may use law as well to exercise authority, they focus on their members as part of a special interest group like the faithful, the workers or the athletes. Political authority focusses on the members of its political community. All of them. The prime example are individual citizens on the state level. International organisations, by contrast, mostly view states as their primary subjects. The notion of membership thus helps to distinguish authority claims on individual regulatory levels internally.

In addition, a focus on the notion of membership hints at a crucial purpose of the whole enterprise. Membership in a political community is impersonal. A typical authority relationship in the public sphere is relatively anonymous in that it cannot rely on strong associative ties between individuals, nor on them recognising their role in and capacity to uphold the political order.[29] Political authorities – in contrast to teachers or parents – simply address a vast number of addressees with no personal ties to the authority or to one another. Political

[28] A John Simmons, *Boundaries of Authority* (Oxford, OUP, 2016).
[29] For a discussion, see Green (n 7) 148 et seq.

authority cannot derive from a special *personal* relationship between authority and subject. Instead, the underlying scenario is the necessity for often millions of citizens to share a territorial and political space while organising their society. This questions associative obligations-theories that extrapolate from the moral relationship between families and local communities to the moral obligation to obey the law between the citizens of a whole state.[30]

Finally, practical authority is relational in the sense that the authoritative directive has a source as well as an addressee. But surely this means that the addressee, ie the member of the political community, plays a role in gauging the nature and scope of the authority claim in question. Relational is, that is the point, a reflexive bond. These considerations make it easy to see how membership functions as primordial criterion for understanding the nature and scope of a political authority claim. Chapter two will put flesh on these bones.

We could summarise the features of my taxonomy in the following way:

Fig 1 Delimiting Authority Claims

	Means (Institutions/Law)	Membership/Addressees	Territoriality
External Delimitation	- Other practical authorities (parents, teachers etc.) use different means - Political authority is attached to an institutional role, not a personal relationship	- Other practical authorities do not address people in their role as members or representatives of a political community	- Other practical authorities lack territorial elements in their exercise of authority
Internal Delimitation	- Different regulatory levels have different kinds of institutions - They use different types of law (hard/soft law) and enforcement mechanisms	- Polities and organisations on different regulatory levels address different agents (citizens, states, peoples)	- Regulatory levels differ in their use of territoriality as part of their authority claim (from territorial sovereignty to functional means)

D. Interim Conclusion

So far, I have presented political authority as a distinct manifestation of practical authority, of providing binding reasons to act. I distinguished it from both coercion as well as from counsel. I then introduced a three-fold analytical framework to differentiate authority in the political realm both from other practical authorities (externally) as well as internally on different regulatory levels. These criteria to evaluate authority claims are: (i) the means and institutions to channel the authority claim: (ii) the use of territoriality to exercise and demarcate authority; and (iii) the members or addressees of the claim. These criteria will form the basis of the identification of the nature and scope of the EU's authority claim in chapter two.

[30] See also Stephen Perry, 'Associative Obligations and the Obligation to Obey the Law' in Scott Hershovitz (ed), *Exploring Law's Empire: The Jurisprudence of Ronald Dworkin* (Oxford, OUP, 2008) ch 8.

Next, I want to provide a broad-brush comparison between a state's and international law's authority claim, in order to apply the above framework and, more importantly, in preparation for locating the EU in Europe's authority landscape.

V. State Sovereignty and International Authority Claims: Two Ends of a Spectrum

A. State Sovereignty and Authority

State sovereignty captures the self-image of the state's authority claim. This conceptualisation avoids a range of terminological and conceptual confusions in debating the distinct authority claims of states and the EU in today's Europe, where claiming political authority is, alas, all too often equated with sovereignty.

Sovereignty wanders like a ghost through any discipline occupied with the study of 'the political' (constitutional and international law, political theory, international relations etc). Sovereignty has thus provided the analytical framework for discussions about the EU's authority claim for decades. Many theorists have tried to update/qualify/broaden the concept's reach to accommodate the EU's authority claim.[31] Although foundational ideas like sovereignty require clarity, this has led to ever murkier conceptual ground. Sovereignty's variegated use has caused despair amongst many and provoked persistent calls for its final burial.[32] Its continued use in academia and the political realm is one reason I join those who resist the claims to give up the study and use of sovereignty, however. Let me explain the others.

Recent scholarly contributions have unearthed a convincing framework of sovereignty and its continued relevance in today's world. I refer to the portrayal of sovereignty as the state's comprehensive authority claim over a distinct territory, accompanied by the practical effort to make good on that claim in reality, that is, for the claim to be effective.[33] This definition captures both elements of state sovereignty, ie the supreme authority to decide about the status and reach of any other authority in its territory (internal sovereignty), and a right to non-interference from external authorities, mostly states (external sovereignty). The practical effectiveness of the claim secures that the state makes good on its claim in the sense that it holds and exercises a variety of vital sovereign rights (de facto authority). In other words, the state claims a comprehensive right to rule and the power to enforce its rule in a demarcated territory.

[31] For a comprehensive overview see Matej Avbelj, 'Theorizing Sovereignty and European Integration: Sovereignty and European Integration' (2014) 27 *Ratio Juris* 344.

[32] Stanley Benn, 'The Uses of "Sovereignty"' (1955) 3 *Political Studies* 109, 122. For a good summary of sovereignty-abandonists, see Martin Loughlin, *The Idea of Public Law* (Oxford, OUP, 2004) 72.

[33] Wouter G Werner and Jaap H De Wilde, 'The Endurance of Sovereignty' (2001) 7 *European Journal of International Relations* 283, 287; Nicholas Barber, *The Principles of Constitutionalism* (Oxford, OUP, 2018) ch 2; Neil Walker, 'Sovereignty Frames and Sovereignty Claims' in Richard Rawlings, Peter Leyland and Alison Young (eds), *Sovereignty and the Law* (Oxford, OUP, 2012).

The claim-structure endorsed earlier helps to elucidate a vital distinction between the abstract idea or claimed *status* of the sovereign state and the *exercise* of a variety of sovereign rights. As long as the state retains the ultimate authority to control the very delegation of sovereign rights by, for example, withdrawing from international arrangements, sovereignty as status and authority claim is left untouched.[34] That notwithstanding, Malcolm poignantly summarises the tension between the possibility for the state to hand over the exercise of sovereign rights without consequences for sovereignty, and the need to retain vital sovereign functions in order to make a credible claim to sovereignty: 'Each time we delegate the exercise of important areas of our authority to Europe, we do not lose sovereignty or become less sovereign; we merely become more likely to lose our sovereignty'.[35]

The state's authority claim leaves open the moral basis of its legitimacy. Sovereignty theory doesn't inquire *why* the state has the right to rule, but rather, *who* has it: the state. It is about allocating decision-making powers (related to the (in)famous *Kompetenz-Kompetenz*). Why the state might legitimately claim and exercise such a right to rule in light of the autonomy of the individual citizen is a quite different question; it is the one theories of authority ask. In other words, sovereignty asks who has the authority, whereas the broader inquiry into political authority is interested in why and to what extent such authority is legitimate. Both inquiries address the same phenomenon (the authority claim of the state) from different angles:

Fig 2 The Link between Sovereignty and Authority

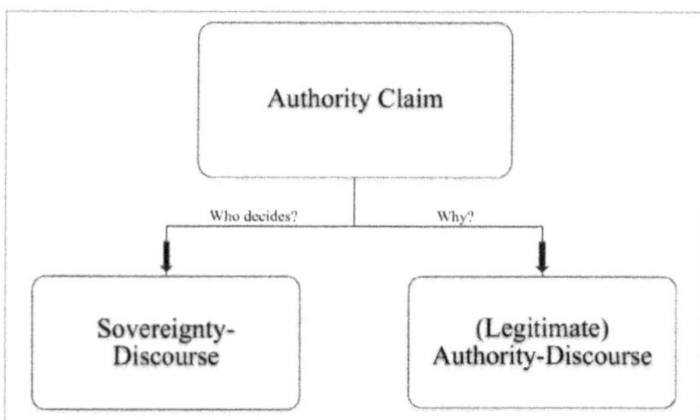

Due to their distinct nature, the two inquiries may yield different results. Raz hit the mark when stating that 'state sovereignty may well apply and prevent external intervention even when the governments of those states act beyond their legitimate authority'.[36] He explicitly linked sovereignty back to the autonomy of the collective which needs to be protected externally against outside influence even if

[34] Werner and De Wilde, ibid, 303; Michel Troper, 'The Survival of Sovereignty' in Hent Kalmo and Quentin Skinner (eds), *Sovereignty in Fragments: The Past, Present and Future of a Contested Concept* (Cambridge, CUP, 2010).

[35] Noel Malcolm, *Sense on Sovereignty* (Centre for Policy Studies 1991) 26 et seq.

[36] Raz, 'Why the State?' (n 4) 159.

its decisions are mistaken. Note that the same is true internally. The state claims that all its laws are an expression of its legitimate authority. If an inquiry based on a chosen moral standard reveals that this claim is exaggerated (answering the *why*-question), however, it has no direct bearing on the question that it is still the state which should decide (answering the *who*-question).

B. International 'Authority' Claims?

In recent decades, Europe has witnessed a significant shake-up of the authority landscape through the emergence of a plethora of new trans- and international fora. Following suit, scholarly attention has shifted to instances of authority beyond the nation state. This section applies the above taxonomy to international authority claims. Before doing that, let me address an issue lingering in the shadows of the previous pages: is it appropriate to use the language of authority in relation to political communities and law-administering organisations beyond the state in the first place?

i. The Applicability of the Concept 'Authority' Beyond the State

Socrates might be responsible for the birth of inquiries into political authority when he declined the offer of his friend Crito to plot his escape from prison and the threat of imminent execution. Socrates refused to flee, arguing that this would violate his moral duty to obey the law of Athens's polis, to which he consented by the way he had led his life.[37] Recalling this anecdote serves as a gentle historical reminder that political authority predates the advent of the post-Westphalian sovereign nation state and is thus analytically independent of statehood.

Some writers like Loughlin, Lindseth and (implicitly) Majone nonetheless want to reserve the language of (political) authority for nation states.[38] I cannot do their accounts justice here, since they emerged in very different debates about constitutional theory and European integration. Let me focus on Loughlin's work as exemplary advocate for this position. Loughlin argues for a distinction between the national, constitutional level as an arena for sovereignty and political authority (*potestas*) on the one hand, and the international level characterised by governance-structures (*potentia*) on the other. *Potentia* refers to the empirically observable powers a government holds and its capacity to exert them, whereas *potestas* denotes

[37] Plato, *Euthyphro. Apology. Crito. Phaedo* (translated by Christopher Emlyn-Jones and William Preddy) (Cambridge (MA), Harvard University Press, 2017) 214 et seq. For a discussion of several accounts of political authority in ancient Greece and Rome, see Benjamin Straumann, *Crisis and Constitutionalism: Roman Political Thought from the Fall of the Republic to the Age of Revolution* (Oxford, OUP, 2016) ch 4.

[38] Peter Lindseth, *Power and Legitimacy: Reconciling Europe and the Nation-State* (Oxford, OUP, 2010) Conclusion; Loughlin, *The Idea of Public Law* (n 32) ch 5; Giandomenico Majone, 'Europe's "Democratic Deficit": The Question of Standards' (1998) 4 *European Law Journal* 5.

the morally relevant political authority, ie the creation of a right to be obeyed.[39] On that view, the (sovereign) authority of a state protects the 'autonomy of the political'. That authority presupposes the 'legal omnipotence' of the state, ie the state as an ultimate source of authority which itself cannot be bound either by the legal obligations it creates or by the constitution.[40] Since the state 'cannot be regarded as the subject of legal rights and duties',[41] it is easy to see how this framework precludes any conceptual space for genuine authority above the state, be it international or supranational. Although Loughlin acknowledges the substantial institutional and substantive impact of the EU on authority-structures in the Member States, for him the impact remains quantitative and merely implies the presence of *potentia* without *potestas* at the EU level.[42] He denies any morally or legally relevant authority-relationship between supra-state institutions and individuals. For Loughlin (and for similar reasons for Lindseth and Majone), in short, there is no *potestas* at the EU level; the EU does not claim nor exercise political authority.[43]

I agree with Loughlin that the state is the exclusive repository for *sovereign* authority. But I reject his idea of confining any authority in the public domain to the state. Whereas the emerging discussion of international authority does not address this issue directly (perhaps anxious that it might become the follow-up to the debate whether international law is really law), a growing body of literature illustrates how the idea of authority claims of international law provides a helpful conceptual lens to ask morally important questions.

Chapter 2 attempts to show that applying the concept of authority to the EU not only provides analytical clarity in relation to the evaluation of the legitimacy of the EU's exercise of public power by law. What is more, the taxonomy proposed above allows one to distinguish the EU's authority claim from manifestations of authority on other regulatory levels. In other words, denying the applicability of the concept of authority to a supranational polity – based on an idealisation of the state as a legally uncontrollable juridical entity – has the undesirable effect of downplaying what is at stake in the EU as a matter of political legitimacy.

As I see it, polities and organisations beyond the state that are not in the business of upholding public order or claiming the monopoly of legitimate force may still claim authority. Authority without an element of coercion, but still authority. Take it from Roughan: 'The nature of authority does not change whether it is exercised by legal or political institutions, or whether it is located in local, national,

[39] Martin Loughlin, 'Constitutional Pluralism: An Oxymoron?' (2014) 3 *Global Constitutionalism* 9, 11 et seq; Martin Loughlin, 'The Erosion of Sovereignty' (2016) 45 *Netherlands Journal of Legal Philosophy* 57, 70.

[40] Loughlin, 'Constitutional Pluralism', ibid, 13 et seq; Loughlin, *The Idea of Public Law* (n 32) 86. Similarly, Raz, 'Why the State?' (n 4) 148 et seq.

[41] Loughlin, 'Constitutional Pluralism' (n 39) 13; Loughlin, *The Idea of Public Law* (n 32) 92 et seq.

[42] Loughlin, 'The Erosion of Sovereignty' (n 39) 73.

[43] More recently, Majone seems to concede that the EU cannot be captured in his earlier narrow regulatory and efficiency-related terms alone: Giandomenico Majone, *Rethinking the Union of Europe Post-Crisis: Has Integration Gone Too Far?* (Cambridge, CUP, 2014) ch 10.

transnational, or international communities. Wherever authority is located, it remains a normative power over subjects'.[44] I agree. The nature of authority doesn't change, only the manifestation of authority claims on different levels. Polities and organisations beyond the state simply fulfil a different function. It does not follow from the fact that states exercise political authority that *only* states claim political authority. Let us now take a closer look at the incipient scholarship on international authority.

ii. Understanding International Authority

Scholars conceptualise international authority in various ways. Some approach it from a legalistic lens, ie with a view to the rather limited instances where international law binds the parties and subjects with 'hard' and enforceable law.[45] For instance, the 'Heidelberg Project on International Public Authority' studies the instantiations of authority in international law, broadly defined as unilateral capacity to determine and reduce the freedom of others.[46] Examples usually include the UN Security Council, the World Trade Organisation (WTO) and sometimes the International Criminal Court (ICC). One obvious consequence of this definitional approach is that it focuses on the international institutions that are closest to the authority exercised by states (binding and enforceable law). Other scholars define international authority more broadly to accommodate various forms of governance beyond the state.[47] Krisch, for example, thinks of international authority as *postnational* or *liquid* authority. For him, authority on the global level involves the use of informal instead of formally binding means, the reliance on substantive rather than formal sources of authority, a diversity of actors instead of unitary authority, and finally a dynamic rather than stable nature of authority relations.[48] Krisch illustrates how international law relies on soft law, recommendations, best practices, etc. Accordingly, whenever international law exercises authority in the statist understanding, ie through binding law, such as the WTO's dispute settlement body or the ICC's judgments, this is the exceptional case. Çali's comprehensive study similarly argues that there is no unified international authority claim nor is there one distinct type of political obligation. In her view, international law

[44] Nicole Roughan, *Authorities: Conflicts, Cooperation, and Transnational Legal Theory* (Oxford, OUP, 2014) 28.

[45] Samantha Besson, 'The Authority of International Law: Lifting the State Veil' (2009) 31 *Sydney Law Review* 343; Buchanan (n 25); John Tasioulas, 'The Legitimacy of International Law' in Tasioulas and Besson (n 25). Raz, 'Why the State?' (n 4) 152.

[46] Armin von Bogdandy, Philipp Dann and Matthias Goldmann, 'Developing the Publicness of Public International Law: Towards a Legal Framework for Global Governance Activities' (2008) 9 *German Law Journal* 1375.

[47] For a great overview see Voelsen and Schettler (n 23) 546 et seq.

[48] Nico Krisch, 'Authority, Solid and Liquid, in the Postnational Sphere' in Maksyimilian Del Mar and Roger Cotterrell (eds), *Authority in Transnational Legal Theory* (Cheltenham, Elgar, 2016).

imposes a variety of duties on national legal orders that make the authority of international law relative and fragmented.[49]

This suggests that the binding force of authoritative directives varies on different regulatory levels and that these instances of governance beyond the state nonetheless fit under the general umbrella of authority in the public domain. International organisations simply seek to bind different actors with different means. In other words, the notable difference between authority at the state and on the international level not only plays out in the means of exercising authority (law versus soft instruments), but also regarding the other tenets identified above. Think of the members/addressees of the organisation. Whereas state authority comprehends citizens as natural subjects of its authority claim, international organisations almost exclusively exercise authority over states: 'International law does not command authority over individuals'.[50] The variegated examples such as the Basel Committee's Banking Regulation Rules, the OECD Council's recommendations or the WTO Dispute Resolution bodies' judgments are all addressed to states only.[51] Consider, finally, the element of territoriality. The jurisdictional reach of international organisations is exclusively defined in functional, rather than territorial terms. This feature marks the precondition for overlapping functional mandates of international organisations in the first place.

The point of these emerging studies of international authority is to acknowledge these areas of international law as authority despite their conceptual divergence from more traditional nation state authority. International authority claims thus differ from political authority at the state level. They mostly depend on deference rather than compliance, address states instead of individual humans, and, therefore, questions regarding their legitimacy and capacity to trigger moral obligations will provoke different answers compared to grounding the legitimacy of state authority.[52] They still raise their own variants of legitimacy questions, however.

C. Interim Conclusion

Thus far, I have proceeded with an analytical microscope, zooming in one step at a time. The chapter started with the moral relevance of *claiming* in the political arena more generally. From there, it moved to the nature of practical and political authority. It then proposed a taxonomy of studying authority claims on different levels, namely based on law/institutions, territoriality, and membership/addressees. Finally, it applied this taxonomy by portraying state sovereignty as the state's particularly strong authority claim and compared it to the incipient scholarship on authority claims of international organisations.

[49] Başak Cali, *The Authority of International Law: Obedience, Respect, and Rebuttal* (Oxford, OUP, 2015).

[50] ibid 75. For a different view, *cf* Besson (n 45).

[51] For these and more examples, Krisch (n 48) Introduction.

[52] Cali (n 49) 13. But *cf* Tasioulas (n 45) 100 et seq.

The gap to be closed in chapter two is how the EU's authority claim fits in. One could visualise our journey so far in the following way:

Fig 3 Authority Claims

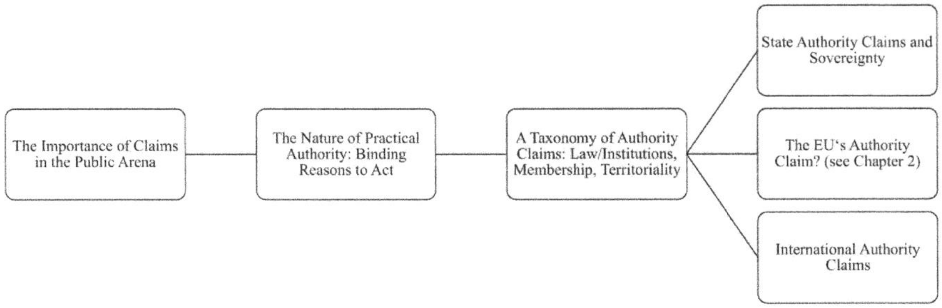

To complement the theoretical groundwork, I now turn to what it means to have legitimate political authority. The point of theories of authority is to establish *objective* moral benchmarks for the exercise of authority. Legitimate authority, in other words, describes the extent to which the self-image of authorities corresponds to objective moral legitimacy standards, the extent to which their claims are true. The remainder of this chapter discusses what it means to have legitimate authority.

VI. Empirical and Normative Legitimacy

The disparate use of numerous notions of political theory (notably sovereignty) makes it difficult to base an argument on them which cannot be swept aside by recourse to terminological disagreement ('I use the concept differently'). Cognitive science would call them 'suitcase-words', because you can pack them with such a variety of meanings.[53] Legitimacy (and, consequently, legitimate authority) is one of those words.

Importantly, moral philosophers and social scientists differ in their use of legitimacy and legitimate authority. While some writings are clear about this analytical distinction,[54] others are more ambiguous and fail to pin down the notion of legitimacy under consideration.[55] I cannot blame institutions like the Commission for blending the two debates into each other (more in chapter three). For political

[53] Marvin Minsky, *The Emotion Machine* (New York, Simon & Schuster, 2006) pt 4.

[54] See Claudia Sternberg, 'Political Legitimacy between Democracy and Effectiveness: Trade-Offs, Interdependencies, and Discursive Constructions by the EU Institutions' (2015) 7 *European Political Science Review* 615, 617–20; Achim Hurrelmann, 'Legitimacy and European Union Politics' in William Thompson (ed), *Oxford Research Encyclopedias: Politics* (Oxford, OUP, 2014).

[55] Lina Papadopoulou, '"All Good Things Come in Threes": From a Double to a Triple Democratic Legitimacy of the European Union' in Lina Papadopoulou, Ingolf Pernice and Joseph Weiler (eds), *Legitimacy Issues of the European Union in the Face of Crisis* (Baden-Baden, Hart/Nomos, 2017). Another example is Giorgio Maganza, 'Can the Authority of EU Law Be Taken for Granted? A Tale of Principles and Realities' in Wolfgang Heusel and Jean-Philippe Rageade (eds), *The Authority of EU Law: Do We Still Believe In It?* (New York, Springer, 2019) 46.

theory, however, conflating these conceptions 'remains a vulgar error',[56] since social and moral legitimacy differ in methodology, aim and moral substance. Instead, remembering Rawls' distinction of concepts and conceptions,[57] it is helpful to understand social/empirical and normative/moral legitimacy as two different *conceptions* of the broader *concept* of legitimacy.

Social legitimacy – as coined by Max Weber –[58] refers to the belief of the bulk of citizens regarding the acceptability of the political regime in place. Legitimacy here means observable acceptance, usefully termed empirical legitimacy. It is about the extent of popular support for the concrete political system and thus system-specific. Legitimacy, in this context, 'derives from people's belief in legitimacy'.[59] The notions of 'acceptance' or 'support' are admittedly ambiguous, since they encompass a range of sociological and psychological factors and cover anything from bare toleration to active adoration.[60] Since this book focuses on moral legitimacy, such ambiguity need not concern us any further.

Normative legitimacy, by contrast, is concerned with the appropriate moral justification of the legitimate exercise of public power. It entails a moral inquiry into the compatibility of legal directives with fundamental reasons, values and principles, notably the overt tension between authority and autonomy.[61] In a nutshell, normative legitimacy allows for and explains a mismatch between our legal and our moral duties. It seeks to establish *universal* moral conditions to evaluate the legitimate exercise of governmental power. This conception of legitimacy, to be clear, informs this book: reflecting on the appropriate normative standard to evaluate the rightfulness of the EU's exercise of authority.

Two major differences should suffice to illustrate the distinct perspective of both inquiries. I already hinted at the first one, relating to the object under consideration. Theories of authority are characteristically abstract. They usually concern a form of organisation or political community per se, for example 'the modern state'. The arguments are supposed to apply *universally* to these forms of government/governance, eg to all modern states. Social (especially political) scientists, by contrast, study the legitimacy of a *particular* political system in terms of what actual members of a discrete political community believe about its legitimacy. Their methodology frames the idea in the context of a given society.[62] The second

[56] Nigel Simmonds, 'Why People Obey the Law by Tom R. Tyler' (1991) 50 *CLJ* 174, 174.

[57] John Rawls, *A Theory of Justice*, Rev edn (Cambridge (MA), Harvard University Press, 1999) 5.

[58] Weber (n 17) 78 et seq where he distinguishes between charismatic, traditional and legal-rational legitimacy.

[59] David Beetham, *The Legitimation of Power*, 2nd edn (Basingstoke, Palgrave Macmillan, 2013) 8, who is extremely critical of Weber's work, to whom he attributes that position.

[60] Michel Troper, 'The Modern State and the Concept of Authority' in Roger Cotterrell and Maksymilian Del Mar (eds), *Authority in Transnational Legal Theory* (Cheltenham, Elgar, 2016) 76.

[61] On the latter, Raz, *The Authority of Law* (n 14) 3; Richard Dagger, *Playing Fair: Political Obligation and the Problems of Punishment* (Oxford, OUP, 2018) ch 2.

[62] Note that this changes when you assess the legitimacy of an individual institution. The social and moral legitimacy of a particular institution, like the ECJ or the European Commission, are both necessarily tied to the concrete role, standing and actions of that institution.

major difference between normative and social legitimacy relates to the assessment of legitimacy, which may yield spectacularly different results. Think only of Weiler's drastic, yet helpful, example of the Nazi dictatorship.[63] A sufficient part of the German population empirically accepted and even supported the regime; therefore, it proved relatively stable. In other words, the belief in the legitimacy of the regime (though perhaps achieved via indoctrination and fear) must necessarily have been widespread. A similar observation applies to past societies with widespread slavery practices. Notice that such regimes in fact claimed legitimate authority in the sense explained earlier, even if that claim was based on despicable theories of slaves as objects or non-Arians as second-class humans.[64] The point is that – despite their empirical legitimacy – no-one argues that such regimes yielded legitimate authority, ie that they ruled rightfully in keeping with any plausible moral standard. The legitimacy claims of such regimes were just false.

To sum up, socially legitimate authority and morally legitimate authority represent two separate inquiries. The former is about actual (subjective) behavioural support, the latter about (objective) justified reasons for such support. Even so, both inquiries also influence each other. A necessary precondition of de jure, ie morally legitimate authority is a sufficient degree of de facto authority. A de facto authority 'claims to be legitimate or is believed to be so, and is effective in imposing its will on many over whom it claims authority'.[65] It does not necessarily have moral authority. The acceptance of the subjects guarantees the stability and effectiveness of a legal order.[66]

Social legitimacy is thus intrinsically related to de facto authority. If political leadership only rarely succeeds in what its subjects expect it to do (eg to deliver policy outcomes), it tends to lose its authority and second-order compliance mechanisms like force need to kick in. Such resources are limited and costly to manage.[67] Conversely, the more popular support a government enjoys the more likely it is that it can govern smoothly, and non-compliance presumably won't be an endemic problem.

Take the following example. If a state imposes a curfew on its entire territory because there is a global pandemic, it must rely on most citizens to stay at home voluntarily. The state simply lacks the police force to enforce it against large-scale non-compliance. This observation is ever more salient beyond the state, where lack of compliance cannot usually be sanctioned by force. If, for example, the national courts would not have followed some remarkable rulings of the ECJ in

[63] Joseph Weiler, 'The Authority of European Law: Do We Still Believe in It?' in Wolfgang Heusel and Jean-Philippe Rageade (eds), *The Authority of EU Law: Do We Still Believe in It?* (New York, Springer 2019) 9.

[64] David Beetham, *The Legitimation of Power*, 2nd edn (Basingstoke, Palgrave Macmillan, 2013) 30.

[65] Raz, *Ethics in the Public Domain* (n 4) 296.

[66] Fritz Scharpf, 'Legitimacy in the Multilevel European Polity' (2009) 1 *European Political Science Review* 173, 173; Beetham (n 64) 33.

[67] Beetham, ibid 28.

the early days of the integration, the EU legal order would look different today, and the lack of actual supranational enforcement means there is nothing the EU could have done (more detail in chapter two). Moral authority thus presupposes a good deal of de facto authority.

That stability and effectiveness social legitimacy brings about in addition constitutes an independent moral achievement in and of itself. Thereby, de facto authority ('legitimation') creates aspects of de jure authority ('legitimacy').[68] Note that this relationship is reflexive. Based on moral psychology, Rawls has shown how more stable moral ideals are likely to muster more social support.[69] De facto and de jure authority thereby become mutually reinforcing, since greater moral authority in turn contributes to more wide-spread social acceptance. Whereas a sufficient degree of social legitimacy is thus necessary but not sufficient for morally legitimate authority, its stability-enhancing effect contributes to morally legitimate authority. To illustrate, see the following table:

Fig 4 Social and Moral Legitimacy

	Social Legitimacy/De Facto Authority	Moral Legitimacy/De Jure Authority
Decisive Criterion	Acceptance by the majority of subjects	Compliance with a particular moral benchmark
Object of Assessment	Concrete: The belief of individuals in a given political system	Universal: Exercise of political power by a generic form of government
Method	Empirical Explanations	Normative Inquiry
Variability	Changes depend on individual beliefs	Changes depend on individual moral benchmark
Interdependence	Social legitimacy supports a political community's de facto authority among its subjects and contributes to its de jure authority (stability, effectiveness, saving resources) as one of its preconditions	

Once again, the focus of this book is morally legitimate authority, the search for a moral benchmark to test the legitimacy of the EU's exercise of authority by law; in short, the extent of the EU's *right* to rule. I focus on the legitimate authority of EU Law, which itself is a subset of the EU's broader moral legitimacy in the terms just described. Rather than a broader justifiability of the EU's institutional framework, the present inquiry specifically seeks to explore the tension between authority claim and autonomy.

Let me turn to the discussion about the vexed relationship of legitimate authority and political obligation.

[68] Raz (n 24) 18 et seq. On their interdependence see Nicole Roughan, 'From Authority to Authorities: Bridging the Social/Normative Divide' in Roger Cotterrell and Maksymilian Del Mar (eds), *Authority in Transnational Legal Theory* (Cheltenham, Elgar, 2016) 283 et seq.

[69] Rawls (n 57) ch 69.

VII. Authority and Political Obligation

The relationship between authority and political obligation, ie a potential moral duty to obey the law, raises the deepest jurisprudential questions about the nature and grounds of law, as it deals with the consequences of legitimate authority for the practical reasoning of the subject.[70]

A. From Legitimate Authority to Political Obligation

I side with most theorists for whom legitimate authority triggers a prima facie moral duty to obey the law. The right to rule correlates to the imposition of a moral duty; they constitute two sides of the same coin. Once the truth of the authority claim, ie its objective legitimacy, is established, the subject has a strong reason, a duty, to do what the authority requires.

This view alone takes the (normative) fact that political authorities make such claims to obedience seriously.[71] It is incompatible with the position that legitimate authority creates no duties, ie that political obligation is independent from authority.[72] Legitimate authority goes beyond the effects of good governance or the moral relationships we might have to political communities to which we are outsiders or mere residents. The right to rule brought about by morally legitimate authority affects our practical reasoning more profoundly. Legitimate authority is necessary and sufficient to create a moral duty. To put it in a slogan, legitimate authority creates a right to rule and a corresponding prima facie moral duty to obey.

I just managed to sneak in an important qualifier: prima facie duties. Let me explain.

B. Prima-Facie Duties: Authority's Internal and External Limits

It seems universally accepted that authority at most triggers a prima facie duty to obey.[73] Legitimate authority doesn't establish an absolute duty. The duty to obey the law, whatever your moral benchmark for legitimacy, is defeasible and limited.

[70] For a discussion Murphy (n 10) 93 et seq.

[71] Edward Song, 'Strong and Weak Legitimacy' (2011) 27 *Southwest Philosophy Review* 167, 170 et seq.

[72] Endorsed by Rolf Sartorius, 'Political Authority and Political Obligation' (1981) 67 *Virginia Law Review* 3; Arthur Isak Applbaum, 'Legitimacy without the Duty to Obey' (2010) 38 *Philosophy & Public Affairs* 215; David Copp, 'The Idea of a Legitimate State' (1999) 28 *Philosophy & Public Affairs* 3; Christopher Wellman, 'Toward a Liberal Theory of Political Obligation' (2001) 111 *Ethics* 735.

[73] See only Murphy (n 10) 97.

The *internal* limits and thresholds built into many accounts are technically not part of this discussion. Think only of the lack of consent for consent theories, or non-democratic procedures for democratic authority theorists. As Perry remarks when discussing political obligation, '(e)very minimally plausible theory sets out certain conditions under which such an obligation is said to arise'.[74] The violation of these conditions simply makes the exercise of authority illegitimate. Consequently, no prima facie duty to obey is created in the first place.

Compare that to *external* limits, for which we need the 'prima facie' qualifier. External limits kick in even if the exercise of authority is legitimate and thus creates moral duties on the part of the subjects. The reason is that independent prudential or moral considerations, aside from the law, can come into conflict with my political obligations. There are always other values that create moral obligations, such as love or friendship. And they may conflict with the law. For example, I might have promised a friend not to reveal compromising information, which law enforcement asks me to divulge during an investigation. Such external limits make it the case that even an existing moral obligation to obey the law may justifiably be set aside.[75] All of that still leaves the notion of duty itself relatively obscure, to which we turn next.

C. The Elusive Notion of Duty

What is the nature of the normative change legitimate political authority triggers in the addressee of its directives? It relates to the level of intrusiveness on the practical reasoning of the addressees. Here, I address both theoretical disagreements as well as how the notion of duty varies across regulatory levels.

Some claim that law requires you to *comply* with it, ie to do as law says for the reason that law says so.[76] In other words, you not only need to act as the law requires, but also because the law tells you to act thus, and for no other independent moral or rational consideration. This triggers the 'paradox of just law', illustrated by the prohibition of murder. Since one has powerful non-legal reasons to refrain from murder, it would be extremely odd to hold that I failed to comply with the legal duty not to murder if I refrained from murder based on independent moral reasons. The paradox is that the more just a law is based on its substance, the less one would comply with the law by acting on it.[77] Others, like Hershovitz, have shown a way out of the paradox by arguing that law demands a less intrusive form of obedience. It merely requires that one *conforms* with it

[74] Perry (n 30) 183.

[75] George Christie, 'On the Moral Obligation to Obey the Law' (1990) 6 *Duke Law Journal* 1311, 1312.

[76] For an elaborate treatment and the relationship to Raz' exclusionary reasons, see Joseph Raz, *Practical Reason and Norms* (Oxford, OUP, 1999) 178 et seq. For a discussion in relation to the notion 'surrender of judgment', see Flathman (n 14) 100 et seq.

[77] For a discussion see Raz, *Ethics in the Public Domain* (n 4) ch 15.

where conforming means to act as the law requires without necessarily basing that action on the legal directive.[78] What matters here are actions, not psychological dispositions.

In my view, the law imposes different moral duties on us, and the most important aspect of any law's authority claim is that you act on it (conformity). I agree with Perry that 'for the most part, the law is indifferent to why one complies with the law so long as one does so'.[79] I am thus sceptical about the viability of a single conceptual kind of duty imposed by the law, no matter in which area, by which entity and on whom. I find it intuitively appealing that law originating on separate regulatory levels entails a variety of duties on a variety of addressees.

This intuition is confirmed by discussions about the difference between domestic political obligation and the duty to obey international law. Based on a very specific concern for the rule of law in the US, Waldron argued that the state officials' duties stemming from international law differ from the duties individuals have towards state law. He grounds that argument in the different value of both agents. Human individuals have inherent moral value and dignity as persons, whereas states and other political communities are artificial institutional structures in the service of humans, so that their value is derivative. According to Waldron, someone's lawyer may legitimately seek to explore potential loopholes in the law, because that is in concordance with the ultimate underlying autonomy of the individual. States, by contrast, enjoy no such natural freedom and thus shouldn't seek to avoid the constraints of the law the precise purpose of which is to guarantee individual autonomy of humans.[80] International law accordingly claims a distinct binding force and imposes a different kind of duty that – at least in part – stems from the fact that it addresses states and not humans qua humans. I agree with this distinction that presupposes the different kinds of authority claims explained above. In her study of the authority of international law, Çali provides a conceptual argument to a similar effect. She refuses to import the above assumption of theories of state authority – namely, that the duty to obey the law on individuals is always of the same kind, to the international arena. Instead, Çali argues that international law imposes three different kinds of duties on state officials: obedience (strong duties, no discretionary space), respect (weak, granting discretion to the states) or rebuttal (balancing with other legal duty to which the international duty might yield).[81] The point these theorists rightly make is that political authority imposes different kinds of duties on individuals qua citizens than on

[78] Scott Hershovitz, 'The Authority of Law' in Andrew Marmor (ed), *The Routledge Companion to Philosophy of Law* (Abingdon, Routledge, 2012).

[79] Perry (n 30) 184.

[80] Jeremy Waldron, 'The Rule of International Law' (2006) 30 *Harvard Journal of Law and Public Policy* 15, 19.

[81] Cali (n 49) ch 2. Similarly, Barnett and Finnemore conceive of the main duty induced by international authorities as one of 'deference', Michael Barnett and Martha Finnemore, *Rules for the World: International Organizations in Global Politics* (New York, Cornell University Press, 2004) 5, 29.

individuals qua state officials.[82] We may visualise the variety of factors that influence the nature of the normative change sought in the following way:

Fig 5 The Criteria that Determines the Nature of Political Obligation

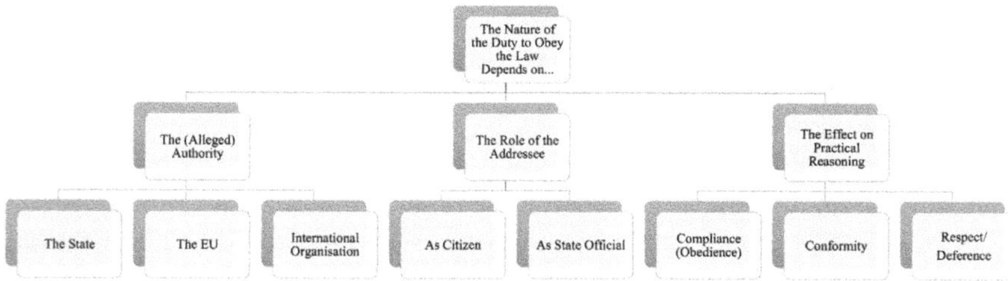

D. Interim Conclusion

I concur with those who see a necessary connection between rightful, legitimate authority and the creation of moral duties on the subjects of said authority. I showed that the moral duties authorities trigger are subject to external limits, such as countervailing independent moral duties, and therefore necessarily defeasible. I then clarified that the character of the duty varies both in nature as well as on different regulatory levels and depending on the role of the addressee.

VIII. Conclusion

In contrast to the flood of literature on the EU's authority claim related to sovereignty and *Kompetenz-Kompetenz*, elaborate and – more importantly – explicit accounts on the legitimate authority of the EU are scarce. I intended this chapter to highlight the crucial theoretical debates that relate to the analytical and normative evaluation of legitimate authority in and beyond the state, precisely to situate the EU in these debates in subsequent chapters.

The remainder of the book spells out the dualism inherent in the framework of analysing claims and evaluating their legitimacy in relation to the EU. Chapter two explores the scope, nature and addressees of the EU's authority claim with the help of the taxonomy explained above (law and institutions, territoriality and membership), ie *how* it seeks to bind *whom where*, before the subsequent chapters search for a moral basis of the EU's authority.

[82] See also Murphy (n 10) 112 et seq.

2

An Authority Claim Over Peoples

I. Introduction

Chapter one grappled with the nature of political authority in and beyond the state. This chapter uses these insights to position the EU's authority claim in the range between national and international authority.[1] In section III, I argue that the EU neither claims sovereignty nor sovereign authority. I then submit that the EU's claim should not be seen as part of international law's authority claims in section IV. Instead, in my constructive interpretation, the EU ultimately addresses and seeks to bind the peoples of Europe (section V). The EU, in short, claims authority over constitutional peoples.

II. The Many Labels of the EU's Authority Claim in the Literature

Up to this point, I have said almost nothing about my primary object of study, the EU. Instead, I looked at authority claims in the political realm more generally. These efforts seemed important both as a foundation for assessing the EU's authority claim and to understand the moral stakes of political authority discourse more broadly. From now on, the focus is on the EU's authority claim, ie on how the EU seeks to bind whom, to depart from there in our search for a possible justification for this claim in the remainder of the book.

The literature on the EU's authority claim is surprisingly ambiguous. It seems very difficult to name the child. They call it: 'autonomy as a proxy for sovereignty';[2] 'sovereignty';[3] 'normative and political authority';[4] 'late sovereignty';[5] 'disguised

[1] I share the approach of Saskia Sassen, *Territory, Authority, Rights: From Medieval to Global Assemblages* (Princeton, Princeton University Press, 2008) 3, namely that 'we cannot understand the x (…) by confining our study to the characteristics of the x'.

[2] Anne Peters, 'Membership in the Global Constitutional Community' in Jan Klabbers, Anne Peters and Geir Ulfstein (eds), *The Constitutionalization of International Law* (Oxford, OUP, 2009) 208 et seq.

[3] Pierre Pescatore, *The Law of Integration* (New York, Springer, 1974) 29 et seq.

[4] Miguel Poiares Maduro, 'How Constitutional Can the European Union Be? The Tension Between Intergovernamentalism and Constitutionalism in the European Union' in Joseph Weiler and Christopher Eisgruber (eds), *Altneuland: The EU Constitution in a Contextual Perspective* (Jean Monnet Working Paper 5/04) 3.

[5] Neil Walker, 'Late Sovereignty in the European Union' in Neil Walker (ed), *Sovereignty in Transition* (Oxford, Hart Publishing, 2003).

claim to sovereignty';[6] 'European authority';[7] 'quasi-national authority';[8] 'supranational authority';[9] or simply 'authority of EU law'.[10] Whereas it is common ground to identify the authority claims of states as sovereignty, there is no agreement on the nature of the EU's authority claim.

As states have historically held the monopoly of expressing political authority claims proper, it is easy to see how the emerging authority claim of the EU led commentators to categorise it as sovereignty claim. But my argument so far indicates that sovereignty is best understood as an authority claim of nation states. I tried to show, moreover, that the very concept of authority is conceptually open to accommodate organisations and political communities beyond the state. The benefit of a closer scrutiny of the EU's authority claim according to the taxonomy of chapter one (means and institutions / territoriality / membership) is two-fold. The first is *analytical clarity*. A better understanding of the EU's authority claim helps to compare the (sometimes conflicting) authority claims of Member States, the EU and international law. For instance, does the EU's authority claim lend credibility to the claim that the EU could 'absorb and replace' states?[11] The second benefit is *normative salience*. The nature of the EU's authority claim informs us about its moral importance, ie which value it affects (individual autonomy or popular or state sovereignty?) and how intrusively it does so. In turn, the standard for evaluating the legitimacy of the EU's authority claim will have to deviate from the rich literature on state and international authority to the extent that the EU's authority claim differs from both. Put differently, answering the question under what conditions the EU has the authority it claims presupposes a thorough understanding of the claim itself.

This *normative* inquiry is of cardinal importance. For it indicates how this book departs from the familiar discussions of the EU's authority claim in relation to decision-making competences. Much ink has been spilt on the allocation of ultimate decision-making power (*Kompetenz-Kompetenz*) in the EU, bending and twisting the concept of sovereignty to accommodate the primacy of EU law and the alleged ultimate authority of the EU.[12] There is, however, only scarce

[6] Jan Willem van Rossem, 'The Autonomy of EU Law: More Is Less?' in Ramses Wessel and Steven Blockmans (eds), *Between Autonomy and Dependence* (The Hague, TMC Asser Press, 2013) 13.

[7] Karen Alter, *Establishing the Supremacy of European Law: The Making of an International Rule of Law in Europe* (Oxford, OUP, 2003) 32.

[8] Christina Eckes and Ramses Wessel, 'The European Union from an International Perspective Sovereignty, Statehood, and Special Treatment' in Takis Tridimas and Robert Schütze (eds), *The Oxford Principles of European Union Law – Volume 1: The European Union Legal Order* (Oxford, OUP, 2018) 89.

[9] Burkard Eberlein and Edgar Grande, 'Reconstituting Political Authority in Europe: Transnational Regulatory Networks and the Informalization of Governance in the European Union' in Edgar Grande and Louis Pauly (eds), *Complex Sovereignty: Reconstituting Political Authority in the Twenty-First Century* (Toronto, University of Toronto Press, 2017) 146.

[10] Damian Chalmers, Gareth Davies and Giorgio Monti, *European Union Law*, 4th edn (Cambridge, CUP, 2019) ch 5.

[11] Joseph Raz, 'Why the State?' in Nicole Roughan and Andrew Halpin (eds), *In Pursuit of Pluralist Jurisprudence* (Cambridge, CUP, 2017) 155.

[12] For a good overview see Matej Avbelj, 'Theorizing Sovereignty and European Integration: Sovereignty and European Integration' (2014) 27 *Ratio Juris* 344.

literature on the appropriate standard for evaluating and underpinning the EU's authority. The claim that this debate is important is not one shared by everyone, however. Eckes and Wessel take the opposite view in an urge to replace authority discussions with a focus on sovereignty:

> Hence, discussing 'authority' offers a convenient way out of the dilemma of how to square the EU's self-conception as a (quasi-) sovereign entity, which is regularly recognised in practice (…) with the basic structures of international law, as well as the national law of the Member States.[13]

This statement has some merit in criticising the literature for its lack of conceptual clarity and failure to engage with the nature of the EU's authority claim. Rarely is there a deeper inquiry into what the EU does in authority terms that goes beyond the above labels. And yet, I do not see how an authority lens 'does not capture the bottom-up or ascending legitimacy that lies as at the core of (popular) sovereignty'.[14] The very purpose of theories of authority is to explain how authority can be legitimate considering each citizen's autonomy and authorship over their lives, both individually and as a collective. To the contrary, it seems that loose talk of sovereignty leaves these fundamental moral questions aside by focusing on the allocation of decision-making powers alone.

III. Why the EU does not Claim Sovereign Authority

Sovereignty has served as *the* analytical lens of any political (primarily the state's) authority claim since the late Middle Ages. As the above list shows, various theorists argue that some form of sovereignty best describes the EU's authority claim. Nonetheless, it is conceptually flawed to argue that the EU claims sovereign authority.

Before expanding on the reasons for this categorical rejection, I want to pause for a moment to focus on the last point. The EU does not *claim* sovereign authority. It literally does not. No European institution *claims* that the EU is sovereign in the sense of articulating such a strong authority claim. And whenever individual national and EU leaders claim 'European sovereignty' outside institutional processes, they use the notion either in an aspirational sense or in a political and informal sense.[15] In fact, they use it exclusively in relation to the wider world externally – carefully avoiding the profound effects a sovereign EU would have

[13] Eckes and Wessel (n 8) 86.

[14] ibid.

[15] Antoine Bailleux, 'The Two Faces of European Sovereignty' (2020) 2020 5 *European Papers* 303, 305. See, eg, Donald Tusk, 'Keynote Speech' (Opening Ceremony of the 2019/2020 Academic Year at the College of Europe, Bruges, 13 November 2019), www.consilium.europa.eu/en/press/press-releases/2019/11/13/keynote-speech-by-president-donal-tusk-at-the-opening-ceremony-of-the-2019-2020-academic-year-at-the-college-of-europe: 'sovereign Europe'. Emmanuel Macron, 'Initiative Pour l'Europe' (Sorbonne, Paris, 26 September 2017), www.elysee.fr/declarations/article/initiative-pour-l-europe-discours-d-emmanuel-macron-pour-une-europe-souveraine-unie-democratique/: 'une Europe souveraine'.

on the realm of authority of Member States.[16] The same is true for the (hitherto) very few and recent appearances of EU sovereignty in institutional documents.[17] European sovereignty is thus a figure of speech, rather than a speech act.[18] That means Walker betrays his own analysis of sovereignty as a claim, as a speech act, when he posits that the EU claims 'late sovereignty'.[19] Speech act theory tells us that words matter, ie that sovereignty is destined to convey a certain normative ideal entrenched in the tradition of political theory. Searle describes this as an 'illocutionary act', intending to achieve a change in the normative position of the addressee by the very speech act itself.[20] In other words, part and parcel of what it means to have sovereign status as a polity is to claim sovereignty in the first place. The EU does not do that.

We will now look at what the other reasons against the use of sovereignty in relation to the EU's authority claim are.

A. Authority and Political Power

One of the crucial points of contact between theories of authority and of sovereignty is political power. By political power, I mean the actual capacity of political institutions to enforce and impose compliance with the given laws (mainly through police and military). For two reasons, the EU's authority claim lacks an intricate relationship to political power.

To start with, the state's monopoly of the legitimate use of force and its accompanying capacity to effectively uphold the authority over its territory is built into the very concept of sovereignty. Both internally and externally, the state has the factual means to uphold its authority claim, ie to enforce compliance through, ultimately, coercion. It disciplines recalcitrant citizens on the inside (using mainly the police) and holds off threats from external actors (using mainly the military). In other words, since states claim to uphold public order, the effective operation of the monopoly of the legitimate use of force must be seen as part of their de facto authority, without which there can be no *legitimate* authority.

The EU can't back up its authority claim with the threat to enforce its laws using force. But it also doesn't claim the monopoly of legitimate force.[21] It entirely

[16] See Thomas Verellen, 'European Sovereignty Now? A Reflection on What It Means to Speak of "European Sovereignty"' (2020) 2020 5 *European Papers* 307, 316 et seq.

[17] See, eg, Commission, *Communication, Secure 5G Deployment in the EU: Implementing the EU Toolbox* (COM(2020) 50 final). European Council, Presidency Conclusions, Brussels, 2.10.2020, Nos. 6, 7.

[18] Ségolène Barbou Des Places, 'Taking the Language of "European Sovereignty" Seriously' (2020) 5 *European Papers* 287, 292.

[19] Walker (n 5) 19 et seq.

[20] John Searle, *Speech Acts: An Essay in the Philosophy of Language* (Cambridge, CUP, 1969) ch 2.

[21] See only Erik Oddvar Eriksen, *The Normativity of the European Union* (London, Palgrave Macmillan, 2014) 95. This obvious fact is often downplayed in authority-related EU-US comparisons. *cf* only Robert Schütze, *European Constitutional Law*, 2nd edn (Cambridge, CUP, 2016) ch 2.

lacks any element of political sovereignty.[22] As we saw in chapter one, political power is intrinsically related to sovereignty, but political power is not a necessary element of authority claims as such. The EU's enforcement portfolio admittedly includes legal sanctions, such as the execution of its laws in national courts, as well as remedies for a failure to do so; financial sanctions (eg the imposition of fines in competition law; or Art 260 of the Treaty on the Functioning of the European Union (TFEU)); and even the loss of voting rights for Member States (Art 7(3) TEU). Since the purpose and mandate of the EU is not to maintain public order however (see Art 72 TFEU), there is simply no need for a police unit to enforce the body of EU law 'on the street', ie outside law-administering authorities like courts and administrations. The *judicial* enforcement of the EU's legal norms suffices. The same is true externally: there is no EU army and the EU's normative architecture doesn't require one.[23] The lack of coercion should thus not be portrayed as deficiency of the EU. Without this basis in and link to political power, we shouldn't express any jurisdictional or legal autonomy in terms of sovereignty.[24] In essence, the authority of the EU hinges on the respect for and efficacy of its 'community of law' alone.[25] This crucial insight also applies in relation to the wider world. There, Bradford has described the 'Brussels-effect', ie how the EU's regulatory standard has a global pull effect and often demands compliance from third-states and private operators.[26] In short, the EU's authority claim lacks any meaningful connection to political power, an intrinsic element of sovereignty.

The EU's institutional architecture downplays another crucial element of sovereign authority, to which institution-centred justifications of political authority at the state level draw ever more attention. I refer to an open political debate about values, policies and the fundamental coordinates of the respective society that underlies and thereby legitimises the democratic state and its decision-making procedures.[27] The EU differs in two important ways. First, in contrast to the state's a priori unconstrained competence to regulate any substantive area, the EU's

[22] But *cf* Gunnar Beck, 'The EU Constitution, Sovereignty and the Problem of Primacy' in Nicholas Barber, Maria Cahill and Richard Ekins (eds), *The Rise and Fall of the European Constitution* (Oxford, Hart Publishing, 2019) 158. He describes EU ultra vires acts as manifestations of political sovereignty in a (Carl) Schmittian sense.

[23] Though it would, in my view, be compatible with an army that pays attention to the EU's theoretical *Gestalt*. See Josef Weinzierl, 'An Army of Peoples? A Demoicratic Perspective on a Future European Army' (2021) 6 *European Papers* 1049.

[24] But see Christina Eckes, 'EU Autonomy: Jurisdictional Sovereignty by a Different Name?' (2020) 5 *European Papers* 319.

[25] Neil Walker, 'The Place of European Law' in Gráinne De Búrca and Joseph Weiler (eds), *The Worlds of European Constitutionalism* (Cambridge, CUP, 2012) 96; Armin von Bogdandy, 'Founding Principles' in Armin von Bogdandy and Jürgen Bast (eds), *Principles of European Constitutional Law*, 2nd edn (Oxford, Hart/Beck, 2010) 30.

[26] Anu Bradford, *The Brussels Effect: How the European Union Rules the World* (Oxford, OUP, 2020).

[27] Jeremy Waldron, *Law and Disagreement* (Oxford, Clarendon, 1999) 99 et seq. Similarly Christopher Wellman, 'Toward a Liberal Theory of Political Obligation' (2001) 111 *Ethics* 735; David Lefkowitz, 'A Contractualist Defense of Democratic Authority' (2005) 18 *Ratio Juris* 346. Scott Hershovitz, 'Legitimacy, Democracy, and Razian Authority' (2003) 9 *Legal Theory* 201.

competences are limited. The conceptual point is that in the EU, debates about regulatory actions are constrained by the scope of EU law. Second, the 'integration through law' paradigm in EU law tips the scale further away from politics (production) towards law (product). Compared to law-making procedures in a state, EU law-making is over-constitutionalised and under-politicised at a foundational level. The substantial reconfiguration of political and legal elements changes the nature of the EU's authority claim.

Summing up, sovereignty combines legal and political components in a special and balanced way. In contrast, the EU's authority claim lacks (for it does not need) the underlying political power associated with the monopoly of force as a core element of sovereignty. The EU Treaties, moreover, do not allow for a substantively unconstrained political debate. These features in the configuration of law and politics mark a qualitative difference between the nature of sovereign state authority and EU authority.

B. Of Distinct Hierarchies

Let's turn to the different conceptions of hierarchy between the EU and sovereign states. Inquiries into the EU's authority claim rarely go beyond primacy, the ECJ's 'new legal order' dogma, and the relation to sovereignty. Here we see a similar trend to conceptualise primacy in terms of sovereignty. Only very recently, Verellen argued: 'In the EU, then, primacy can plausibly be reformulated as a weak claim to internal sovereignty'.[28]

This framing is a conceptual mistake. I agree that primacy implies a demanding authority claim over the legal systems of the Member States. For one, it operates as a conflict-resolution tool and sets aside conflicting national law, which is rendered inapplicable (not invalid!) within the scope of EU law.[29] Primacy moreover encompasses an autonomy-driven element, meaning that EU law doesn't allow standards of national (even constitutional) law to dispute its validity.[30] Finally, primacy has an institutional component which the Court employs to strengthen its own role in the preliminary reference procedure (Art 267 TFEU). For example, on the one hand, *Foto Frost* established the monopoly of the ECJ to invalidate EU law. *Achmea*, on the other, exemplifies the Court's monopoly of the binding interpretation of any EU law.[31] Taken together, primacy as constructed by the ECJ represents the metaphorical knight who uses sword and shield to protect the normative integrity of the EU legal order.

[28] Verellen (n 16) 313. See also the discussion in Nicholas Barber, *The Constitutional State* (Oxford, OUP, 2010) ch 10; Nicholas Barber, *The Principles of Constitutionalism* (Oxford, OUP, 2018) 48.

[29] See only Case C-106/77 *Amministratione delle finanze dello Stato v Simmenthal* EU:C:1978:49; Case C-198/01 *CIG* EU:C:2003:430, para 48; Case C-614/14 *Ognyanov* EU:C:2016:514.

[30] Case C-11/70 *Internationale Handelsgesellschaft* EU:C:1970:114; Case C-273/15 *Ezernieki* EU:C:2016:364, para 53; Case C-201/15 *AGET Iraklis* EU:C:2016:972, paras 105 et seq.

[31] Case C-314/85 *Foto Frost* EU:C:1987:452, para 15; Case C-284/16 *Achmea* EU:C:2018:158, para 37.

Indeed, primacy serves as a *functional* equivalent to the *legal* component of sovereignty by representing the EU's version of how the legal orders interrelate.[32] That does not, however, mean that the EU claims sovereignty. The fact that the two tools fulfil similar functions does not make them identical. Limited functional equivalence does not necessarily imply the applicability of the same concept.

In addition, sovereignty entails a hierarchy of norms that includes the capacity of higher norms to *invalidate* lower norms. By contrast, the primacy of EU law does not create such a hierarchy since conflicting national law is (merely) declared inapplicable *in the scope of EU law*. For that reason, terminology like 'legal monism' is misguided since it suggests such an unqualified top-down hierarchy at the EU level.[33] Well beyond the important principle of conferral (Art 5 TEU), no element of the EU's authority claim can be understood without the serious engagement and sometimes critical input from national institutions. Most importantly, national courts ensure the full application of EU law and administer it in their daily practice.[34] The implication for our purposes is that EU law does not claim to establish a sovereign hierarchy of norms.[35] It is thus mistaken to suggest that 'the Union does claim to be the supreme authority within its territory'.[36]

The above qualifier *in the scope of EU law* makes plain that EU law does not constitute the highest law of the land in the EU territory. In contrast to national constitutions, EU law does not claim the right to determine or even extend to every single regulatory aspect that appears under God's European sun. EU law has limits.[37] The EU has limits and often depends on national institutions for enforcing its laws. True, hard red lines for the outer limits of the scope of EU law quickly fade when examined in their practical environment of functional competences and the wide reach especially of negative integration. The theoretical point remains, however: EU law has tangible limits and – unlike states – does not claim universal authority in its territory.[38] In essence, primacy represents a (limited) functional equivalent – but, crucially, a conceptual *aliud* to the legal component of sovereignty.

[32] I assume this is what Peters (n 2) 208 et seq means in the external realm by 'autonomy as a proxy for sovereignty'.

[33] In more detail, see Pavlos Eleftheriadis, *A Union of Peoples* (Oxford, OUP, 2020) ch 4. But see Mattias Kumm, 'Rethinking Constitutional Authority: On the Structure and Limits of Constitutional Pluralism' in Matej Avbelj and Jan Komárek (eds), *Constitutional Pluralism in the European Union and Beyond* (Oxford, Hart Publishing, 2012) 43 et seq.

[34] See only Case C-430/21 *RS* ECLI:EU:2022:99, para 39.

[35] See also Julio Baquero Cruz, *What's Left of the Law of Integration?: Decay and Resistance in European Union Law* (Oxford, OUP, 2018) 45. But *cf* Walker (n 5) 21.

[36] Barber, *The Constitutional State* (n 28) 179.

[37] Similarly Turkuler Isiksel, 'Constitutionalism as Limitation and Licence' in Tom Ginsburg, Mark D Rosen and Georg Vanberg (eds), *Constitutions in Times of Financial Crisis* (Cambridge, CUP, 2019) 19 et seq. See also recent developments in the case law on purely internal situations, the very existence of which proves my point. Case C-497/12 *Gullotta* EU:C:2015:168, Opinion of AG Wahl, paras 30 et seq.

[38] Kaarlo Tuori, *European Constitutionalism* (Cambridge, CUP, 2017) 319.

C. Membership and Territory Beyond the State

Theorising about the EU often encounters the following issue: since various notions for conceptualising the EU piggyback on and imitate their national counterparts, their usage invites confusion. The concepts sound familiar, but their content often is not. I can illustrate what I mean by taking a closer look at the notions of citizenship and territoriality.

EU membership for citizens does not amount to an exclusive political relationship that grants essential rights in and against the supranational polity itself in exchange for imposing heavy burdens on the subject. The EU does not constrain individual autonomy as such. Instead, it mostly grants rights against other states and against your home state. The disruptive character of EU citizenship, in a nutshell, stems from the observation that it facilitates transnational integration and extends the political space for EU citizens horizontally.[39] A visual illustration might help to grasp this disruptive potential:

Fig 6 The EU Citizen's Normative Relationships

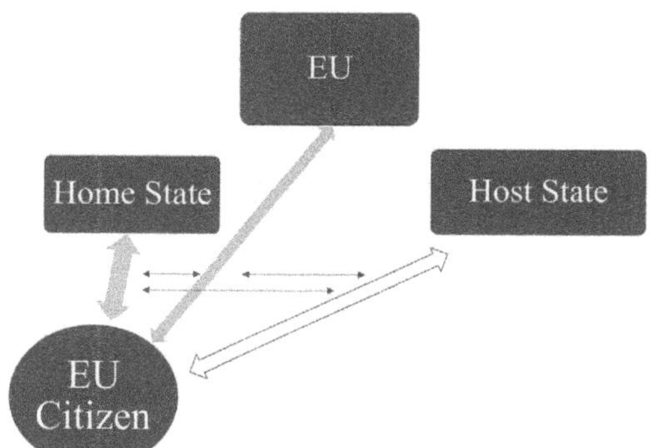

While EU citizenship thus mainly plays out transnationally, the link between the EU citizen and the host state is the only contingent one (transparent arrow). In other words, it is optional and needs activation through movement. By contrast, the home state link (thick vertical arrow) is necessary to gain EU citizenship in the first place, and the status in the EU polity is parasitic yet automatic (thin diagonal arrow). These individual bonds between the EU citizen and the political communities interact and often create tensions (horizontal arrows). A direct relationship between the EU and 'its' citizens thus not necessarily enhances the legitimacy and authority of the European project. On the contrary, the EU's authority claim seemingly creates a legitimacy problem by cutting into the

[39] Päivi Johanna Neuvonen, *Equal Citizenship and Its Limits in EU Law: We the Burden?* (Oxford, Hart Publishing, 2016) 36.

state-citizen nexus and by granting rights to the citizen in question without necessarily providing a justificatory compensation beyond rights-individualism at the supranational level.[40] The EU establishes a membership status in a qualitatively distinct supranational polity, which facilitates access to and integration into the combined territory of the Member States of the EU. EU citizenship thus escapes the bilateral logic of dual citizenship. It is less intrusive than dual citizenship, since its status as an addition to national citizenship differs from the zero-sum game between competing states (with ensuing questions of military conscription, handing on citizenship, etc).

Second, in relation to territoriality, think only about *secession* – the prevention of which constitutes one paradigmatic manifestation of the territory- and membership-related aspects of state sovereignty.[41] Things could not be more different in the EU. Any Member State has an absolute and unconditional right to leave the EU according to Art 50 TEU, which corroborates its sovereign status. The EU's lack of control over its members (and consequently over its territory) excludes the attribution of sovereignty.[42] While leaving the EU is never easy – the messy business of Brexit testifies to that – the conceptual point remains: it is possible.

So, the EU doesn't claim sovereign authority. A final step is missing, however. Students of EU federalism are aware that the remarkable development of the EU revived the old idea of divided sovereignty.[43] Let me offer my scepticism about describing the EU's authority claim in terms of divided sovereignty.

D. Some Doubts about Divided Sovereignty

What does divided sovereignty mean? Unsurprisingly, this notion proves almost as elusive as sovereignty itself.[44] As a lowest common denominator, divided sovereignty must allow each composite entity of a federal polity to claim and exercise ultimate authority within its sphere of competences. Political theorists

[40] Joseph Weiler, 'Van Gend En Loos: The Individual as Subject and Object and the Dilemma of European Legitimacy' (2014) 25 *European Journal of International Law* 83, 94, 99; Neuvonen, ibid, 38.

[41] For a famous judicial treatment, see Canadian Supreme Court, Reference re Secession of Quebec [1998] 2 SCR 217, 1998 CanLII 793. For a philosophical study see David Lefkowitz, 'On the Foundation of Rights to Political Self-Determination: Secession, Nonintervention, and Democratic Governance' (2008) 39 *Journal of Social Philosophy* 492.

[42] But *cf* Jean-Victor Louis, *The Community Legal Order*, 2nd end (EC Official Publications, 1993) 14.

[43] John Temple-Lang, 'Chapter VII – The Draft Treaty Establishing the European Union and the Member States: Ireland' in Roland Bieber, Jean-Paul Jacqué and Joseph Weiler (eds), *An Ever Closer Union: A Critical Analysis of the Draft Treaty Establishing the European Union* (Office for Official Publications of the European Communities; European University Institute, 1985) 247: 'Sovereignty is a bundle of powers, and so it is divisible. In the Community it is divided between the MS and the Community itself'.

[44] For an overview see Daniela Obradovic, 'Community Law and the Doctrine of Divisible Sovereignty' (1993) 20 *Legal Issues of Economic Integration* 1.

are overwhelmingly sceptical about the very possibility of divided sovereignty, because ultimate authority denotes a sense of hierarchy that only leaves room for one sovereign on a given territory.[45] I share this scepticism, since this book understands sovereignty as the state's comprehensive claim to ultimate authority over a given territory and the accompanying powers and efforts to make good on that claim (chapter one, section V.A).

Even if – for the sake of argument – one accepts the general possibility of divided sovereignty, the EU's idiosyncratic normative architecture escapes its conceptual realm.[46] First, consider speech act theory (already consulted above), where many have pointed out that not even the ECJ claimed divided sovereignty between the Member States and the EU.[47] The Court in *van Gend* and *Costa* declared a 'limitation of sovereign rights' or a 'limitation of sovereignty', as well as a 'transfer of powers', but not a 'transfer of sovereignty' to the then Community. The terminological difference is important and often ignored.[48] But the Court thereby implicitly acknowledges that not even the far reaching 'new legal order' amounts to a divided sovereignty claim.

Second, the concept of divided sovereignty – as its earliest defender Waitz explained in relation to the nineteenth century German *Reich* – limits the *scope* but not the *content* of each level's sovereignty.[49] It requires a true *Bundesstaat*, ie that neither of the regulatory levels, which supposedly divide sovereignty between them, can depend on the institutions or even funding of the other level; and that – ultimately – the citizen stands in the same relationship to each divided sovereign. None of this applies to the EU, whose capacity to rely on national institutions to enforce its law, combined with the absence of the use of force to do so itself define its authority claim. And so does the qualitatively different relationship a citizen has to their home state on the one hand, and to the EU on the other.

Again, the theoretical leap from observing institutional expressions of a composite architecture of political authority in a non-unitary polity, to concluding that it *therefore* constitutes an instance of divided sovereignty is a leap too far. I thus find it hard to understand why Schütze insists on positioning the EU in the tradition of divided sovereignty, since that only undermines his admirable attempt to take the specific federalism of the EU out of its historical straitjacket of sovereignty.[50] The EU's authority claim, in my view, is no manifestation of divided sovereignty.

[45] For a summary of the arguments see Stefan Oeter, 'Federalism and Democracy' in von Bogdandy and Bast (n 25) 63 et seq.

[46] Similarly, though for different reasons Obradovic (n 44) 10–14, 17; Dieter Grimm, *Sovereignty: The Origin and Future of a Political and Legal Concept* (New York, Columbia University Press, 2015) ch 5.

[47] See only van Rossem (n 6) n 59.

[48] For example Louis (n 42) 11 et seq; Obradovic (n 44) 7; Grimm (n 46) 113.

[49] Georg Waitz, 'Das Wesen Des Bundesstaats', *Grundzüge der Politik* (Nürnberg, Homann, 1862) 166 et seq.

[50] Schütze (n 21) 73.

E. Interim Conclusion

To portray the EU's authority claim in terms of sovereignty has no explanatory value. It either misrepresents the content of the EU's authority claim, or the concept of (divided) sovereignty beyond recognition.[51] Put differently, such attempts suffer from the mimetic bias to seek at the supranational level what the EU seems to take away from the national level. But the helpful analysis of sovereignty as a communicative framework for statist political authority is not distorted if we accept that the EU's supranational authority claim participates in this representation and communication, while it cannot and should not be subsumed under the conceptual heading of sovereignty. It helps analytical clarity a great deal to disassociate sovereignty from authority claims on other regulatory levels.

Let me move on to explain what distinguishes the EU's authority claim from international authority.

IV. Why the EU does not Claim International Authority

The ongoing solidification of international law prompts scholars to question the assumption that political relationships above the state level represent a system of anarchy.[52] This has resulted in the emerging discussion about instances of international authority mentioned in chapter one. Do I make things more complicated than they are? Does the EU not constitute an – albeit sophisticated – international organisation, which situates its authority comfortably in the international realm? My aim from the outset was to depart from what the EU claims and does in practice, rather than from familiar labels such as international/constitutional/(con-)federal in interpreting the EU's authority claim. The conceptual lens through which I chose to study authority claims enables me to point to important differences between international authority claims and the EU.

A. On Mandates and Means of Authority

EU law and international law differ in the degree of exclusiveness of their mandate. International law is creatively fractured. It consists of a plethora of

[51] Similarly Bailleux (n 15) 303 et seq. For a recent example of the latter see Matej Avbelj, 'A Sovereign Europe as a Future of Sovereignty' (2020) 5 *European Papers* 299. See, generally, for advice to avoid these fallacies in political theory, Joseph Lacey, 'Conceptually Mapping the European Union: A Demoi-Cratic Analysis' (2016) 38 *Journal of European Integration* 61, 62.

[52] See only David A Lake, 'Rightful Rules: Authority, Order, and the Foundations of Global Governance' (2010) 54 *International Studies Quarterly* 587, 587.

individual organisations which often overlap in their mandate. Take the well-known example of international trade, where the WTO, the OECD, and many regional and bilateral trade agreements plough through the field side by side. For that reason, Sand rightly doubts whether the entirety of international law is capable of being evaluated by recourse to one single normative standard.[53] Compare that to the 'autonomy of EU law', which defines EU law as a self-sufficient normative framework, excluding unilateral alterations by other legal regimes, be they national or international. This idea of 'autonomy' conveys the claim that the EU legal order is self-referential, meaning that it excludes the possibility for international law to call into question the validity of or impose an external interpretation of EU law on the Union.[54] Neither Member States nor other international organisations may legitimately act within the scope of EU law. According to the ECJ, it is part of 'the very nature of EU law, which … requires that relations between the Member States be governed by EU law to the exclusion, if EU law so requires, of any other law'.[55] The validity and interpretation of EU law ought to be assessed exclusively against review standards internal to the EU legal order. Since we already saw above how the notion *scope of EU law* confirms the limited, non-sovereign character of the EU's architecture, we now see that it distinguishes the EU's authority claim from both state sovereignty and international authority.

The polity-formation via membership contributes moreover to a non-fragmented, coherent political community. The complex web of citizen, state and people as 'members' distinguishes the EU from international organisations: Because EU law mostly obligates the collective as such (EU peoples), citizens qua citizens gain more rights than duties through EU membership. Moreover, Member State relations are the catalyst for the moral relations of peoples when we, for example, counterbalance free movement with extradition of criminals, or internal freedom with external borders. According to the ECJ, mutual trust between Member States is based on the premise that every Member State complies with the values of Art 2 TEU.[56] Mutual trust among the Member State officials thus serves to facilitate the joint government of their peoples. We can illustrate these findings in the following way:[57]

[53] Inger-Johanne Sand, 'Varieties of Authority in International Law' in Patrick Capps and Henrik Palmer Olsen (eds), *Legal Authority Beyond the State* (Cambridge, CUP, 2018) 169.

[54] For eg in relation to the WTO (Opinion 1/94 *WTO Accession* EU:C:1994:384), to the ECHR (Opinion 2/13 *Accession to the ECHR* EU:C:2014:2454) and to Investment Treaties (*Achmea* (n 31)); Opinion 1/17 *CETA* EU:C:2019:34.

[55] Opinion 2/13 (n 54) para 212.

[56] Case C-156/21 *Hungary v Parliament and Council* ECLI:EU:2022:97, paras 125, 129.

[57] For a similar reflection on many of these relations, see Pavlos Eleftheriadis, 'The Idea of a European Constitution' (2007) 27 *OJLS* 1.

Fig 7 The Legal Manifestations of the EU's Authority Claim

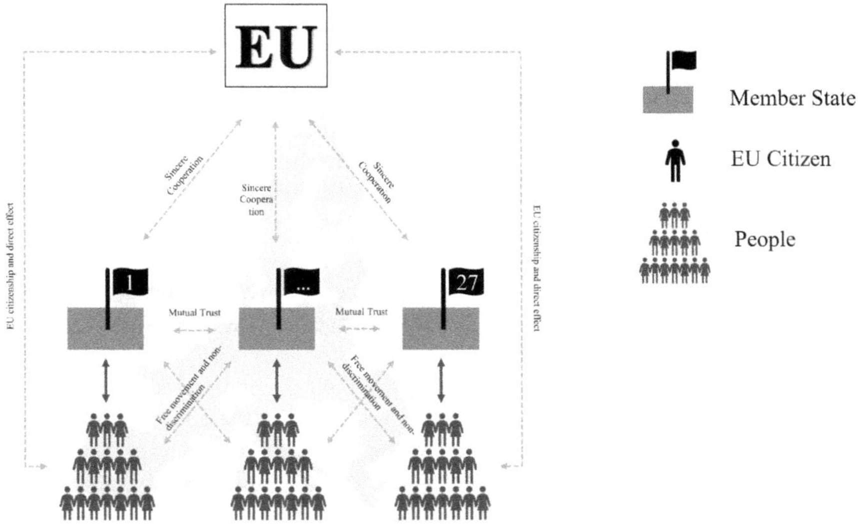

Figure 7 shows the complex web of legal duties and authority relations in the EU's governance structure, annotated with a few of the notions integral to EU law. The EU exercises political authority through creating and maintaining these individual relationships. Its character is thus far from a bilateral, top-down arrangement between polity and citizens well-known from the state level. In its place, we find a complex interplay of meaningful vertical, horizontal and diagonal political relationships among the EU and its citizens, Member States and peoples.

There is no such political community in any meaningful sense in an international organisation. In addition, the difference between being inside and outside the EU is striking. As I explain elsewhere in more detail, it has a huge normative impact that leads to a distinct understanding of territoriality.[58] One fundamental difference between international organisations and the EU is that the latter has a place and that it differentiates between insiders and outsiders. The recent discussions about Frontex as well as the pivotal role of the EU's borders in regulating migration underline this finding.

Recall, finally, the means to exercise authority discussed in chapter one. The exercise of political authority through binding and enforceable law remains, in international law, the exception to the rule. Most of the rules on the international

[58] Josef Weinzierl, 'Territoriality beyond the State: The EU's Territorial Claims and the Search for Their Legitimacy' (2021) 22 *German Law Journal* 650.

level are soft-law, such as commitments and standards, and international law's compliance mechanisms are often legally non-binding.[59] Even some of the most sophisticated international legal authorities, like the WTO, do not have an independent standing judiciary and must have recourse to exclusively international enforcement mechanisms.[60] Importantly for theories of authority, international law does not impose the same or even a similar type of duty on those it addresses (in my view, states). The discussion in chapter one showed that the moral duties international law imposes on state officials come in various forms, such as obedience, respect, deference and rebuttal – all of which differ conceptually from a citizen's political obligation.[61]

In contrast to these variegated institutions, the authority of the EU is not only based on law but also exercised and enforced through law. The EU's authority claim marks a qualitative and quantitative difference, even to instances where international institutions emancipate themselves from their original mandate and claim a certain authority over its founders.[62] This results from the combination of the following features: (i) the enforcement of EU law on the national level by national (!) courts; (ii) the supranationalisation of decision-making powers traditionally left to states (the status of EU law (primacy) and its invocability (direct effect)); and (iii) the breadth and scope of EU law.

In addition to these characteristics, EU law presents itself as a 'seamless-web' invokable by individuals in national courts. The EU puts national legal orders in the service of EU law as it expects them to adapt not only the handling of entrenched legal concepts – such as limitation periods and remedies for breach of contract – but also their individual legal cultures as a whole and, indeed, their constitutions.[63] Any legal and moral duties stemming from these features relate to the EU in its entirety. The EU accordingly maintains a coherent and complete set of law-administering institutions, rather than a narrow, functional and non-exclusive mandate on the international plane. These elements corroborate the qualitative difference in scope and force between the authority claims of international organisations and of the EU.

These reflections explain why I reject Tasioulas' argument according to which the fact that international law is law means that it enjoys the same legitimacy as

[59] See in more detail, Jutta Brunnée and Stephen J Toope, *Legitimacy and Legality in International Law: An Interactional Account* (Cambridge, CUP, 2010) 108 et seq.

[60] Those who do, such as the International Court of Justice (ICJ) or the ICC, depend on the actual and continuous consent of the concerned Member State. For a discussion of the authority of the WTO *cf* Lake (n 52) 602 et seq.

[61] Similarly Andreas Follesdal, 'The Legitimate Authority of International Courts and Its Limits' in Patrick Capps and Henrik Palmer Olsen (eds), *Legal Authority beyond the State* (Cambridge, CUP, 2018) 192.

[62] Mikael Madsen, 'Bolstering Authority by Enhancing Communication : How Checks and Balances and Feedback Loops Can Strengthen the Authority of the European Court of Human Rights' in Joana Mendes and Ingo Venzke (eds), *Who Should do What in European and International Law?* (Oxford, Hart Publishing, 2018).

[63] Eriksen (n 21) 90 et seq.

national law (since any law claims the same authority by virtue of its nature, by virtue of being law).[64] I accept the premise that international law is law, but not the conclusion. The reason I distinguish between the authority claim of the state, of international law, and of the EU is not only analytical clarity. Authority is, both etymologically (from the Latin origin *auctoritas*: 'author'), and in terms of its legitimacy inseparable from its respective author and institutional legal system. Political authority is concerned with the status of the respective legal regime in its entirety, which – *pace* Tasioulas – is not 'invariable'. Otherwise, the *Codex Juris Canonici* (the law of the Catholic Church), or any national sports federation's statutes *qua law*, would enjoy the same status and legitimate authority as any national criminal law code: because they are law. The idea that law *qua* law necessarily claims the same authority/legitimacy would moreover leave no room for the conflicting authority claims in Europe since the claims on both levels are based on law. No-one argues that the mutually incompatible claims of the ECJ on the one hand, and the national constitutional courts on the other, rely on identical legitimation strategies because they are law-based. A crucial argument this book makes is that just as the nature of authority claimed and exercised differs on various levels, so does the appropriate standard for its respective normative legitimacy.

Recent scholarly emphasis on the relational character of authority, ie its expression of a distinct normative relationship between authority and subject, reveals yet another distinguishing factor between the EU's and international authority claim: the main addressee.

B. Identifying the Addressee

A crucial part of understanding authority claims on different regulatory levels is identifying their main addressee. There is no doubt that the overwhelming majority of international law scholarship, as well as the practice of international law, works under the assumption that international law is law among ('inter') nations ('national'), ie among states.[65] While I agree that international law addresses and obligates states, this view is not accepted by everyone.

Besson's rich account of international authority urges us to 'lift the state veil' and realise that individual citizens are self-standing subjects of international law. In her view, individuals constitute the ultimate reference points for duties on states who merely represent these individuals. In my understanding, her argument is that: (i) a service conception of authority presupposes a valuable autonomy of the

[64] John Tasioulas, 'The Legitimacy of International Law' in John Tasioulas and Samantha Besson (eds), *The Philosophy of International Law* (Oxford, OUP, 2010) pt I.

[65] See only Thomas Christiano, 'The Legitimacy of International Institutions' in Andrei Marmor (ed), *The Routledge Companion to Philosophy of Law* (Abingdon, Routledge, 2012) 380.

agent whom the authority claim addresses; (ii) this autonomy is unique to human individuals and not applicable to state sovereignty/autonomy; and (iii) it follows that international law ultimately binds state officials as proxy subjects of their autonomous citizens, not as self-standing subjects of international law.[66]

I find it difficult to accept any of the steps of this argument. As will become clearer in chapter four, despite Raz's impressive intellectual achievement of providing a universal account of theoretical and practical authority, the service conception is most vulnerable when explaining authority in the public realm.[67] That renders it a problematic candidate to assess international authority in the first place. While I agree that individual autonomy is conceptually as well as morally distinct from state sovereignty, the moral intuition underlying this distinction reinforces the point that authority over individuals cannot be explained by the same structure as authority over states. It seems to overshoot the mark to posit that the state's autonomy has no independent, even instrumental value and needs to be erased from the equation to give way to the individual citizen. Finally, I cannot see how international law binds states only as proxy subjects. For example, international tribunals do not usually grant legal standing to individuals, but only solve disputes between states, because – in general – they do not exercise authority over individuals. I believe that Besson's example of the duty to prevent genocide is not representative for international law and its authority claim but constitutes an exception. Finally, I have difficulty in understanding how the mere transposition of international law into domestic law, as well as the fact that contributions to international organisations bind resources affect 'the balance of a citizen's reasoning'.[68] In other words, it seems to have little basis in social reality to legitimise a duty of individuals to obey international law, if international law for the most part does not obligate individuals.[69] International law obligates states. The few cases where it imposes direct duties on individuals cannot be the benchmarks for its authority.

Since this chapter is not about providing a self-standing account of international authority, let this suffice to indicate my scepticism about giving up the traditional focus of international law on states as agents distinct from the represented citizens. It would, nonetheless, be a mistake to think of this as an infant disease – a flaw that needs to be overcome. The authority of international law differs from national (and in my view the EU's) authority because it serves a different function.

[66] Samantha Besson, 'The Authority of International Law: Lifting the State Veil' (2009) 31 *Sydney Law Review* 343, 364. More concisely also in Samantha Besson, 'Sovereignty, International Law and Democracy' (2011) 22 *European Journal of International Law* 373.

[67] Especially because it has nothing to say on the role and value of institutions. See Andrei Marmor, 'The Dilemma of Authority' (2011) 2 *Jurisprudence* 121, 133.

[68] But *cf* Besson, 'The Authority of International Law' (n 66) 364.

[69] Başak Cali, *The Authority of International Law: Obedience, Respect, and Rebuttal* (Oxford, OUP, 2015) 44 et seq explains why political philosophers tend to focus on individual autonomy in discussions of international law.

C. Interim Conclusion

In its central case, international law's primary subjects are states, not individual humans. International law is organised in a fragmented web of international organisations with purely functional, often overlapping mandates. Moreover, international organisations overwhelmingly do not use enforceable legal norms, but resort to soft law and persuasion. I am not saying there are no exceptions, only that these cannot underwrite an account of the legitimate authority of international law.

The EU, in contrast, addresses both states and citizens directly, and it does so with binding laws that are enforced in a curious mix of national and supranational institutional cooperation. Notions of membership and territoriality construct an inside-outside distinction mostly irrelevant in international organisations. Finally, the autonomy of its legal system claims a normative self-determination towards both national and international law that is alien to international law. The EU's authority claim, in sum, differs qualitatively from international law. In short, 'International Law can neither explain nor legitimate the reality of Community life'.[70]

In the remainder of this chapter, I will provide my constructive interpretation of the EU's authority claim as 'Authority claim over peoples'. I will also offer an explanation of the relationship between peoples, citizens and state officials in the EU's normative architecture, and describe whom the EU's authority claim addresses: the constitutional peoples of Europe.

Before doing that, this seems a good place to remember the sceptics of chapter one, according to whom the nature of the constitutional state makes authority beyond the state a theoretical impossibility. According to writers from Loughlin to Majone, sovereignty and political authority are both confined to the national level, while the EU constitutes a form of non-authority related joint government. For them, the EU and international law in general lack the capacity for political authority. Consequently, the constitutional state remains the sole repository of authority in the public domain.

The above inquiry suggests that these views are mistaken. I agree with Wilkinson that they misrepresent the normative reality by downplaying the transformations brought about by the EU.[71] To deny that the EU claims a distinct kind of authority, you would not only have to portray the institutional arrangements in the EU as mere quantitative – not qualitative – difference to international law and reject that the concept of membership has any meaning apart from the relationship between the EU and the Member State institutions. It would also require

[70] Joseph Weiler, *The Constitution of Europe: 'Do the New Clothes Have an Emperor?' And Other Essays on European Integration* (Cambridge, CUP, 1999) 336.

[71] Michael Wilkinson, 'Constitutional Pluralism: Chronicle of a Death Foretold?' (2017) 23 *European Law Journal* 213, 222 et seq.

you to downplay the transformational effect of autonomy, primacy and direct effect as structural principles of how EU law relates to other legal regimes, as well as to argue that the scope and breadth of EU law don't alter the nature of the EU's authority claim.

The language of authority is appropriate because the authority exercised through EU law involves the claim to moral rightfulness. This claim demands a form of political obligation, ie moral duty to obey, on the part of the various addressees.[72] By avoiding the language of authority, we would ignore the questions this raises for the legitimate authority of the EU. We could do that, but I think we shouldn't.

V. An Authority Claim Over Peoples

Long gone is the overall rather short period when the relationship between state and citizen constituted the only meaningful political bond. Of course, on the national level, we are still subject to the state's authority as individual citizen and, simultaneously, as member of the respective national people. In addition to ever-expanding international law, however, the emerging picture in present-day Europe represents a complex matrix of vertical, horizontal and diagonal relations among a variety of actors. The EU does not address individuals as unmediated members of the EU polity, because there is no single European (constitutional) demos, understood as a 'group of human individuals engaged in generally binding collective action through common institutional practices'.[73] Instead, the EU's supranational authority claim essentially hovers between national and international authority.[74] In my view, the best way to construct the EU's authority claim is in relation to the peoples of Europe as ultimate addressees. They remain distinct but open their communities to each other to accept European standards of legality instead of their idiosyncratic national standards. They mutually recognise each other's policy choices and together form part of this supranational and transnational institutional framework. Put differently, the supranational authority claim is the result of the commitment of the EU peoples to institutionally binding collaboration. The EU claims a right to rule over the peoples of Europe as such, as well as in their more day-to-day manifestations and roles as citizens and Member State institutions/officials.

We will only be able to fully grasp this dual role of the peoples as source and subjects of the EU's authority at the end of chapter five, but the findings so far allow me to explain the role of the European peoples as ultimate addressees of the EU's

[72] Similarly Eriksen (n 21) 87.

[73] Francis Cheneval, *The Government Of The Peoples: On The Idea And Principles Of Multilateral Democracy* (London, Palgrave Macmillan, 2011) 57.

[74] Similarly Walker (n 25) 60.

authority. Let me start by focusing on the moral value that the EU's authority claim affects: popular self-determination.

A. The EU's Authority Claim and Popular Self-Determination

Claims are relational. Authority implies a claim-right directed at addressees whose autonomy it affects by changing their normative position. It is essential to identify the correct subject/addressee, which underscores the central notion of membership in a political community once more.[75]

Individual autonomy has hitherto constituted the starting point of any political authority discussion, simply because most theories of authority focused exclusively on the state.[76] 'Individual autonomy' means the equal moral value of every human being, expressed by the capacity to be free and accept responsibility for one's actions.[77] In that context, theories of authority attempt to evaluate the compatibility of individual autonomy with the state's authority.

Note how state sovereignty seems to play an equivalent role as foundational value of theories of international authority. State sovereignty almost seems an end in itself, like individual autonomy. Sovereign states, however, cannot have any moral value which is entirely independent of the human beings they represent and whose wellbeing and security is in their hands.[78] In a sense, sovereignty occupies a hinge function between national and international authority. It represents the autonomy of the state in relation to international law at the same time as it represents the state's authority claim over its citizens. That is no paradox, but the manifestation of the idea that the state claims independence from external authority and interference *to* exercise internal authority over its citizens and be fully responsible for them. As I argued before, that is not to say that states cannot have moral value at all, or that the value of sovereign self-determination is inept to influence political authority discussions. That would be to throw out the baby with the bathwater. But the value of state sovereignty is derivative and thus morally less weighty compared to individual autonomy, which matches our moral intuition of the different quality of national and international authority.

Distilling the ultimate addressee of the EU's authority claim is rather complicated. Because of the role of Member State institutions and EU citizens in the EU's governance, individual autonomy as well as state sovereignty are potential values which the EU's authority claim affects. Instead of viewing the duality of subjects

[75] The *pouvoir constitué* is usually coextensive with the citizenry, Cheneval (n 73) 76 et seq.

[76] See only Robert Paul Wolff, 'The Conflict between Authority and Autonomy' in Joseph Raz (ed), *Authority* (New York, New York University Press, 1990) 25 et seq.

[77] ibid 26.

[78] In more detail Carmen E Pavel, 'The International Rule of Law' (2020) 23 *Critical Review of International Social and Political Philosophy* 332.

(state institutions/officials and citizens) as separate addressees, I argue that the EU ultimately addresses the peoples of Europe as underlying entities. The EU constrains the self-determination of the constitutional peoples of Europe, which has distinct (but secondary) effects on individual autonomy and state sovereignty. Conversely, what should be protected from illegitimate EU interference is not state sovereignty per se, but the constitutional space and the collective freedom of a constitutional people to organise itself. The peoples are entitled to self-rule by virtue of setting up the state as the institutional refugium to self-determine their affairs in the first place.

How is this different from focusing on individual autonomy and state sovereignty? An exclusive focus on the individual citizen and their autonomy misrepresents the normative and social reality in the EU. This view is not uncommon, however. For example, von Bogdandy argues that '(i)t is theoretically more convincing to conceive only the individuals, which are national as well as Union citizens, as the sole subjects of legitimacy'.[79] Similarly, Somek's search for the hypothetical EU citizen who is envisaged by and would consent to the EU's authority presupposes that the EU's authority claim addresses the citizen and their individual autonomy in the first place.[80] Admittedly, *van Gend* made the fact that EU law imposes rights and duties on EU citizens clear very early on. EU citizenship also involves legal and moral duties. But these duties only distinguish the EU from a vast array of international law. In fact, EU law purports to vindicate the very shortcomings scholars have identified to deny any authority to international law, viz. the lack of influence of individuals in international law-making as well as the lack of enforcement.[81] Whereas on the national level one is usually subject to the state's authority as an individual citizen, this is not the case in the EU. The derivative nature of EU citizenship and its mostly transnational effects for integrating into host states testifies to that. A state, for example, tells you not to build a house without permission, to pay income tax, or not to trespass on someone else's property. That affects your autonomy as a citizen. The EU, by contrast, tells you not to discriminate against other EU citizens or regulates the terms of doing business. The European Arrest Warrant illustrates this regulatory effect. EU law here 'merely' facilitates the conditions of surrendering EU citizens to another Member State. It has nothing to do with the criminal law procedure and the substance of any crime. The latter is still regulated by the Member States as part of their authority claim that stands in tension with individual autonomy. EU law, by contrast, mostly addresses individuals as a member of their people that is collectively constrained by these rules. Note how we teach EU law. We speak about Italian traders, Belgian companies, Polish families, because the interrelationship of these individuals as members of different peoples matters.

[79] Bogdandy (n 25) 43 et seq.

[80] Alexander Somek, *Individualism: An Essay on the Authority of the European Union* (Oxford, OUP, 2008).

[81] Jack L Goldsmith and Eric A Posner, *The Limits of International Law* (Oxford, OUP, 2005) 193 et seq.

Hence, proclaiming the European courts' judgments 'in the name of the Citizens of the European Union'[82] would pretend a single source of authority that neither reflects social reality nor the normative architecture of the current EU. The EU imposes duties on EU citizens as representatives and members of a collective people that is constituted in a Member State.

An exclusive focus on state sovereignty as value affected by the EU's authority would also be insufficient. The EU of course imposes most duties on Member State institutions and their officials. EU membership entails many primary and secondary (remedial) duties for Member States in relation to the enforcement of EU law and the required adaptions to national law.[83] But a focus on state sovereignty cannot account for the duties on EU citizens. EU citizens not only have explicit legal duties in all the scenarios where EU law is applicable horizontally – in their roles as employers, service-providers, students or just citizens. EU law also requires a minimum duty to integrate on the part of the migrant citizen who exercises free movement rights.[84]

While the continued existence of states is a precondition for the continuation of the EU as it stands, EU membership transforms state institutions by integrating them in supranational governance structures which ensure the national implementation and trans- as well as supranational policing of EU law. EU law curtails states' unilateral choices by withdrawing certain pivotal decisions about the effect of 'foreign' law from their authority as well as obliging them to justify their way of governing their territory (eg derogations from fundamental freedoms). At its core, the EU is designed to bind its Member States by subjecting them to binding rules in relation to each other and by giving them a common (not always single) voice in international relations. To do so, the EU goes beyond constraining state sovereignty alone and involves citizens and peoples more directly.

Both Member States institutions and EU citizens are thus subject to a supranational authority in a bounded political community. The EU is neither a community of states nor of citizens alone, but a community of constitutional peoples. They act themselves whenever the very roots of EU integration are affected, viz. its core architecture, composition and future.

It follows that the value affected by the EU's authority claim is ultimately the autonomy or self-determination of the individual peoples. This impact on popular self-determination manifests itself legally through powers (eg to determine their own powers, join and exit organisations beyond the state, etc) and corresponding immunities not to have these powers removed against their will.[85]

[82] Stephan Wernicke, 'Au Nom de Qui? The European Court of Justice between Member States, Civil Society and Union Citizens' (2007) 13 *European Law Journal* 380, 407.

[83] Paul Craig, 'EU Membership: Formal and Substantive Dimensions' (2020) 22 *Cambridge Yearbook of European Legal Studies* 1, 6 et seq.

[84] Loïc Azoulai, 'The (Mis)Construction of the European Individual Two Essays on Union Citizenship Law' (EUI Department of Law Research Paper No 2014/14) 11 et seq; Neuvonen (n 39) ch 2.

[85] Francis Cheneval, 'Demoicratic Self-Government in the European Union's Polycentric System: Theoretical Remarks' in Josephine van Zeben and Ana Bobić (eds), *Polycentricity in the European Union* (Cambridge, CUP, 2019) 54 et seq.

The way in which the peoples of current and aspiring EU Member States deal with their EU membership reveals EU law's impact on self-determination as well. For one, various EU peoples have amended their constitution to accommodate EU integration and have thereby rewritten the very document and narrative that constitutes them as a constitutional people in the first place (take only Art 23 German *Grundgesetz*; Art 23a-k Austrian Federal Constitutional Law; Art 29 Constitution of Ireland; and Art 7 (6) Constitution of Portugal). They thereby recognise the importance and transformative impact of EU integration for their own identity. For another, think only of the widespread use of national referenda in major treaty revisions, as well as in the decisions to join or withdraw from the EU. For example, nine out of 10 accession candidates of the EU's 2004 enlargement round held referenda (only Cyprus didn't). France even requires referenda for the accession of other Member States.[86] This illustrates that EU membership is a decision affecting the core of a national people's self-determination.[87] I don't claim that the EU legally requires these referenda as part of its authority claim. Instead, the fact that the peoples individually enshrine referenda requirements in their national constitutions reflects the salience of EU membership from their perspective. These referenda are a reaction to and acknowledgment of the EU's authority claim. Outside of the EU context, compulsory referenda for external affairs are extremely rare.[88] The direct involvement of the constitutional peoples via referenda reveals the profound impact of the EU on popular self-determination, which an exclusive focus on state sovereignty and state officials would be unable to grasp.

The EU's authority claim affects how the national peoples constitute and govern themselves because of their mutual integration in the EU.[89] Morally, the value of popular sovereignty manifests itself in a collective right to non-domination, which I will dive into in chapter five. Popular sovereignty as a right to non-domination allows for binding laws and an institutional framework beyond the state precisely to protect collective autonomy in an interdependent world. For present purposes, the important take away is that the EU addresses both citizens and state institutions/officials, as well as their respective autonomy and sovereignty only on a secondary level – namely as members and representatives/agents of constitutional peoples.

[86] See Christophe Hillion, 'EU Enlargement' in Paul Craig and Graínne De Búrca (eds), *The Evolution of EU Law*, 2nd edn (Oxford, OUP, 2011) 208 et seq.

[87] Referenda are also part of the debate on the UK's and Denmark's permanent opt-outs from the eurozone, see Rebecca Adler-Nissen, 'Opting Out of an Ever Closer Union: The Integration Doxa and the Management of Sovereignty' (2011) 34 *West European Politics* 1092, 101 et seq. More generally, see Hillion (n 86) 208 et seq.

[88] Notably, Ireland would require a referendum to join NATO. See Ireland Department of Foreign Affairs, *Challenges and Opportunities Abroad: White Paper on Foreign Policy* (Stationery Office, 1996) para 36.

[89] Similarly Signe Larsen, *The Constitutional Theory of the Federation and the European Union* (Oxford, OUP, 2021) 21 et seq.

To summarise, only state authority relates directly to an individual citizen. The core tension that interests theories of state authority exists between individual autonomy and state law, ie the collective decisions of the people. By contrast, the EU claims authority over a collective, a constitutional people. Here, the core tension exists between the collective autonomy (popular sovereignty) of one people on the one hand and collective decisions of several peoples on the EU level on the other. That manifests a different *conception* of authority, which nonetheless fits within the *concept* of authority. Let me put the distinction in a chart, illustrating the individual regulatory levels and the main agents and values these respective authority claims affect.

Fig 8 Authority and Autonomy on Different Regulatory Levels

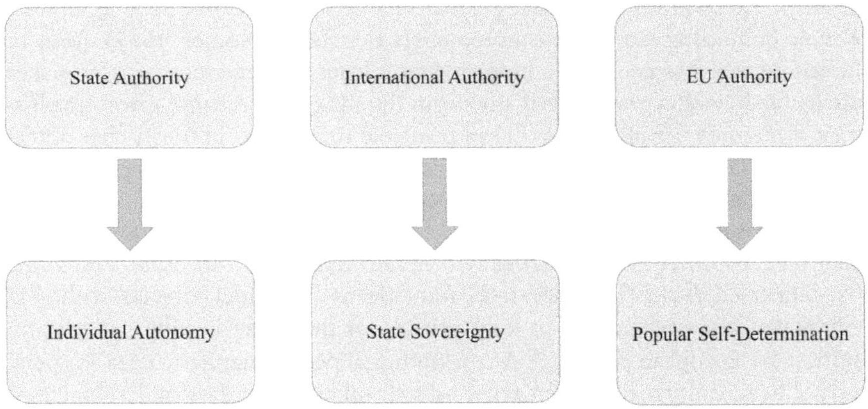

B. Why the Peoples

The EU's constitutional peoples are the ultimate addressee of the EU's authority claim. To clarify, it is important to note what distinguishes the focus on peoples from the focus on (Member) States and state sovereignty. To begin with, the focus on peoples enables one to explain the involvement of the EU citizen in the EU's normative architecture. As Papadopoulou notes: 'European citizens are referred to as a source of EU legitimacy neither as an integrated European people nor as individuals, but rather as citizens organized in peoples'.[90] Indeed, each individual people remains constituted in separate states, which through their institutions play a vital role in the EU's governance. But the focus on peoples enlarges the theoretical toolbox for the idea that the peoples jointly author a

[90] Lina Papadopoulou, '"All Good Things Come in Threes": From a Double to a Triple Democratic Legitimacy of the European Union' in Lina Papadopoulou, Ingolf Pernice and Joseph Weiler (eds), *Legitimacy Issues of the European Union in the Face of Crisis* (Baden-Baden, Hart/Nomos, 2017) 87.

supranational arrangement that is conceptually distinct but not independent from their separate states.[91] I don't understand the EU as a union derivative of *states* with no direct normative relationship to the constitutional peoples and their citizens. Instead, the EU complements states, which are themselves but an instrument for the self-determination of an individual people.

Next, the focus on peoples reflects that the EU affects self-determination at a deeper level and is more demanding compared to international organisations. On the one hand, the focus on peoples takes into account that the EU impacts on the agency and autonomy of citizens at all compared to international organisations. On the other, international approaches to the EU put the people in the back seat. As *pouvoir constitué* of the Member State, the demos then plays no active role. Legitimation from Member States' executive representatives alone would be sufficient. By contrast, emphasising 'the people' as *pouvoir constituant*, as authors of their political community, conceptualises the state as secondary: as agent of the self-determined people. An independent role for the European peoples makes intelligible how they normatively underpin the EU polity. A more direct involvement of the peoples allows the EU in principle to exercise authority that differs qualitatively from other international organisations.

The focus on peoples puts the people in the driving seat. It thereby (re-)conceptualises how the individual entities (citizens, state officials, peoples) relate to each other in a theoretically coherent framework. In other words, the well-rehearsed duality between states and citizens as distinct subjects of the EU only makes sense when seen as joint proxies for the underpinning constituting entities: the European peoples.[92] A constitutional people manifests itself in social and political reality mainly as citizens and state officials. But those individual legal obligations of the Member States and EU citizens reflect a commitment of their underlying constitutional people. While the respective obligations of citizens and state officials to obey the law might differ in moral force, they still emanate from the participation of their people in the EU as a political community.

There will of course be tensions between the interests of Member States and EU citizens. Not only in virtue of the vertical configuration of individual rights and duties between the national and the supranational level,[93] but also in relation to the powers of citizen and state representatives in different EU institutions. Think only of the inter-institutional deliberations about the economic package to combat the COVID 19 crisis, which ever more openly reflected the balancing of interests between political families, regional representation and individual

[91] Francis Cheneval and Kalypso Nicolaidis, 'The Social Construction of Demoicracy in the European Union' (2017) 16 *European Journal of Political Theory* 235, 236 et seq. Cheneval (n 73) 58.

[92] Similarly Case C-105/03 *Pupino* EU:C:2004:712, Opinion of AG Kokott, para 26. For a discussion of the theoretical interrelationship of both, see Jelena Von Achenbach, 'Verfassungswandel durch Selbstorganisation: Triloge im europäischen Gesetzgebungsverfahren' (2016) 55 *Der Staat* 1, 416.

[93] Nicole Bolleyer and Christine Reh, 'EU Legitimacy Revisited: The Normative Foundations of a Multilevel Polity' (2012) 19 *Journal of European Public Policy* 472, 479.

Member States. Institutionally, such a discourse reflects the competition between the interests of an independent *demos* (national leaders in the European Council) and interdependent *demoi* (MEPs), which forms part and parcel of the EU's very architecture.[94]

Note that I am not dismissive of states as such. They continue to be the primary repositories of authority in today's world. I also recognise the pivotal role of state institutions, especially the executive branch, in making and enforcing EU law or in acceding to or seceding from the EU. My theoretical claim remains, however, that the Member States as such (and their sovereignty) are not the ultimate addressees of the EU's authority claim. Instead, the EU affects popular self-determination and the collectives of constitutional peoples themselves that ultimately put their state institutions in the service of a political community beyond the state. The peoples are the principals; the state institutions are the agents.

Roughly, statist authority addresses individual citizens and international authority obligates states. The EU's authority claim addresses both Member States and their citizens as agents of the peoples of Europe. It ultimately seeks to obligate constitutional peoples. The constitutional peoples underwrite two types of political communities: their states (each on their own), and the EU (jointly, but not as one). It is true that, ultimately, the EU Treaties constitute an 'agreement between the *peoples* of Europe'.[95] The EU's authority framework as constructed here takes the heritage of the Treaty of Rome's Preamble (now enshrined in Art 1 TEU) seriously. After all, does it not proclaim the creation of a 'union among the peoples of Europe'?

While this ought to suffice to characterise the peoples as addressees of the EU's authority claim, the remainder of the book will provide more detail on the flipside: namely, the peoples as source and authors of EU law's normative authority.

VI. Conclusion

This chapter made the case that the EU claims a distinct kind of political authority. The EU's authority claim shouldn't be conceptualised as (even divided) sovereign authority. At the same time, the EU's authority claim differs from international authority claims. I see enough evidence that the EU claims authority over and seeks to bind the peoples of Europe. It thereby complements their individual organisation (*Verfasstheit*) in separate sovereign states and transcends international authority and its exclusive focus on states as addressees. Whereas, methodologically, others start from preconceptions and fully-fledged theories about the nature

[94] Similarly Eriksen (n 21) 92 et seq.

[95] Case C-415/05 P *Al Barakaat International Foundation (Kadi)*, Opinion of AG Maduro, EU:C:2008:30, para 21.

and relationship between national and international law, I analysed the EU's authority claim by dissecting the EU's manifestation of core concepts of political authority: means and institutions, territoriality and membership. This allowed me to avoid taking a stance on many disputed concepts (such as constitutionalism, federation, confederation).[96]

The focus on peoples best reflects social reality (ie what the EU does in authority terms) as well as the normative ambition of the European project. The EU requires the peoples to open up their respective national spaces and experience a loss of control over their territory. It mandates to prioritise their EU law obligations over national obligations to respect their commitments at the supranational level. Further, it facilitates their integration into a common European space that will be policed both trans- and supranationally. Through the EU, the various European peoples constrain each other by setting up supranational institutions.

What comes next and what distinguishes chapter two from the following chapters? To answer that, recall the claim-structure in chapter one that provides conceptual clarity in two crucial respects that both stem from the capacity of claims to be right or wrong.

First, think about the distinction between the nature of the authority claim, ie what kind of authority does the EU claim over whom (addressed in this chapter) and its actual legitimate authority, ie why and to what extent does the EU have legitimate authority (addressed in the remainder of the book). Here, we first need to understand the claim in order to say something useful about its legitimacy, ie whether the claim is true or false. The scope of the authority claim can be false in the sense that it is too far reaching as evaluated considering the appropriate normative basis. Because a polity claims authority of a certain scope and force does not mean it legitimately has this authority. The remainder of the book searches for this normative basis to evaluate the EU's claims.

Second, this claim structure helps to distinguish between the claimed basis for the EU's authority and its actual, normatively preferrable basis. 'Wrong' is here understood in the sense that the claimed basis for the authority is wrong. For example, I will argue that consent is the wrong basis to evaluate the EU's authority so that those institutions and academics who support it are wrong. This observation will shape the inquiry in various ways. First, I analyse what the EU institutions view as the basis of the EU's authority (chapter three). Second, I evaluate the viability of these institutional proposals considering the relevant literature on the basis for the EU's authority (chapter four). And third, I try to rectify the shortcomings of these accounts by proposing my own account of the appropriate normative basis of the EU's authority (chapters five and six). Thus, not only can the scope of the authority claim be 'wrong', but also the EU institutions' view concerning the normative basis to evaluate the EU's authority.

[96] See for a concise overview of these debates, Barber, *The Constitutional State* (n 28) ch 10. For a literature review see Lacey (n 51) 65.

3

Institutional Reflections on the EU's Authority

I. Introduction

This chapter occupies a hinge function between chapter two and chapters four to six. Whereas chapter two brought the contours of the EU's authority claim to light, ie its nature, scope and addressees, the present chapter introduces the search for the moral basis of that authority. The remainder of the book is about evaluating on what basis and to what extent the EU's authority claim is (morally) true.

The present chapter focuses on social-institutional reality. That is, it investigates how the EU Treaties and institutions construct the moral basis for the EU's right to rule. Since the EU often asserts its position and, in particular, the authority of EU law in relation to its Member States (as well as their citizens) and international law, statements to that effect are not uncommon. Here, I am looking for traces of theories of authority in social reality.

This chapter scrutinises each institution's view in relation to two distinct elements. First, it seeks to uncover the substantive moral standard (or moral benchmark, or normative standard) they use to evaluate the EU's authority in the respective institutional statements. Second, it asks who – in their view – underwrites the EU's authority, ie which entity is viewed as the source of the EU's authority. Note the limited scope. This chapter is a forensic exercise aiming to understand how the Treaties and institutions ground the EU's authority. The assessment, how viable and convincing their views are, is reserved for the next chapter.

At the outset, let me stress the important distinction between the EU's authority on the one hand, and the authority of individual institutions (the Commission, the ECJ, etc) on the other. These are two distinct subject matters. My project is exclusively concerned with the former: the authority of the EU and its laws. This chapter does not enquire into the authority of individual EU institutions.[1] Instead, I look at how individual EU institutions and the Treaties themselves reflect on the authority of EU law.

[1] A project others have pursued. See Martijn van den Brink, 'Justice, Legitimacy and the Authority of Legislation within the European Union' (2019) 82 *MLR* 293. Uwe Puetter, *The European Council and*

There is one more caveat. We will find that many institutions use a broader notion of legitimacy. Whereas chapter one distinguished between moral legitimacy (normative compliance with an independent moral benchmark) and social legitimacy (empirical acceptance by the subjects), some institutions often use moral and social legitimacy/authority interchangeably. Institutional practice is simply messier than theoretical literature. This requires appropriate caution when imputing legitimacy standards to these institutions. Nonetheless, chapter one also showed that the two legitimacy debates are intrinsically connected. First, both relate to the broader question of rightful rule. Second, social legitimacy supports a political community's de facto authority and contributes to its de jure authority (stability and effectiveness). Accordingly, if an institution uses the same moral standard consistently, that gives us prima facie reason to believe that this standard informs both the empirical and normative component of legitimacy, even if political theory rightly distinguishes them.

Let's kick off the discussion with the EU Treaties.

II. Traces of Authority in the Treaties

Quite predictably, the Treaties reveal their conception of the ground for the EU's authority in their Preambles. Though it might come as a surprise to some, there are noticeable differences between the two foundational Treaties.

A. The TFEU Preamble: Nucleus of a Union of Peoples

The TFEU Preamble reproduces the Preamble of the founding Treaty of the then European Economic Community (EEC), namely the 1957 Rome Treaty. The Preamble's most conspicuous aspect is the early focus on peoples, as well as states, suggesting that the Treaty and its drafters even then imagined the authority of the EEC to go beyond the one of traditional international organisations. The Preamble refers to peoples as distinct from states no less than four times, most prominently by invoking the 'ever closer union among the peoples of Europe' at the outset.[2] The Treaty thereby emphasises that the integration project is about the interdependence of those self-determining collective entities and their prosperity in post-war Europe.

the Council: New Intergovernmentalism and Institutional Change (Oxford, OUP, 2014) ch 3, especially at 147; Vivien A Schmidt, *Europe's Crisis of Legitimacy: Governing by Rules and Ruling by Numbers in the Eurozone* (Oxford, OUP, 2020) chs 5–8.

[2] Even the Preamble of the 1951 Treaty establishing the European Coal and Steel Community refers to the hope for it to be a 'basis for a broader and deeper community among peoples'.

In substance, the Preamble mentions instrumental benefits (economic and social progress), but the emphasis is clearly on the value of institutional cooperation among the participants. For example, the Preamble intends the recognition of the EU as an instrument for joint action of the Member States to eliminate barriers or remove obstacles between them (also expressed in Arts 1, 2 EEC-Treaty). More to the point, cooperative notions like 'common action' and 'concerted action', 'pooling resources' pervade the Preamble.

This institutional-cooperative basis for moral authority has both intrinsic and instrumental value. Transnational cooperation of states-peoples intrinsically advances peace and stability.[3] This is especially true regarding the EU's institutional architecture, which from the outset went beyond any traditional international set-up.[4] Binding institutional cooperation by its very nature fulfils an ordering function that has been a core value of political communities for millennia. The mere existence of the institutional architecture makes future especially military conflicts among the participating peoples less likely.

Simultaneously, such cooperation is *instrumental* for achieving – as Art 3 TEU reminds us today – the Union's aim to 'promote peace … and the well-being of its peoples'.[5] In a nutshell, an institutional arrangement that fosters peace can also be used to promote peace. This broader emphasis on peace and well-being questions portrayals of the then EEC as yet another international organisation with economic goals. Admittedly, the means to achieve these aims were economic. Nonetheless, economic integration between European states only years after World War II was deeply political. Not only because economic integration is inherently political,[6] but because economic means were used to achieve political ends. The Member States supranationalised crucial defence-related industries in the European Coal and Steel Community and sought to establish an internal market through the EEC.

The idea of promoting peace and institutionalised political relations among states through primarily economic means did not just pop up after World War II. Ever since Kant's theoretical groundwork for portraying commercial interdependence as the main driver of a 'cosmopolitan constitution', the use of economic means to further political ends presented itself as an option for political leaders

[3] Claudia Sternberg, 'Political Legitimacy between Democracy and Effectiveness: Trade-Offs, Interdependencies, and Discursive Constructions by the EU Institutions' (2015) 7 *European Political Science Review* 615, 626.

[4] For a list of the remarkable institutional novelties, see Julio Baquero Cruz, *What's Left of the Law of Integration?: Decay and Resistance in European Union Law* (Oxford, OUP, 2018) 13.

[5] The Monnet-Plan and the Schuman-Declaration stressed this aspect early on. See ibid ch 2, called Law after Auschwitz'. Claudia Sternberg, 'Public Opinion in the EU Institutions' Discourses on EU Legitimacy from the Beginnings of Integration to Today' (2016) 54 *Politique Européenne* 23.

[6] Turkuler Isiksel, 'The Dream of a Commercial Peace' in Luuk van Middelaar, Philippe van Parijs and Herman van Rompuy (eds), *After the Storm: How to Save Democracy in Europe* (Tielt, Lannoo, 2015); Jussi Jaakkola, 'Enhancing Political Representation Through the European Economic Constitution? Regressive Politics of Democratic Inclusion' (2019) 15 *European Constitutional Law Review* 194.

and academics alike.[7] Due to the instrumental value of cooperation in economic areas to achieve broader political aims, economic integration is thus intrinsically connected to political legitimacy.

To sum up, the 1957 EEC Treaty – confirmed by various treaty revisions over the past decades to end up as the TFEU Treaty – envisages the authority of the EU as focusing on the European peoples as ultimate reference entity. Yet, Member States play a noticeable role in the TFEU Preamble's vision of the EU's authority as well. In terms of substantive normative basis, the Treaty Preamble derives the EU's authority from cooperation and integration through a sophisticated set of institutions that – both inherently and instrumentally – seek to guarantee peace and prosperity.

B. The TEU Preamble: Enriching Values

Is there any reason to think that the TEU, which marks the creation of the EU through the 1992 Maastricht Treaty, differs from the TFEU's vision of the EU's authority? At first glance, the answer is no. Various paragraphs of the TEU Preamble in its Maastricht-version confirm the TFEU's focus on institutional cooperation as decisive value of the EU. They emphasise a new stage in EU integration, ending the division of the European continent, enhancing the democratic and efficient functioning of the institutions, and economic progress. In addition, the current post-Lisbon Preamble puts a visible emphasis on substantive values, which the Treaty of Lisbon added to the Preamble as well as to the Treaty text itself (Arts 2 and 6 et seq TEU).[8] Three distinct paragraphs engage with the 'cultural, religious and humanist inheritance of Europe', emphasise the 'attachment to the principles of liberty, democracy and respect for human rights and fundamental freedoms and of the rule of law' and mention social rights separately. This indicates a shift in the Treaty-makers' perspective from contractarian notions and their oft instrumental benefits towards substantive values. We will see below that various EU institutions reacted to this new prominence of values in the TEU and adjusted their conception of the EU's authority accordingly.

Regarding the relevant agents, an apparent hierarchy of states over peoples in the TEU Preamble gives the impression that the underlying rationale is integration and cooperation between states and not primarily peoples. For example, Art 1(1) TEU prioritises the EU as a vehicle of the 'High Contracting Parties' over the 'ever closer union among peoples' which, incidentally, moved to the end of the Preamble. Similarly, the Lisbon-amendments to central treaty provisions such

[7] Immanuel Kant, 'Toward Perpetual Peace' in Pauline Kleingeld (ed), David Colclasure (tr), *Toward Perpetual Peace and other Writings on Politics, Peace, and History* (New Haven, Yale University Press, 2006) 67 et seq. For a very insightful discussion, see Turkuler Isiksel, 'Cosmopolitanism and International Economic Institutions' (2020) 82 *Journal of Politics* 211.

[8] Earlier, the Treaty of Nice had already added social rights to the Preamble.

as Arts 3 (6), 4, 5 TEU confirm the renewed sensitivity for the derivative nature of the EU and the respect for the integrity of the Member States and their competences. The Preamble – like the TFEU's – nonetheless mentions the European peoples four times. Moreover, the introduction of EU citizenship broadens the perspective well beyond Member States as main actors. Considering these findings and the ever more salient competences of the EU (chiefly the common currency), there is no indication that the creation of the EU in 1992 marked an 'international turn'. Nonetheless, the focus on Member States is noteworthy in comparison to the TFEU Preamble, where the peoples take precedence.

To sum up, the TEU Preamble is ambiguous when it comes to the relevant agent(s) as source of the EU's authority. Member States, peoples and citizens play a distinct role and interact in grounding the EU's authority. There are two key differences to the TFEU. First, the citizens play no part in the original EEC-Treaty Preamble and its successors. Second, whereas Member States seem to be secondary to the EU peoples in the TFEU Preamble, the TEU puts three agents (Peoples, Member States, EU citizens) on a roughly equal level. Regarding the substantive moral standard to evaluate legitimate authority, the continuity of the TFEU's cooperative elements (integration through functioning institutions and achieving common projects) is enriched with substantive elements, ie the values enshrined in Art 2 TEU.

Let us move on to consider the ECJ's vision as the institution that played a vital part in shaping the authority of EU law over the past decades. But on what basis?

III. The Court: From Effective Contracts to Institutional Integrity

Although historians often twitch at the sight of counterfactuals, it is almost certain that the 'Authority claim over Peoples' described in chapter two would not exist but for the audacity of the ECJ. Its central role in interpreting and shaping the EU legal order inevitably prompted various pronouncements on the source of the EU's legitimate authority.

A. Effective Integration and a Role for the Citizen

It is no surprise that the story of the Court's vision of the EU's authority begins with *van Gend*.[9] In *van Gend*, the ECJ derives the distinct authority of EU law from the idea that the Treaties structurally and institutionally transcend purely inter-state relations. It takes the mentioning of the peoples in the Preamble, the

[9] Case C-26/62 *Van Gend en Loos* EU:C:1963:1.

precursor of the EP, and the preliminary reference procedure to herald a qualitatively new form of public institutional arrangement with a noticeable role for individuals.[10] Ever since, the calibration of a network of individuals and states through institutions underpinned the ECJ's reasoning.

Overall, *van Gend* revealed more about the relevant subjects of the EU's authority than about its substantive moral justification. That is not only due to the doctrinal question at hand: namely, the direct effect of primary law in national courts. More theoretically, in order to support the 'new legal order' the Court sought to boost the role of the individual citizen in that legal order ('… Treaty is more than an agreement which merely creates mutual obligations between the contracting states', '… institutions endowed with sovereign rights, the exercise of which affects Member States and also their citizens', '… the nationals of the states brought together in the Community are called upon to cooperate in the functioning of this Community through the intermediary of the EP and the Economic and Social Committee', '… the task assigned to the Court of Justice under Article 177 … confirms that the states have acknowledged that Community law has an authority which can be invoked by their nationals before those courts and tribunals').

The substantive moral basis for the EU's authority in the eyes of the ECJ was added in *Costa v ENEL*.[11] *Costa* provided two main arguments to support EU law's authority, one instrumental and one contractarian, whereby the combination of both generates a distinct normative force.[12] The instrumental argument comes to the fore ever since the formation of the central idea of *effet utile*, according to which a Member State's unilateral deviation from EU law would call into question the pursuit of the Treaties' objectives.[13] *Effet utile* expresses the idea that EU law is there to be implemented and enforced to its fullest extent. As will become clearer in chapter four, this cannot serve as a self-standing argument for EU law's authority, since the EU's multilevel system is characterised by the interaction of EU law and national law. Unsurprisingly, each of the legal orders 'wants' to be fully effective. The Court's combination of this instrumental argument with a contractarian angle adds force to the argument, however. The ECJ simply reminds the Member States that they have created the Community 'on a basis of reciprocity' so that Community law, if open to unilateral deviations, would lose its binding force and thus its character as, well, *Community* Law. A potentially varying force of EU law would moreover lead to 'discrimination' of

[10] For an analysis of the broader implications, see Franz Mayer, 'Van Gend En Loos: The Foundation of a Community of Law' in Miguel Poiares Maduro and Loïc Azoulai (eds), *The Past and Future of EU law* (Oxford, Hart Publishing, 2010).

[11] Case C-6/64 *Costa v ENEL* EU:C:1964:66.

[12] See also Paul Craig and Gráinne De Búrca, *EU Law: Text, Cases, and Materials*, 7th edn (Oxford, OUP, 2020) 316. They identify four core arguments (contractarian, functional, egalitarian, analytical).

[13] *Costa* (n 11). Confirmed in Case C-106/77 *Amministratione delle finanze dello Stato v Simmenthal* EU:C:1978:49, paras 17 et seq. More recently Case C-378/17 *Garda Síochána* EU:C:2018:979, para 36.

(EU) law-abiding Member States. The Court thus reminds the Member States of the obligations they incurred towards each other.

These broadly contractarian arguments resonate in fair-play accounts of authority that we will scrutinise in the next chapter in more detail: you bind yourself by agreeing to the Treaty or by acceding to the Union. Not keeping the bargain by unilaterally deviating from EU law would unfairly discriminate others.[14] This explains the subsequent coupling of primacy and uniformity in the case law.[15] The Court not only assumes that Member States want to always abide by EU law. It uses this assumption to help the enforcement of EU law by empowering EU citizens and the institutions of other Member States.

To sum up, the early ECJ shifted the emphasis from Member States to individual citizens when discussing the relevant source of the EU's authority. In substance, a contractarian notion, combining fairness (uniform and binding application) and instrumental efficacy (*effet utile*), underwrites the ECJ's vision in this phase.

B. After Lisbon: The ECJ's Restatement of EU Law's Authority

The evolution from the EEC to the EU in its post-Lisbon form happened in the same two decades in which information technology (IT) progressed from the first 'notebook style'[16] laptop to the mass-distribution of smartphones (1989–2009). It seems only a slight overstatement to label both as quantum leaps in their respective sectors. The EU 'upgrade' in the Treaty of Maastricht; ever more salient competences; the major treaty revisions around the new millennium; an enlargement by 15 new Member States; a failed Constitutional Treaty; and a binding Fundamental Rights Charter barely left a stone unturned. The impact of this development on the Court's self-image of the EU's authority is discernible in *Kadi*[17] but received its canonical formulation in *Opinion 2/13*. There, the Court recalled the institutional structure and special characteristics of EU law (especially primacy and direct effect), before proclaiming:

> These essential characteristics of EU law have given rise to a structured network of principles, rules and mutually interdependent legal relations linking the EU and its Member States, and its Member States with each other, which are now engaged, as is recalled in the second paragraph of Article 1 TEU, in a 'process of creating an ever closer union among the peoples of Europe'.[18]

[14] For an explicit endorsement of fair play, see Case C-39/72 *Commission v Italy* EU:C:1973:13, paras 24, 25. There is, however, a noticeable consent-flavour in these statements.

[15] For example Case C-11/70 *Internationale Handelsgesellschaft* EU:C:1970:114, para 3. Case C-369/96 *Arblade* EU:C:1999:575, para 31. Case C-316/05 *Nokia* EU:C:2006:789, para 43.

[16] Mary Bellis, 'The History of Laptop Computers' (*thoughtco*, 4 October 2019), www.thoughtco.com/history-of-laptop-computers-4066247.

[17] C-415/05 P *Al Barakaat International Foundation (Kadi), Opinion of AG Maduro*, EU:C:2008:30199.

[18] Opinion 2/13, *Accession to the ECHR* EU:C:2014:2454, para 167.

The Court later ties this rationale to the pursuit of the EU's objectives (Art 3 TEU) by declaring the 'implementation of the process of integration' to be the '*raison d'être* of the EU itself'.[19] Not unlike the TFEU Preamble, the Court grounds the EU's authority in the intrinsic and instrumental value of EU institutions for the cooperation among states/peoples. The second argument for the authority of EU law builds on this and complements the contractarian notion with substantive values:

> This legal structure is based on the fundamental premiss that each Member State shares with all the other Member States, and recognises that they share with it, a set of common values on which the EU is founded, as stated in Article 2 TEU. That premiss implies and justifies the existence of mutual trust between the Member States that those values will be recognized and, therefore, that the law of the EU that implements them will be respected.[20]

In the early period, the value of law-administering institutions was covered by the emphasis on equality and fair play as well as the instrumental value of EU law. Here, the Court not only emphasises the value of the EU's institutions and ties it to normatively rich concepts such as mutual trust. What is more, the Court uses the Art 2 TEU values to corroborate EU law's authority with moral/constitutional substance. While the focus in *Kadi* and *Opinion 2/13* is on *fundamental rights*, the Court would later broaden its use of the arsenal of values in Art 2 TEU. It used *liberty* and *democracy* to reconcile the voluntary nature of the EU with the obligations involved in its membership.[21] The *rule of law* then served as a conceptual basis to discipline Member States' attempts to curtail the independence of their national judiciaries.[22] In sum, the ECJ increasingly ties the integrity of the Treaties' institutional system to the values enshrined in Art 2 TEU.

The third step in the Court's reasoning is to link this institutional architecture and normative foundation firmly to the enforcement of EU law.[23] In the eyes of the Court, the enforcement of EU law represents not just a matter of output-related technical effectiveness of a single market, but rather the value-based interaction of self-governing collectives, which participate in this supranational community. The Court's self-understanding of the EU's authority shifted from technical notions – such as effectiveness and uniformity – to an emphasis on the value of institutions and procedures cloaked with thoroughly normative concepts that have formed the bedrock of its jurisprudence ever since.

Regarding the relevant agent, we meet the tripartite structure of citizens, peoples and Member States, which has informed ECJ jurisprudence since the

[19] ibid para 172. See also Case C-621/18 *Wightman* EU:C:2018:999.

[20] Opinion 2/13, *ibid* para 168. Confirmed only recently in Case C-156/21 *Hungary v Parliament and Council* EU:C:2022:97, para 125.

[21] *Wightman* (n 19) para 62.

[22] Case C-619/18 *Commission v Poland* EU:C:2019:615, paras 42 et seq. Case C-430/21 *RS* EU:C:2022:99, paras 38 et seq.

[23] Opinion 2/13 (n 18) paras 170, 173.

1960s. In terms of theoretical architecture, the ECJ interestingly derives the *hierarchical* authority of the EU from the *horizontal* relationships among these constituent entities. The idea is that the political communities' institutions and laws gain their moral value from how they facilitate and concretise the mutual moral relationships among the members.

C. Interim Conclusion

To this day, the Court doesn't employ a 'clean', ie one coherent theory about the moral backbone of the authority of EU law. The overarching focus, nonetheless, is on the value of EU institutions to facilitate cooperation. In that regard, law-enforcing institutions (courts) have always taken a more prominent role than law-making institutions. Even the early contractarian arguments remain abstract, and the Court rarely appreciates the value of EU law-making openly. This emphasis on the value of law-enforcement is alien to theories of national authority, but understandable beyond the state, where this very enforcement is often far from given. In addition to its institution-focus, the ECJ has used instrumental arguments (*effet utile*) in the past, and increasingly relies on substantive values (Art 2 TEU) to corroborate EU law's authority.[24] Yet, neither serves as a stand-alone basis for the EU's authority. They have always been secondary to institutional-procedural elements.

Note, finally, that the ECJ's own position in the EU's architecture as guarantor for EU law's coherence and effectiveness very likely plays a part in its reasoning as well. For the Court thereby puts its own role as institutional guardian of EU law and its enforcement in the spotlight. Such a connection between an institution's function in the EU's governance and its view of the ground of the EU's authority can be drawn in relation to various other institutions under consideration here. One of them is our next candidate: the Commission.

IV. The Commission: Delivering Benefits between Social and Moral Legitimacy

As we turn to the Commission's viewpoint, recall the words of caution in the Introduction. It is rather difficult to discern the Commission's view, especially in the early days. For one, there is a substantial risk of selection bias considering the breadth and diversity of Commission publications.[25] For another, the Commission's discourse is one of legitimacy, not of authority. Those two are of

[24] For an instructive recent example see *Hungary v Parliament and Council* (n 20) para 129.
[25] Similarly Sternberg (n 3) 618 et seq.

course intrinsically linked, but the present focus is on legitimacy as normative standard for authoritative, rightful rule. A great share of the Commission's views and significant parts of the relevant literature undoubtedly relate to the empirical conception of legitimacy, ie mustering public support for political rule.[26] Rare mentions of the concept of authority as well as overwhelming evidence of a specific focus on a single legitimation strategy nonetheless allow for the tentative conclusion that the Commission would readily view that standard as moral standard for rightful rule as well.

The Commission's benchmark to assess the EU's legitimate authority has always been output-centred. Already the earliest Commission pronouncements on justifying the then EEC's *right to exist* more than its *right to rule* focused on economic prosperity as a primordial means of improving the living conditions in the Member States. Unlike the EEC-Treaty Preamble, the Commission seems to confine the instrumental value of the EU to economic goals narrowly understood.[27] In other words, the legitimacy of the integration project is based on its instrumental capacity to deliver (economic) benefits. According to the early Commission, the EEC and its Common Market were about 'the *effects* and the expected *results* of the process of integration along with the *benefits* from that general economic expansion' (emphasis added).[28]

As the White Paper on the Single Market of 1985 shows, the Commission's perspective remained unchanged for quite some time. The Commission reflects on the achievements of a common customs tariff with 'pride' and, so it informs us, the 'benefits to an integrated Community economy of the large, expanding and flexible market are so great that they should not be denied to its citizens because of difficulties faced by individual Member States'.[29] The legitimacy of the EU and its law, which facilitates these benefits, is thus based on its instrumental capacity to deliver a single market. The contrast to the – albeit tentative – normative language of the Rome Treaty's Preamble is striking.

In the early 2000s, the Commission opted to confirm its instrumental justification for the European project, while tying it to the expectations of the individual stakeholders. It singled out policy areas in which 'people expect the Union to lead' and demanded 'more effective and relevant policies' to enhance the legitimacy of

[26] For one example see Dominika Biegoń, 'Specifying the Arena of Possibilities: Post-structuralist Narrative Analysis and the European Commission's Legitimation Strategies' (2013) 51 *Journal of Common Market Studies* 194.

[27] Commission, *Seventh General Report on the Activities of the Community* (1 April 1963–31 March 1964) 21–22. Commission, *Tenth General Report on the Activities of the Community* (1 April 1966–31 March 1967) 30. Commission, *Third General Report on the Activities of the Community* (1 April 1959–31 March 1960) 25–26 states the temporal priority of the economic over the political. See also Commission, *Fourth General Report on the Activities of the Community* (16 May 1960–30 April 1961) 18. Sternberg (n 3) 627.

[28] Commission, *Fourth Report*, ibid 11.

[29] Commission, *Completing the Internal Market: White Paper from the Commission to the European Council*, 28–29.6.1985 (COM/85/0310) No 15. This seems to be in line with public choice models of the EU's legitimacy. For a discussion see Gráinne De Búrca, 'The Quest for Legitimacy in the European Union' (1996) 59 *MLR* 349, 353 et seq.

the EU.[30] So citizens expect the delivery of results. For that reason, reflections on the past achievements of the EU are dominated by listing 'results which would not have been possible by individual Member States acting on their own'. Even democracy and the rule of law seem only relevant to the extent they contributed to achieving results.[31]

This strategy often amounts to mere window-dressing, however, since it imputes these wishes to the European citizens without consulting them. In other words, the Commission's agenda was to tell the people that they really wanted output legitimacy, ie to change the citizen's expectations rather than its own benchmark for legitimacy and authority.[32] The longing for more popular support clearly appeals to the social aspect of legitimacy, namely its ability to attract support by the populace.[33] Whereas the Commission's efforts thus do not seek to establish a moral benchmark for the exercise of rightful rule, the overwhelming focus on instrumental outcomes leaves no doubt about its broader vision of how to evaluate the authority and legitimacy of the EU.

In 2017, after the tectonic changes in the EU's form mentioned earlier, the Commission reminded everyone of its fundamental yardstick for the legitimacy of EU integration, displaying its fondness for pathos: 'The images of battles in trenches and fields in Verdun, or of a continent separated by the Iron Curtain and the Berlin Wall, have been replaced by a Union standing out as a beacon of peace and stability'.[34] Instead of the earlier focus on market and economy, the ulterior motives are now (and always have been?) directly political: namely peace and stability. Interestingly, in tandem with the Treaties and the ECJ's recent judicial pronouncements, the Commission also embraced the ever more prominent values of Art 2 TEU: 'Even if the attachment to peace is not one that all of today's Europeans can relate to in the same way as their parents or grandparents, these core values continue to bind us together'.[35]

[30] Commission, *European Governance – A White Paper*, 12.10.2001 (2001/C 287/01), Executive Summary. See also Commission, *White Paper on a European Communication Policy*, 1.2.2006 (COM (2006) 35) 2: 'Citizens expect Europe to offer them prosperity, solidarity and security in the face of globalization'. Myrto Tsakatika, 'Claims to Legitimacy: The European Commission between Continuity and Change' (2005) 43 *Journal of Common Market Studies* 193, 204, 207. For an overview of the fierce academic criticism of the 2001 White Paper see ibid 195.

[31] Commission, *European Governance* (n 30) 5, 8. This hasn't changed. See Commission, *Communication, Further Strengthening the Rule of Law Within the Union: State of Play and Possible Next Steps*, 3.4.2019 (COM(2019)163) 2.

[32] Sternberg (n 5) 34 et seq; Tsakatika (n 30) 210. On this relationship, see Anna Davidson, 'Through Thick and Thin: "European Identification" for a Justified and Legitimate European Union' (2008) 4 *Journal of Contemporary European Research* 32.

[33] De Búrca (n 29) 351.

[34] Commission, *White Paper on the Future of Europe: Reflections and Scenarios for the EU 27 by 2025*, 1.3.2017 (COM(2017) 2025) 2. Baquero Cruz (n 4) 22 agrees and argues that the 'possibility of war … should be the basis for the value we must give to the law of integration'.

[35] Commission, *Future of Europe* (n 34) 2. See also Commission, *Report on the Operation of the TEU*, 10.5.1995 (SEC(95) 731) 3.

But make no mistake. The instrumentalist output-related justification is still alive and kicking. The emphasis is on serving ulterior interests, determined by the Member States as ultimate constituent actors, in line with the familiar earlier image. Headlines like 'Strengthening the Rule of Law: A Priority for an Effective Functioning of the Union' vividly illustrate that.[36] In the eyes of the Commission, the authority of EU law is intrinsically related to its capacity to deliver the benefits of the EU to its stakeholders. The added value of, for example, the single market, does 'not materialise if Member States do not apply or implement single market rules, or if the rules are undermined by other barriers'.[37] Driving this analogy with law as service for consumers to the extreme, the Commission thinks it has to do everything so that the '*end-users* of EU law … can fully enjoy their rights'.[38]

In my view, the Commission's perspective on the EU's authority should be understood as an instrumental account of authority. Although the notions of output legitimacy and instrumental accounts of authority are used in different contexts, their justification strategy is structurally equivalent. That is, they focus on ulterior ends that justify the practice under concern. I think the substantive outputs envisaged by the Commission – especially delivering economic prosperity – is one example of an instrumental account of the authority of EU law, in the sense that the latter is conducive to achieving these economic ends. Hence, I don't wish to suggest that output legitimacy is identical to instrumental authority; instead, I think that output-centred legitimacy strategies can be translated into a particular kind of instrumental justification for authority. The Commission's view of the EU's authority is instrumental since it is based on the capacity of EU law to serve more or less clearly defined ends: to deliver benefits to Europeans and especially the Member States.[39]

Note the stark contrast between this vision, and the one of the Treaties and the ECJ. While the latter overwhelmingly focus on the moral value of institutions and procedures in administering a political community, the Commission emphasises outputs and benefits. For the Commission, the way laws are made and enforced is irrelevant as long as the result can be delivered. Finally, the Commission's focus on Member States as primary agents also departs from the Treaties' and ECJ's eclectic combination of peoples, states and citizens.

[36] Commission, *Communication, 2020 Rule of Law Report: The Rule of Law Situation in the European Union*, 30.9.2020 (COM(2020) 580) 2.

[37] Commission, *Monitoring the Application of European Union law, 2017 Annual Report*, 12.7.2018. See also Commission, *Monitoring the Application of European Union law, 2018 Annual Report*, 4.7.2019 Foreword. Commission, *Communication, EU Law: Better Results through Better Application*, 19.1.2017 (2017/C 18/02) 1. Commission, *Communication, Strengthening the Rule of Law within the Union: A Blueprint for Action*, 17.7.2019 (COM(2019) 343) 1: 'The European project relies on permanent respect of the rule of law in all Member States. It is a prerequisite for the effective application of EU law' or the 'effective delivery of its policies'.

[38] Commission, *EU Law: Better Results* (n 37) p 12.

[39] See only Commission, *White Paper On Artificial Intelligence: A European Approach to Excellence and Trust*, 19.2.2020 (COM(2020) 65) 2.

Like the ECJ, the Commission's normative vision acutely reflects its position in the EU's architecture. The Commission itself is *instrumental* in promoting, guarding and enforcing EU law (for example, through its legislative initiative monopoly, the infringement procedure, or its pivotal role in Competition Law and Policy). As the quasi-executive of the EU, moreover, outcomes will always be more important to the Commission than to other institutions. There is a direct correlation between the institution's own role in administering EU law, and its view of the normative basis of EU law's legitimacy.

Next, the European Parliament (EP) enters the stage with a very different appraisal of the basis for the EU's authority which is, nonetheless, also related to its own role and standing.

V. The EP: Input Legitimacy First

The institutional standing and self-confidence of the EP have both grown significantly since its humble beginnings, which the ECJ used in *van Gend* to support EU law's authority. At the same time, the EP's vision of the EU's authority remained fairly consistent. It has regularly offered an intrinsically democratic-institutional account that centres on the value of institutional arrangements to solve transnational coordination problems and disagreements. According to the EP, only the universal free election of the EP can provide the authority to face the 'contingencies, divergences and particularities of the moment'.[40] This 'new political authority',[41] therefore, is rooted in the authorisation by the peoples.[42] European integration – so the EP argues – is so fundamental, so intrusive and so important, that it must involve the voices of citizens as subjects, rather than objects of the law.[43] The focus is on input, not output. While that must have sounded optimistic and aspirational in 1960, the EP has ever since repeated the argument that the European project is about the links among the peoples of Europe.[44] In contrast to the Court's focus on enforcement, the EP emphasises law-making.

[40] My translation from the European Parliamentary Assembly, 'Rapport fait au nom la commission des affairs politiques et des questions institutionelles sur l'élection de l'Assemblée parlementaire européenne au suffrage universel direct', 30.04.1960, 16.

[41] Leo Tindemans, Report to the European Council, 27.12.1975, Bulletin of the European Communities Supplement 1/76, 29.

[42] But *cf* Sternberg (n 3) 630 for more references but the opposite conclusion. She argues this is intrinsically connected to output legitimacy by helping the European Communities to 'do their job well'. If that were correct, however, there would be no conceptual space for any purely input-centred account of legitimate authority.

[43] European Parliamentary Assembly, 'Rapport' (n 40) 17.

[44] For example, EP, Resolution on the European Parliament's Guidelines for a Draft Constitution for the European Union, 11.7.1990 (1990 OJ C231/91) No 1; EP, Resolution on the 60th Anniversary of the End of the Second World War in Europe on 8 May 1945, 12.5.2005, Nos 6, 8.

The EP has more recently enriched its notion of the EU's authority. In line with the general post-Lisbon emphasis on values encountered throughout this chapter, the EP opined, rather boldly, that the values enshrined in Art 2 TEU made up one of the original drivers of European integration as a whole.[45] Similarly, the emphasis on values represents one of the key normative underpinnings of the EP's resolutions on the current rule of law problems in Eastern European Member States,[46] as well as in its appraisal of the EU's relations to external partners.[47] We should not, however, conceptualise this focus on the EU's values as a self-standing, sufficient justification for the EU's authority. Instead, they operate as a supplementary force and are often combined with democratic elements,[48] or the founding ideas of peace and prosperity.[49]

In relation to the relevant agent, the EP emphasised early on input-based features by invoking the peoples' (by which it means citizens) contribution to the 'European building'.[50] This is hardly surprising since it is in the EP's self-interest to bolster its own institutional role as the main forum of representation for the EU citizens. Nonetheless, the EP offers no unified account of the relationship between citizens, states and peoples in the EU's theoretical architecture. Especially due to its substantive emphasis on citizen representation, the persistent role for Member State cooperation as an element of justification for the EU's authority is astonishing.[51]

Summing up, while the EP leaves room for Member States and peoples as distinct entities, the focus on EU citizens as agents in the EU's governance framework distinguishes the EP from many other institutions. Regarding the normative standard based on which it evaluates the EU's authority, the EP consistently focuses on the democratic value of the EU as supranational forum in which the European peoples author the decisions which subsequently affect them through elected representatives. It increasingly complements this democratic idea(l) with substantive values (Art 2 TEU).

[45] EP, Resolution on the Situation of Fundamental Rights in the European Union of 8.9.2015 (2014/2254(INI)) No A.

[46] EP, Resolution on Ongoing Hearings under Article 7(1) of the TEU Regarding Poland and Hungary, 16.1.2020 (2020/2513(RSP)) No A-B; EP, Resolution on the Rule of Law in Romania, 13.11.2018 (2018/2844(RSP)) No A-C; EP, Resolution on the Situation in Hungary, 17.5.2017 (2017/2656(RSP)) No A-B; EP, Resolution on the Rule of Law and the Consequences of the ECJ Ruling, 10.03.2022 (2022/2535(RSP)).

[47] EP, Resolution on the State of EU-US Relations, 12.9.2018 (2017/2271(INI)). Also EP, Resolution on EU-NATO Relations, 13.6.2018 (2017/2276(INI)) No A; EP, Resolution on the Role of the EU in Promoting a Broader Transatlantic Partnership, 13.6.2013 (2012/2287(INI)) No B.

[48] See for an earlier combination with democratic elements, EP, Resolution on the Declaration of Fundamental Rights and Freedoms 12.4.1989 [1989] OJ C120/51); EP, Resolution on Guidelines for a Draft Constitution of the European Union (n 44) Nos 1–14.

[49] See EP, Resolution on the 60th Anniversary (n 44).

[50] Textes relatifs à l'Assemblée parlementaire européenne au suffrage universel direct, 2.6.1960, 834.

[51] See only EP, Resolution on the Mutual Defence Clause (Art 42(7) TEU), 2.11.2016 (2015/3034(RSP)) No C.

VI. The European Council: International Instrumentalism[52]

The European Council has step by step raised its profile in the EU's institutional architecture. Treaty reforms (like its first formal recognition as a consequence of the Lisbon reforms) cannot, however, sufficiently explain this development. Much is instead due to the European Council's formal and informal reinterpretation of its own role in the past decades, especially since the crisis-ridden times of 2008.[53] Today, the Treaty description of its role to 'define the general political directions' (Art 15(1) TEU) is a glaring understatement. Chiefly due to its non-legislative role, it proves difficult to decipher the European Council's views of the EU's authority. And yet, the various turning points in European integration provided ample opportunity for it to reflect, albeit implicitly, on the moral basis for the EU's right to rule.

A. Legitimacy Through Economic Output

Early statements in European Council Conclusions emphasise the EU's instrumental capacity to achieve the economic goals identified in the Treaty. When reflecting on the 25th anniversary of signing the Rome Treaty, the only element the European Council recalls is 'the importance of the contribution made by the European Community over a quarter of a century to the achievement of the objectives of economic and social progress in the member countries'.[54] Regarding the decisive actor, the focus is clearly on the Member States and their task to design the then Communities in a way that it is 'capable of meeting the challenges with which Europe is confronted today'.[55]

The European Council subsequently linked the economic prosperity and stability in Europe to the citizen's legitimate expectations.[56] Similar to the Commission's statements, however, this shouldn't be understood as a shift in

[52] The findings of this section are based on a comprehensive survey and constructive interpretation of the European Council Conclusions.

[53] See only Puetter (n 1) ch 3. In the early days, it was a very informal meeting. For example, in European Council, Presidency Conclusions, London, 29/30.6.1977, the European Council professionalised and institutionalised its own meetings for the first time. The European Council's increasing role came mostly at the expense of the Commission. See Anchrit Wille, *The Normalization of the European Commission: Politics and Bureaucracy in the EU Executive* (Oxford, OUP, 2013) 207 et seq.

[54] European Council, Presidency Conclusions, Brussels, 29/30.3.1982, No 1. For as early as 1955 see the founding Member States' Messina Declaration of 2.6.1955.

[55] European Council, Presidency Conclusions, Lisbon, 27.6.1992, 2.

[56] European Council, Presidency Conclusions, Cannes, 26/27.6.1995, Introduction. European Council, Presidency Conclusions, Corfu, 24/25.6.1994, Introduction. European Council, Presidency Conclusions Brussels, 15/16.6.2006, Nos 4 and 38. The EU ought to be at the 'service of its citizens', see European Council, Presidency Conclusions, Brussels, 17/18.6.2004, No 5. … or to the 'benefit of the Union's citizens', see European Council, Presidency Conclusions, Brussels, 8/9.3.2007, 1.

perspective towards more input-focused legitimation strategies. The terminological shift instead constitutes little more than an advertising measure to give output legitimacy an allure of deriving from the populace.[57] The point is that instrumental output continues to serve as normative standard to evaluate the EU's legitimacy, independently of its role in the beliefs of EU citizens.

B. From Enlargement to Strategic Autonomy: The More, the Merrier?

Substantial political developments in the early 1990s – such as the downfall of the Soviet Empire and the German reunification – prompted the European Council to update its view of the EU's authority, in search for the basis of a more 'political' community. Already in 1990, it emphasised the common European values (later enshrined in Art 2 TEU), thus intending to invite the ex-Soviet states to join the EU.[58] Those values are once again mentioned at a time when the Russian invasion of Ukraine has revitalised the discussion of the EU's renewed enlargement towards the East.

Since the European Council's discussions of the EU's authority have often been linked to a push for enlargement, it is illuminating to briefly reflect on the relation between authority and size. The European Council often associates size and number of Member States with greater authority, especially internationally. For example, in 2006, it opined that enlargement has helped to overcome the division of Europe and contributed to peace and stability throughout the continent. It has inspired reforms and has consolidated common principles of liberty, democracy, respect for human rights and fundamental freedoms and the rule of law, as well as the market economy. The wider internal market and economic cooperation have increased prosperity and competitiveness, enabling the enlarged Union to respond better to the challenges of globalisation. Enlargement has also enhanced the EU's weight in the world and made it a stronger international partner.[59]

Perhaps this reflects a common assumption in international relations, according to which 'right follows might', ie that population and economic size corresponds to the polity's geopolitical influence.[60] That, incidentally, is also present in the EU's internal discourse in relation to different-sized Member States: for example, the preeminent role of France and Germany as drivers of

[57] Sternberg (n 5) 35 et seq. See, eg, European Council Laeken-Declaration on the Future of the European Union, Annex I to European Council, Presidency Conclusions, Laeken, 14/15.12.2001, 20, stating that the European Council's vision of the EU 'admirably matches citizens wishes'.

[58] European Council, Presidency Conclusions, Dublin, 28.4.1990, Nos 1 and 3.

[59] European Council, Presidency Conclusions, Brussels, 14/15.12.2006, No 5. For earlier examples, see European Council, Presidency Conclusions, Helsinki, 10/11.12.1999, No 3. European Council, Presidency Conclusions, Nice, 7-10.12.2000, No 4. The Commission seems to agree, see Commission, *Third General Report* (n 27) 11.

[60] See only Federico Fabbrini, 'States' Equality v States' Power: The Euro-Crisis, Inter-State Relations and the Paradox of Domination' (2015) 17 *Cambridge Yearbook of European Legal Studies* 3, 6.

integration or the permanent guarantee of an Advocate General position for the big Member States. In any event, empirical evidence suggests that enlargement does indeed contribute to more compliance with EU law.[61] An influential recent study on the 'Brussels-Effect' confirms this relation between size and authority. It suggests that the EU's global regulatory authority derives its normative force, among others, from the sheer scale of assembling and regulating (currently) 27 individual nation states.[62] Politically, the recent debates between Europe and the US (eg between the Biden Administration and the EU regarding industrial policy) illustrate the advantage of debates on equal footing between the two, which seem impossible to achieve for individual Member States. These considerations play a concrete role for our object of study: the moral authority of EU law. The weight of any associational or contractarian justification, ie one based on the horizontal institutional integration of the participants, increases in relation to the authority of individual Member States with a growing number of EU members, since the nominal weight of each individual entity shrinks. In short, the greater the number of Member States and EU citizens, the more normative weight for EU law passed by all of them.

At the dawn of a new millennium, the European Council kindly summarised its view of the EU's authority in the Tampere Conclusions. It portrays a dual source for the EU's legitimacy, combining *instrumental economic goals* and *substantive values*. According to the European Council, EU integration is based on a 'shared commitment to freedom based on human rights, democratic institutions, and the rule of law. These common values have proved necessary for securing peace and developing prosperity in the European Union'.[63]

The European Council's most recent take still grounds the legitimacy of the EU in its ability to tackle contemporary challenges. In substance, a sound economic system, curiously connected to values, forms the heart of the European Council's view of the *raison d'être* of the EU.[64] This is evident in the reflections on the challenges for the EU as an autonomous and strategic player. The considerable development of the Area of Freedom, Security and Justice since Tampere, combined with permanently looming terrorism threats and the questioning of the post-war transatlantic defence alliance, prompts the European Council to increasingly view the EU as instrumental to protect EU citizens and their freedom as a whole:

> The common values underpinning our democratic and societal models are the foundation of European freedom, security and prosperity. The rule of law, with its crucial role

[61] Tanja Börzel and Ulrich Sedelmeier, 'Larger and More Law Abiding? The Impact of Enlargement on Compliance in the European Union' (2017) 24 *Journal of European Public Policy* 197.

[62] Anu Bradford, *The Brussels Effect: How the European Union Rules the World* (Oxford, OUP, 2020).

[63] European Council, Presidency Conclusions, Tampere, 15/16.10.1999, No 1. Similarly, European Council, Presidency Conclusions, Brussels, 25/26.3.2004, Nos 6–8. See also European Council, Presidency Conclusions, Brussels European Council, 10/11.12.2008, No 1. European Council, Presidency Conclusions, Brussels, 11.12.2020, No 1.

[64] See only European Council, Conclusions, Brussels, 2.10.2020, Nos 7 and 9.

> in all our democracies, is a key guarantor that these values are well protected; it must be fully respected by all Member States and the EU.[65]

The common values are not portrayed as ends in themselves. And neither is European integration. Instead, they serve the aim of maximising the impact of the Member States in the world. As so often in Europe's history, the common identity on the inside is nurtured by a perceived external threat, or at least significant challenges in the external environment.[66] For example, the call for the EU to become digitally or technologically 'sovereign'[67] links political theory to a modern version of threat (cyber warfare, powerful digital companies).

It is questionable whether the combination of instrumental benefits and substantive values as main reasons for the EU's authority match with political reality or whether they can coexist without friction. According to widespread academic criticism, the emphasis on common values and the well-being of the citizens have been sacrificed on the altar of economic viability during the financial crisis.[68] There, the European Council resorted to mechanisms outside the EU legal order (European Financial Stability Facility (EFSF), European Stability Mechanism (ESM), etc), where democratic and legal accountability, to put it mildly, are scarce. Whilst this is no place to assess the implications of these crisis mechanisms (wait for chapter six), it shows how the European Council prioritised economic and financial stability over institutional legitimacy and substantive accountability.

This short digression illustrates that employing a broader arsenal of normative standards increases the risk that they clash with each other. This is additional evidence that social reality is simply messier than academic models. In any case, the discrepancy between political theory and institutional reality contributes to the theoretical debate whether political theory ought to give up unitary models of legitimacy to stay closer to social reality, despite the risk of conflict among these standards. Alternatively, it could be precisely the task of political theory to provide a 'clean' analytical framework as an ideal standard for institutions and their social reality. As I will explain in chapter five, the truth lies in between. Whereas theories of political authority ought to provide a unitary ideal guideline for evaluating the rightful exercise of public power, this is compatible with non-monistic – viz. various parallel – assessment vehicles internal to a single standard (such as elements of input, output and throughput).[69]

[65] European Council, Guidelines following the United Kingdom's Notification under Article 50 TEU, 29.4.2017. See also Informal Meeting of Heads of State or Government, Sibiu Declaration, 9.5.2019.

[66] See, in more detail, Josef Weinzierl, 'Territoriality beyond the State: The EU's Territorial Claims and the Search for Their Legitimacy' (2021) 22 *German Law Journal* 650.

[67] European Council, Conclusions, Brussels, 2.10.2020, Nos 6 and 7.

[68] In European Council, Presidency Conclusions, Brussels, 19/20.3.2009, 1, the European Council still had an eye on EU citizens, when declaring: 'By acting together, the EU can put its financial sector on a sound footing, get credit flowing to the real economy and protect its citizens from the worst impacts of the crisis'. Compare that to European Council, Presidency Conclusions, Brussels, 17.6.2010, and European Council, Presidency Conclusions, Brussels, 14/15.3.2013.

[69] For a discussion in relation to democratic authority on the national level, see Thomas Christiano, 'The Authority of Democracy' (2004) 12 *Journal of Political Philosophy* 266.

C. Interim Conclusion

In line with other institutions, the European Council does not offer a unified moral benchmark for evaluating the authority of the EU. This is not a criticism. Apart from the fact that institutions are not bound by academic models, the European Council is a political body involved in the governance of the EU. Its conclusions reflect the political environment of the day as much as the compromise between the leaders of multiple sovereign states.

Nonetheless, two things can be discerned. First, the European Council almost exclusively relies on the Member States as relevant agents and reference points for the legitimate authority of the EU. Neither peoples nor citizens play a vital role in legitimising the EU's authority. Citizens are mostly used in proclamations to enhance and proclaim the social legitimacy of the EU. Second, the overall trend for offering a substantive moral benchmark is and always has been instrumental. The European Council judges the EU's authority by way of the advantages it has for the Member States. Although those are primarily economic, the more visible geopolitical standing of 27 states united in a supranational political community plays an ever-greater role in recent years. The common values of Art 2 TEU figure in many, especially recent, Council Conclusions. Yet, they never assumed a self-standing legitimising function. In other words, the European Council employs an *international-instrumentalist* justification strategy. Like the Commission, the EU's right to rule is justified here because it provides the service for these Member States of increasing their individual economic well-being as well as their voice internationally while adhering to common values.[70]

With that, let us finally address the perspective of actors that, while not EU institutions in the narrow sense of Art 13 TEU, have influenced the debate of EU law's authority for decades: national constitutional courts.

VII. National Constitutional Courts: Popular Consent

It should have become apparent by now that this book is not about the intensely debated theoretical disagreement between the ECJ and the national constitutional courts. It leaves the (sovereignty-related) question of ultimate decision-making authority mostly to one side and studies the EU's authority claim regarding the correct moral standard to evaluate its legitimacy.

National constitutional courts nonetheless have a say in debating the moral basis for the EU's authority. This is not only due to the EU's unique institutional architecture, where the law-administering institutions of its Member States play a vital role in enforcing EU law. National constitutional courts are 'EU institutions'

[70] This is deliberately phrased in terms of Joseph Raz's service conception, which will be discussed in chapter 4.

in at least two important ways. For one, they are vital parts of the EU's normative architecture (as explained in chapter two) and pronounce on the theoretical implications of EU membership for their own constitutional arrangement. For another, they have historically been the main actors in reconciling the EU's emerging authority claim with their respective constitutions for which they act as ultimate guardians.

National constitutional courts overwhelmingly base the authority of the EU and its laws on the consent of their constitutional people, since they treat certain core guarantees in their national constitutions as expressions of popular sovereignty. As one of their most prominent representatives, the German Constitutional Court (*Bundesverfassungsgericht* or BVerfG) argues that the

> democratic legitimation by the people of public authority exercised in Germany belongs to the essential contents of the principle of the sovereignty of the people and thus forms part of the Basic Law's constitutional identity … It follows that the Basic Law does not authorise German state organs to transfer sovereign powers to the European Union in such a way that the European Union were authorised, in the independent exercise of its powers, to create new competences for itself.[71]

Put differently, the legitimation strategy of 'the people's consent' is derived from the national constitution, which enshrines the possibilities for as well as the limits to integration beyond the state. The constitution and, more precisely, the will and consent of the *pouvoir constituant* informs the national constitutional court's authority basis.

The constitutional courts focus on the self-determining people instead of Member States as the relevant constituent entity.[72] This shift has important theoretical implications. First, it distinguishes their approach from the classic state-consent justification in international law, which downplays any theoretical impact of international arrangements on individuals or their fate as a collective people. The focus on peoples constitutes a bottom-up acknowledgement of the qualitative difference in EU law's intrusion into the national constitutional arena. Second, the focus on their people allows constitutional courts to impose limits on EU integration, even if Member State officials would consent to them.[73] For there to remain sufficient space on the national level to allow a people to self-determine its affairs in a proper democracy, various salient competences can't be transferred to the EU and the national parliament's scope of action itself must not be substantially

[71] BVerfG, Judgment of 05 May 2020–2 BvR 859/15 (*Weiss*), para 101.

[72] Similarly Eva-Maria Tieke, *Das Subjekt Demokratischer Legitimation in Der Europäischen Union* (Baden-Baden, Tectum, 2016) 303 et seq.

[73] For an overview of the evolving disagreement between the ECJ and national constitutional courts, see Andrew Oppenheimer, *The Relationship between European Community Law and National Law: The Cases* (Cambridge, CUP, 1993, 2003) vols 1 and 2. Instructive also is Bruno De Witte, 'Direct Effect, Primacy, And the Nature of the Legal Order' in Paul Craig and Gráinne De Búrca (eds), *The Evolution of EU Law*, 2nd edn (Oxford, OUP, 2011).

eroded.[74] It follows that the attempt to transfer non-transferable competences (elements of national constitutional identity) violates the constitution. In other words, the state institutions cannot validly transfer certain competences to the EU because the *demos* as constituted power (*pouvoir constitué*) is constitutionally obliged to retain them at the national level.[75] Other national constitutional courts operate with similar *controlimiti*, so that national popular self-determination sets absolute limits to EU integration and consequently to the legitimate exercise of public power by the EU.[76]

The viability of the constitutional courts' theoretical edifice is not under consideration here (wait for chapters four to six). The take-away for our purposes is the exclusively derivative nature of the EU's authority in that picture. It seems like a supranational adaption of the historically quite popular benchmark for political authority on the national level, ie the notion of normatively meaningful *consent* of individual citizens. Actual constitutional authorisation by the people entails the necessary consent from which the EU's moral authority and its limits derive. Even more important is that the national constitutional courts' notion of legitimate authority focusses exclusively on a single unit. It relies on each national constitution and people individually, with no concern for how they interrelate as a European political or moral community. The BVerfG's limits on the EU's legitimate authority derive from the German Constitution, the Czech Constitutional Court's limits from the Czech Constitution, the Spanish Constitutional Court's limits from the Spanish Constitution, and so on. Put differently, in contrast to referring to a 'union of peoples', the constitutional courts focus on their individual constitutional people alone. And yet, the national constitutional courts remarkably perceive the national people – instead of Member States – as the ultimate constituent entity of the EU polity. Their argumentative edifice rests on the normative requirement that, ultimately, the national people needs to author any public rule exercised over that people.

To sum up, the constitutional discourse in national supreme courts is unambiguous. The EU's authority is anchored in – and simultaneously limited by – the consent of each individual people as expressed in the respective constitutions.

[74] BVerfG, Judgment of 21 June 2016–2 BvR 2728/13 (*Gauweiler*) paras 115 et seq. BVerfG, Judgment of 30 June 2009–2 BvE 2/08 (*Lisbon*) para 249 contains a list.

[75] Only the constituent power can do that. See, also for other examples, Michel Troper, 'The Modern State and the Concept of Authority' in Roger Cotterrell and Maksymilian Del Mar (eds), *Authority in Transnational Legal Theory* (Cheltenham, Elgar, 2016) 89.

[76] For example, Spanish Constitutional Court, judgment 26/2014 of 13 February 2016 (*Melloni*), sec II.3 refers to the 'sovereignty of the Spanish people' as the ultimate reference entity. Moreover, the Italian Constitutional Court since the 1970s has derived its 'controlimiti-doctrine' from Art 11 Italian Constitution, which speaks of the 'limitations of sovereignty' Italy agrees to. See only *Italian Constitutional Court, Frontini v Minister delle Finanze* [1974] 2 CMLR 372. For a similar approach of the French Constitutional Court and insights on other Member States, see De Witte (n 73) 354 et seq. The Polish Constitutional Court, K32/09, 24 November 2010 confirmed this view by relying mainly on the consent of the nation to bind Poland to the EU (the word *consent* appears no less than 58 times in the judgment).

VIII. Conclusion: Theoretical Purity vs Institutional Reality

The following summary shows that the institutions hold divergent views in relation to the moral standard for and relevant actor concerning the EU's authority. In that, at least, they imitate their academic counterparts. A striking difference between the two perspectives, however, is that academics strive for uniform and coherent accounts, whereas the institutions are happy to take leaves out of various books:

Fig 9 Institutional Visions of the EU's Authority

	Substantive Moral Standard	**Relevant Agent**
Treaties I: TFEU	Overall focus on the (intrinsic and instrumental) value of binding institutional cooperation to achieve peace and prosperity among the EU peoples	European peoples as joint entities; prominent subsidiary role for Member States
Treaties II: TEU	Combination of cooperative (integration through functioning institutions) and substantive values (Art. 2 TEU)	Ambiguous. Noticeable focus on Member States
ECJ	Developed over time. Post-Lisbon: Institutional elements (the integrity of and respect for supranational law-making and enforcement procedures) firmly conjoined with substantive values (Art. 2 TEU)	No explicit account. Important roles for citizens, states and EU peoples, mostly focusing on their respective relation to each other
Commission	Emphasis on instrumental value of delivering various outcomes	Ambiguous, mainly Member States
European Parliament	Emphasis on democratic elements (value of EU institutions to enable European cooperation by allowing input of all Europeans). Subsidiary role for substantive values (Art. 2 TEU)	Not entirely clear, but noticeable focus on role of EU citizens
European Council	Mainly instrumental: EU law's capacity to deliver outputs through coordination among stakeholders. Subsidiary role on substantive values (Art. 2 TEU). Focus on enlargement as tool to increase EU's authority	Member States
National Constitutional Courts	Consent of national people, each individually	Constitutional Peoples

This cautious summary depicts institutional reality. Neither is any given institution's perspective necessarily internally coherent, nor are the different views of individual institutions compatible with each other. Due to the looming threat of

selection bias and the often murky blend of social and moral legitimacy, I had to proceed with appropriate caution when imputing these views to the institutions. Note in that context also the variegated use of notions such as 'people', which might mean self-determined national *demoi* to some, the citizens or an individual citizen to others, or even constitute a synonym for states. The following conclusions are thus only tentative.

Seeing theories of authority applied in practice results in a rather convoluted picture. Many individual considerations are at play, sometimes capable of being traced back to well-known authority literature, sometimes idiosyncratically derived from the specifics of the EU polity. This theoretical patchwork quilt illustrates how different conceptions of the EU's authority inform institutional practices. The same applies to the disagreement about the underlying agent. That is, whom does the EU ultimately concern and who is the source of its authority? Its Member States? EU citizens? The European peoples? All of them together? In one way or another, the moral standards focus on a mix of constituent entities, thereby reflecting the lack of a European *demos*, the composite architecture of the EU, and the still unresolved question of the EU's constitutional nature. While the absence of any discussion seems to suggest that the institutions don't disagree about the nature and scope of the EU's authority claim in the sense of chapter two, they all disagree on the moral basis and relevant agent underlying the legitimate authority of EU law. This chapter shows that there is no such thing as 'the EU's view of its authority basis'. Each institution has formulated its own, often dynamic and developing conception. Deciphering this polyphony of institutional conceptions on the right moral standard and agent for grounding the EU's authority constitutes the first lesson of this chapter.

The second lesson stems from the interesting links between the institutional position and the institution's view of the EU's authority. To a varying degree, the conceptions of the institutions studied in this chapter mirror the standing of these institutions in the EU's architecture. Recall only the EP's focus on the peoples' input or the Commission's emphasis on economic benefits. There seems to be a reflexive relationship between institutional standing and authority conception.

The third lesson emerges from connecting the dots, from discovering interesting alliances and frictions among the Treaties and institutions studied above. For example, the substantive convergence between the European Council and the Commission's instrumental accounts might be due to the 'executive spirit' in both institutions. Both have executive responsibilities at the national and EU level respectively. Yet, the reasoning of both institutions differs sharply. While the heads of states and governments in the European Council intend to justify the added value of the European project to their home constituents, the Commission's instrumental outlook can be traced back to its crucial role in delivering and monitoring the EU's policies. Furthermore, there is a palpable tension between the European Council's rather lax attitude towards regulatory fragmentation resulting from enlargement on the one hand, and the Court's and Commission's usual emphasis on institutional unity, coherence and integrity on the other. This reflects the political character of the European Council as opposed to the Court's and Commission's overall more juridic nature. Finally, the vision of each institution either consisted in a patchwork of different moral ideas from the outset or changed over time to adjust to internal or external developments. The exception is national constitutional courts. They have consistently relied on the people's consent to underwrite the EU's legal and moral authority. This can be explained by the fact that they are not EU institutions in the narrow sense (Art 13 TEU), but first and foremost national institutions. Consequently, whenever the EU evolved, either through Treaty amendments or a shifting geopolitical environment, this didn't affect national constitutional courts directly. They simply continued to rely on their home constitutions.

At the end of this chapter, I can only hope that the juxtaposition of the institutions' views on the EU's authority fulfilled the hinge function I promised at the beginning of the chapter. Whereas chapter two explored the nature, scope and addressees of the EU's authority claim (and where it ought to be located in the range between national and international authority), chapter three led us to the core question of the remaining chapters, namely to identify the correct moral standard to evaluate the EU's legitimate authority. It showed that the Treaties and institutions disagree about both the moral basis for the EU's authority and about the underlying agent and source. The rich collection we encountered here serves as background for the ensuing analysis of each model's cogency.

In chapter four, I complement this institutional reality by turning to academic accounts of the EU's authority (some of which I hinted at above). That is, I portray implicit and explicit models of the appropriate moral baseline for the EU's authority in the literature, link them to the view of the institutions, and assess their theoretical soundness. This marks the penultimate step before I propose my own view of how to evaluate the grounds and limits of the EU's right to rule, or – in other words – of how to assess the truth of the EU's authority claim.

4

Potential and Limits of Current Models on the EU's Authority

I. Introduction

This chapter puts the institutional perspectives of the previous chapter into their theoretical context and evaluates the viability of existing – implicit or explicit – accounts of the EU's authority. At the outset, however, let me reflect on the appropriate agent: on who is the source of the EU's authority, since this aspect affects each of the substantive accounts that follow.

II. Identifying the Source of the EU's Authority

In chapter two, I argued that the EU barely affects the individual autonomy of an EU citizen qua individual human, especially when compared to states and their monopoly of force. The EU's authority thus cannot be based on ideas such as EU citizen consent or maintaining a fair distribution of benefits and burdens between them as individual agents, since that would be at odds with the EU's authority structure. Chapter two moreover showed that an exclusive focus on states and their officials fails to appreciate the distinct normative architecture of the EU. In other words, Member States are not the appropriate source of the political authority of the EU. Yet, some authors insist on the Member States as the primary and exclusive source for the EU's authority:

> Whatever authority the EU claims … must be rooted in a grant made to it by the Member States, as the principal site of recognized political authority in Europe. And, provided this is maintained, the Member States come to the rescue of the EU by supplying it with the political legitimacy to act which on its own it lacks.[1]

I disagree. I think that ultimately the constitutional peoples themselves as self-determining collectives underpin the EU's moral authority. Indeed, each individual people remains constituted in and as separate states, which through their institutions

[1] Stephen Weatherill, *Law and Values in the European Union* (Oxford, OUP, 2016) 9; Anand Menon and Stephen Weatherill, 'Transnational Legitimacy in a Globalising World: How the European Union Rescues Its States' (2008) 31 *West European Politics* 397, 398.

play a vital role in the EU's governance. But the focus on peoples enlarges the theoretical toolbox for the idea that the peoples jointly author a supranational arrangement that is conceptually distinct, but not independent from the states they each make up separately.[2] I don't understand the EU as a union derivative of *states* with no direct normative relationship to the constitutional peoples and their citizens. Instead, the EU complements states, which are themselves but an instrument for the self-determination of an individual people.

Precisely because of ever-growing inter-, trans- and supranational developments, political theory ought to acknowledge that peoples may entrust political agency to non-state polities. While the peoples in social reality act mostly as state officials and citizens, they intervene themselves to take important decisions through referenda, when amending their constitutions, or via their representatives in the EP. A constitutional people is conceptually prior to state institutions, which derive their legitimacy from popular (constitutional) authorisation and implement the will of a self-determined collective.

While it is true that the Member States are the principal sites of political authority, this does not apply to areas beyond their legitimate jurisdiction, however. In many ways, the EU does for the European peoples what their states can't. Since the EU's tasks thus escape the legitimate authority of the individual state, it is hard to see how states could act as the main repository for legitimate authority in precisely those areas. As Craig remarked re the widespread use of terminology such as democracy and legitimacy, it 'bears testimony to the acceptance by the major players that the Community requires a form of legitimation which can no longer be found purely in the traditional language of state agreement and state control'.[3] In short, we ought to focus on the constitutional peoples themselves as a source of the EU's political authority.

The EU enables the peoples to deliberate and resolve tensions between the two levels (state and EU), via which they exercise their self-determination.[4] The point is that states lack the normative power to bind their peoples in the way the EU purports to do, because the EU affects the self-determination of the European peoples from which the states themselves originate.[5] In the EU's architecture, state institutions do not 'own' their citizens in the sense that they alone could represent their interests and political agency. Think of the current

[2] Francis Cheneval and Kalypso Nicolaidis, 'The Social Construction of Demoicracy in the European Union' (2017) 16 *European Journal of Political Theory* 235, 236 et seq. Francis Cheneval, *The Government of the Peoples: On the Idea and Principles of Multilateral Democracy* (London, Palgrave Macmillan, 2011) 58.

[3] Paul Craig, 'Democracy and Rule-making Within the EC: An Empirical and Normative Assessment' (1997) 3 *European Law Journal* 105, 112 et seq.

[4] Nicole Bolleyer and Christine Reh, 'EU Legitimacy Revisited: The Normative Foundations of a Multilevel Polity' (2012) 19 *Journal of European Public Policy* 472, 479.

[5] One reason why state consent fails as an appropriate framework. See Daniel Bodansky, 'The Legitimacy of International Governance: A Coming Challenge for International Environmental Law?' (1999) 93 *American Journal of International Law* 596, 610.

developments in some Member States, where authoritarian governments face pro-European opposition: not through their institutions, but via their own civil society. Such movements would have no voice in the debate about the EU's legitimate authority if we focused on state institutions and officials alone. Neither would their national judges, who intend to apply EU law faithfully, or the Members of the European Parliament (MEPs), who derive their mandate directly from their national people as well. There are thus both analytical and normative advantages to focusing on the constitutional peoples.

Chapter five builds on the insight that we should view the EU's constitutional peoples as ultimate agents and source of the EU's authority more fully. For now, however, let's focus on the literature on the moral grounds for the EU's authority.

III. Taking Stock: The Obscure Debate on the Moral Basis of the EU's Authority

I call the debate on the correct moral standard to evaluate the EU's authority obscure because it is hard to find fully-fledged accounts of the moral authority of EU law. One aim of the ensuing pages is to uncover the normative assumptions behind these contributions in the literature. To start, let's focus on a value that has informed theories of authority for centuries: consent.

A. The Role of Consent in the EU's Authority Architecture

i. Authority Through Consent

Based on an intuition derived from private relations (think of promises or contracts), consent has long played an important role in understanding the authority of the state. My state may legitimately obligate me if and to the extent to which I have signed up for that scheme.[6] Consent is attractive, since it protects autonomy (my decision), equality (adults relate to each other as equals, which only consent can change to a hierarchy of authority) and establishes an accountability relationship between authority and subject.[7] Mainly due to the realisation that individuals rarely consent actively, some theorists resorted to qualifications such as hypothetical or tacit consent. Locke famously insisted that everyone who does not decide

[6] Proponents of this *actual consent* view (though with notable differences) include Thomas Hobbes, *Leviathan* (Continuum, 2005); Leslie Green, *The Authority of the State* (Oxford, Clarendon, 1988); Robert Nozick, *Anarchy, State and Utopia* (Oxford, Blackwell, 1974).

[7] Thomas Christiano, 'The Legitimacy of International Institutions' in Andrei Marmor (ed), *The Routledge Companion to Philosophy of Law* (Abingdon, Routledge, 2012) 383.

to escape the jurisdiction of a state and leave gives tacit consent to its authority.[8] Consent theorists accept that this moral benchmark is high and that the legitimacy of most laws is questionable.[9]

Many theorists translate this idea to the international sphere and anchor the authority of international law in the consent of the (state) parties to international treaties.[10] This stems from the traditional understanding of state sovereignty explained in chapter one. Since sovereign states can only incur obligations by actively consenting, their consent is the only available legitimacy source for international authority. Attempts to curtail sovereign states' room for manoeuvre by creating and enforcing binding legal norms independently of the everyday consent of the affected state are often considered hugely problematic.[11] To this day, most international lawyers intuitively subscribe to the view that the authority of international law and its institutions is based on state consent. That is why Çali calls it the 'standard account'.[12]

The ingenuity of consent theory is that I bind myself voluntarily. The source of authority is the individual citizen's/state's normative powers, which enable them to overcome the core difficulty of reconciling autonomy with authority. But now to the EU.

ii. Primary Law-Making as a Plausible Starting Point

Considering this success story of consent, it is unsurprising to find traces of it in reflections on the EU's authority. After all, aren't the Member States the 'Masters of the Treaties', who fully control the constitutional basis of the EU? Even the ECJ itself mentioned this phrase not so long ago when summarising party arguments in AG Sharpston's appeal against the decision of the Representatives of the Member State Governments to replace her early.[13] MacCormick echoes this idea when he invokes *pacta sunt servanda* as the normative consequence of state

[8] John Locke, *Two Treatises of Government and A Letter Concerning Toleration* (edited by Ian Shapiro) (New Haven, Yale University Press, 2003).

[9] Green (n 6) 165 et seq.

[10] For a discussion, see Allen Buchanan, 'The Legitimacy of International Law' in Samantha Besson and John Tasioulas (eds), *The Philosophy of International Law* (Oxford, OUP, 2010) 90 et seq. For a recent nuanced defence see Richard Collins, 'Consent, Obligation and the Legitimate Authority of International Law' in Patrick Capps and Henrik Palmer Olsen (eds), *Legal Authority Beyond the State* (Cambridge, CUP, 2018).

[11] See only Martin Loughlin, *The Idea of Public Law* (Oxford, OUP, 2004). For a discussion focused on sovereignty and EU membership, see Michel Troper, 'The Survival of Sovereignty' in Hent Kalmo and Quentin Skinner (eds), *Sovereignty in Fragments: The Past, Present and Future of a Contested Concept* (Cambridge, CUP, 2010). From an international perspective, see Buchanan (n 10) 86 et seq; John Tasioulas, 'The Legitimacy of International Law' in Tasioulas and Besson (n 10) 113 et seq.

[12] Başak Cali, *The Authority of International Law: Obedience, Respect, and Rebuttal* (Oxford, OUP, 2015).

[13] Case C-424/20 P(R) *Sharpston* EU:C:2020:705, para 17. See also Dieter Grimm, 'Sovereignty in the European Union' in Johan Van der Walt and Jeffrey Ellsworth (eds), *Constitutional Sovereignty and Social Solidarity in Europe* (Baden-Baden, Nomos, 2015).

consent in the search for the legitimacy of EU law.[14] What is more, one of the strongest counterarguments to consent theories on the national level, namely the empirical absence of actual consent,[15] does not apply in the EU. Member State consent is ubiquitous at the level of the EU's constitutional foundation, such as primary law-making and accession.

There is thus prima facie a good case for a consent-based justification of the EU's authority. I am nonetheless sceptical about the viability of consent as the correct standard to evaluate the EU's authority. Let's take Çali's great questions as a starting point:

> If European Union law aims to integrate 28 states more deeply, does this mean its authority should be understood in ways that match the normative intentions of its creators? Are European Union member states under a more profound duty to respect the authority of European Union law? Does European Union law have authority on grounds other than the binding nature of the treaty? In other words, does it attract obedience for reasons beyond the standard account?[16]

While you will find my answers to these questions in the remainder of the book, my answer to the last question is: Yes, it does. The standard account of state consent doesn't do the trick in the EU. Let me explain why.

iii. *The Normative Limits of Member State Consent*

The notion of voluntariness lies at the heart of consent theory.[17] This in itself is morally questionable, however, since it prioritises voluntary obligations over involuntary ones without good reason, especially in the public realm.[18] Even if we grant the importance of voluntariness, the picture in the EU is murky. EU membership is indeed voluntary for the European states and their peoples (Arts 49 et seq TEU). This formal observation nonetheless obscures that – in substance – the EU in many ways resembles a non-voluntary scheme. For the individual citizen the EU is non-voluntary as it takes the collective decision of a majority of one's people to enter and exit the EU. More importantly still, on a collective level Brexit provides many years of evidence about the substantive costliness of exit.[19]

[14] Neil MacCormick, *Questioning Sovereignty: Law, State, and Nation in the European Commonwealth* (Oxford, OUP, 1999) ch 9.

[15] David Estlund, *Democratic Authority: A Philosophical Framework* (Princeton, Princeton University Press, 2008) 9.

[16] Cali (n 12) 35.

[17] On the relationship between voluntariness and consent, see Andrei Marmor, 'An Institutional Conception of Authority' (2011) 39 *Philosophy & Public Affairs* 238, 250.

[18] Ronald Dworkin, *Justice for Hedgehogs* (Cambridge (MA), Harvard University Press, 2011) 318 et seq.

[19] Leslie Green, 'Rights of Exit' (1998) 4 *Legal Theory* 165.

These reflections raise doubts about the theoretically meaningful voluntariness of EU membership. The point is that consent falsely suggests that it is easy to revoke consent at any time. The breadth and depth of the EU's authority claim explained in chapter two make it all but impossible to foresee the future avenue of EU integration and how the individual peoples will be affected by the mutual opening of their territories. In other words, it is implausible to assume that consent at a given time legitimises the daily workings and future developments of the EU.[20]

The second reason for doubting a primary role of consent is the widespread overestimation of the moral work consent can do in underpinning political authority. The doubts result mainly from the idea that the reasons for consent are actually more important than the consenting act itself, and that consent is in itself insufficient to establish political legitimacy, given that one can consent to morally atrocious regimes.[21] Applied to the EU, this shows that consent as a basis for the EU's authority is normatively unattractive, as it puts unwarranted emphasis on the exit right of states and their peoples. Consent is unable to establish tangible substantial limits on the EU's authority beyond legality (ie conformity with the Treaties) as long as they remain members. In a nutshell, one would have to accept any EU law in accordance with primary law as legitimate if one doesn't leave. A consent-focus has the counterintuitive implication that the EU can legitimately increase the burden on the collective autonomy of its peoples as long as they remain in the EU. In that sense, exit rights only pretend that there is an easy moral way out.

Third, many theorists rightly criticise the failure of individual consent to account for interactive concerns, especially the cooperative enterprise a political community necessarily is.[22] A multilevel polity like the EU highlights this failure. The exclusive fixation of consent on one individual source of authority (for example a citizen's consent on the state level or state consent on the international level) belies the various horizontal, diagonal and vertical elements that underly the EU's authority architecture and its various actors. Whose consent matters? Consent can't accommodate the nature of the EU as a collective enterprise of peoples acting mainly through state institutions and citizens. It would obscure that the *raison*

[20] More generally see Christian Volk, 'The Problem of Sovereignty in Globalized Times' [2019] *Law, Culture and the Humanities* 1, 10. For a parallel critique in international authority theory, see Cali (n 12) 100.

[21] Joseph Raz, 'Government by Consent' in Joseph Raz, *Ethics in the Public Domain: Essays in the Morality of Law and Politics*, Rev edn (Oxford, Clarendon, 1995); Jeremy Waldron, 'Theoretical Foundations of Liberalism' (1987) 37 *Philosophical Quarterly* 127, 136–40; Scott Hershovitz, 'Legitimacy, Democracy, and Razian Authority' (2003) 9 *Legal Theory* 201, 215; Christiano (n 7) 385.

[22] Thomas Christiano, *The Constitution of Equality: Democratic Authority and Its Limits* (Oxford, OUP, 2008) ch 7; Samantha Besson, 'State Consent and Disagreement in International Law-Making. Dissolving the Paradox' (2016) 29 *Leiden Journal of International Law* 289, 291; Nicole Roughan, *Authorities: Conflicts, Cooperation, and Transnational Legal Theory* (Oxford, OUP, 2014) 33.

d'être of the EU is based on a plural: on the horizontal political, economic and historical links between the peoples of Europe and their states. How they relate to each other must play a role in grounding the authority of EU law, and individual consent leaves no room for that.

Beyond these structural features, basing the EU's authority on consent (most obviously Member State consent) has various normative consequences I am reluctant to accept. For example, national constitutions would necessarily have primacy over EU law. That holds true even if they consented to the primacy of EU law, since that consent would ultimately derive from and be determined by their national constitutions. Consequently, Member States would be allowed to derogate from EU law based on their interpretations of their constitutions, which alone form the basis and thus also the limit of state consent. Remember that the survey of the institution's vision of the EU's authority (chapter three) showed that national constitutional courts are the only institutions which openly argue for consent-based authority. Even in their frameworks, however, consent is not a 'super-value' that gives the EU unlimited authority in the sense consent theory suggests. Quite the contrary. Consent has absolute substantive limits, chiefly among them national constitutional identity. There are sectors so central to statehood and national democracy that they may not be transferred to the EU. In other words, their transfer to the EU would be illegitimate, quite apart from the presence of a consenting act by state officials. This shows, first, that consent alone can't do the moral work expected from it and, second, that the necessary focus of consent on one individual entity would render the binding force of EU legal acts up for grabs.

What is more, procedures, accountability and substantive guarantees don't matter in a consent-based account. Each Member State – as represented by its current government – would individually constitute the ultimate source of authority of the EU, thus shutting out any normatively interesting horizontal moral relationship between the European peoples, civil societies and individuals. Consent's utter disregard for the value of political institutions and the moral reasons for setting up political communities in the first place makes it an unattractive benchmark for legitimate authority.

To sum up, consent is the wrong moral standard to evaluate the authority of EU law. For one, the notion of voluntariness fails to grasp the deeper normative architecture of the EU. For another, various structural features (focus on exit rights and each agent individually), as well as unattractive normative consequences (no concern for the EU's multilevel architecture and accountability mechanisms), and the lack of endorsement by the Treaties or EU institutions, suggest that we ought to look elsewhere for a viable basis of the EU's authority.

Before moving on, let me 'de-radicalise' my claim. I don't suggest that consent is irrelevant for the present discussion. I have tried to show previously that the more consent an authority enjoys, the more effective the governance (chapter one). Consent is a crucial ingredient of *social* legitimacy, of a political regime's de facto acceptance by the bulk of its subjects. That, however, only impacts on a ruler's moral authority to the extent that it makes it more stable. It creates an 'extra reason' to obey and expresses 'confidence' in the abilities of the government of the day.[23] In short, consent of the bulk of subjects is necessary for the de facto authority of a government but can only function as supporting consideration for moral legitimacy. That is the real importance of Member States' renewed consent at moments of treaty amendment.[24] Their consent denotes trust and establishes accountability. Conversely, the negative referenda in France and in the Netherlands, which killed the Constitutional Treaty in 2005, constituted remarkable illustrations of the widespread lack of trust in how the EU was run. But it does not follow that consent should be considered the moral basis for the EU's authority.

B. Beyond Instrumentalism Beyond the State

Let's now look at the potential of instrumental accounts to ground the EU's authority.

i. Instrumental Authority

Raz's service conception is the starting point for instrumental justifications of authority. According to Raz, authority is normally justified (Normal Justification Thesis) if and to the extent its directives help the agent to conform to reasons which apply to them independently (Service Conception). Therefore, it would be better if we treated these directives as authoritative.[25] Raz himself expanded his view beyond the state. In his view, states as well as super-state organisations (he mentions the UN and the EU) 'are justified by the results, by the quality of their character and life'.[26] In that sense, a doctor's advice and a legal directive are functionally similar. In both cases, the authority provides a service to the subject, helping them to do what they have reason to do anyway. Raz later introduced the 'independence condition' which restricts the authority of law to instances where it is more important to decide correctly than to decide for oneself.[27] This results

[23] Joseph Raz, *The Morality of Freedom* (Oxford, Clarendon, 1986) 88 et seq; Raz, 'Government by Consent' (n 21) 367; Liam Murphy, 'The Normative Force of Law: Individuals and States' in Leslie Green, John Gardner and Brian Leiter (eds), *Oxford Studies in Philosophy of Law* (Oxford, OUP, 2018) vol 3, 120.

[24] See Erik Oddvar Eriksen, *The Normativity of the European Union* (London, Palgrave Macmillan, 2014) 91 for a fuller appreciation of the value of authorisation in the EU's architecture.

[25] Raz, *The Morality of Freedom* (n 23) 53. See also Joseph Raz, 'The Problem of Authority: Revisiting the Service Conception' (2006) 90 *Minnesota Law Review* 1003, 1014.

[26] Joseph Raz, 'The Democratic Deficit' (King's College London Dickson Poon School of Law, Legal Studies Research Paper Series) 2018–07, 10.

[27] Raz, 'The Problem of Authority' (n 25).

in piece-meal authority, the legitimacy of which is contingent on the individual's own expertise in the area under concern. The duty to obey the law is here first and foremost a rational one, which becomes moral if the underlying reasons are moral.[28]

Murphy uses an instrumental account to evaluate the authority of international law in its entirety. In Murphy's view, compliance with international law is morally mandatory because the limited enforcement of international law increases the destabilising effects of non-compliance and because it makes the world a better place.[29] Similarly, Tasioulas provides an elaborate instrumental account of international authority. He endorses Raz's service conception to 'normally justify' the authority of international law.[30] For him, international law has legitimate authority to the extent that it makes its subjects better conform to independent reasons if they treat international law as authoritative. For Tasioulas, the piece-meal nature of authority reflects social reality in relation to actors (international law has varying authority on different states) and domains (international law's authority varies according to the underlying issues) as much as it reflects the normative value that states should be unbound by international law where they can foster global goods better individually.[31]

These instrumental theorists thus ground the authority of law in its ability to help us to achieve ulterior, often moral ends. They focus on the quality of the outcome for the agent subjected to authority.

ii. Traces of Instrumental Authority in the EU

Any account of legitimate authority that focuses exclusively on outputs can, in fact, be characterised as instrumental. The family of instrumental accounts is thus much broader than Raz's service conception.

Many social scientists and political theorists understand and interpret the EU through an instrumental lens. I refer to the belief that the EU is legitimate to the extent it delivers (mostly economic) outputs which improve the lives of Europeans. In chapter three, for example, I argued that the Commission and the European Council focus on the benefits and output the EU brings for its participants (mostly the Member States) in their discussions of the EU's legitimacy, and I translated that into an instrumental account of authority. Relatedly, various early theories about the broader rationale for EU integration, especially

[28] David Lefkowitz, 'The Duty to Obey the Law' (2006) 1 *Philosophy Compass* 571, 593.

[29] Murphy (n 23) 118 et seq. Andreas Follesdal, 'The Legitimate Authority of International Courts and its Limits' in Patrick Capps and Henrik Palmer Olsen (eds), *Legal Authority beyond the State* (Cambridge, CUP, 2018) applies Razian instrumentalism limited to the role of international courts.

[30] Tasioulas (n 11) 100 et seq.

[31] ibid 103 et seq.

neo-functionalist and liberal intergovernmental approaches, focused exclusively on outcomes, especially economic prosperity and efficiency.[32] Today, Scharpf seems to be the most ardent defender of the view that the EU should be legitimised in terms of output alone.[33] He argues that the EU lacks the preconditions for input legitimacy and warns that the EU's output legitimacy ought to be aware of its impact on input legitimacy on the national level. In my view, output legitimacy thus understood can be translated into one subcategory of instrumental authority that focuses directly on substantive ends.

The institutional developments after the 2008 Financial Crisis led scholars more recently to note critically that, if anything, the EU's authority can currently be justified with reference to economic prosperity and shared benefits alone, rather than, say, input legitimacy.[34] Notably, Isiksel has characterised the EU's normative architecture as 'functional constitutionalism', where functionalism ought to 'convey the EU's purposive mode of legitimation'.[35] The EU's legitimate authority, in her view, is grounded on the effective delivery of goods, especially an economic union. That means 'its legitimacy depends on the successful realization of these substantive objectives; that is to say, its basis of legitimacy is functionalist'.[36] Especially because the goal of an economic union is entrenched in primary law and thereby removed from easy amendment, the EU's authority depends on the 'desirability and successful realization of these aims'.[37] Instead of making an argument for the attractiveness for such a normative vision, Isiksel interprets the EU's normative architecture. That, according to her, simply is the EU's nature: a constitutional arrangement beyond the state that bases its right to rule on delivering an economic union to its Member States and their citizens. In short, the EU relies on *finalité economique* rather than *finalité politique*.[38]

This *tour d'horizon* illustrates that instrumental visions pervade contemporary writing on the EU's authority without even the need for a proper normative defence. It seems so obvious. Should we thus assess the legitimacy of the EU's authority claim based on its instrumental value? I don't think so:

[32] Paul Craig, 'Integration, Democracy, and Legitimacy' in Paul Craig and Gráinne De Búrca (eds), *The Evolution of EU Law*, 2nd edn (Oxford, OUP, 2011) 16 et seq.

[33] See only Fritz Scharpf, *Governing in Europe: Effective and Democratic?* (Oxford, OUP, 1999). Fritz Scharpf, 'Legitimacy in the Multilevel European Polity' (2009) 1 *European Political Science Review* 173, 178.

[34] Michael Wilkinson, 'The Specter of Authoritarian Liberalism: Reflections on the Constitutional Crisis of the European Union' (2013) 14 *German Law Journal* 527, 548; Turkuler Isiksel, 'Constitutionalism as Limitation and Licence' in Tom Ginsburg, Mark D Rosen and Georg Vanberg (eds), *Constitutions in Times of Financial Crisis* (Cambridge, CUP, 2019) 195.

[35] Turkuler Isiksel, *Europe's Functional Constitution: A Theory of Constitutionalism Beyond the State* (Oxford, OUP, 2016) 72 et seq, 45.

[36] ibid 78. See also Signe Larsen, *The Constitutional Theory of the Federation and the European Union* (Oxford, OUP, 2021) 97 et seq.

[37] Isiksel (n 35) 220.

[38] ibid 18.

iii. The Case against Instrumental Authority

The important yardstick of instrumental theories of authority is to what extent law helps the members of a political community to achieve certain ends. Such an instrumental structure is inadequate, however, to ground authority.

Firstly, I take issue with the way in which instrumental accounts cloud the underlying moral issues by shifting the focus from morality to prudential reasons and rationality. That feature alone makes instrumental theories an odd case for justifying authority, since the underlying problem of authority is moral: namely, how to reconcile binding laws with individual or collective autonomy. That, of course, can easily be remedied by only counting moral reasons as enablers of instrumental authority, ie by narrowing down the category of reasons that underpin instrumental authority. There is no such easy remedy for the next point, however.

I suggest that instrumental benefits of rule-following can't ground legitimate authority, let alone political obligation. Rule-following for its own sake is morally empty, especially in a multilevel system in which individual legal orders compete. The well-known doctrine of *effet utile* in EU law helps me to make my point. *Effet utile* means that the effectiveness of EU law as such is an argument for its normative force. An interpretation which leads to a 'better' implementation of EU law is preferable because it helps EU law to be effective.[39] And yet, national constitutional orders want to be effective as well. *Effet utile* cannot explain why (a hypothetically conflicting) national law should not be effective. Its normative force is necessarily constrained to intra-systemic arguments, which serve the rule of law of a given legal system.[40]

This weakness of *effet utile* in theoretical terms corresponds to criticism of Raz's service conception. The idea that it would be better for my compliance with the reasons that apply to me independently to treat law as authoritative, does not establish that law is, in fact, authoritative.[41] It seems as if instrumental accounts miss the point of the moral problem authority poses by failing to translate a rational advantage into moral authority. It remains open how a rational 'would be good' turns into a moral 'ought to'. The example of the EU as a multi-level order with competing legal systems illustrates this defect powerfully.

Secondly, instrumental accounts (like consent theories) focus on a single agent, such as the citizen in the state context, or the state in the international context.

[39] See, prominently, Case C-106/77 *Amministrazione delle finanze dello Stato v Simmenthal* EU:C:1978:49, para 18. For a comprehensive survey of the case law, see Urška Šadl, 'The Role of Effet Utile in Preserving the Continuity and Authority of European Union Law: Evidence from the Citation Web of the Pre-Accession Case Law of the Court of Justice of the EU' (2015) 8 *European Journal of Legal Studies* 18.

[40] Armin von Bogdandy, 'Founding Principles' in Armin von Bogdandy and Jürgen Bast (eds), *Principles of European Constitutional Law*, 2nd edn (Oxford, Hart/Beck, 2010) 29 et seq.

[41] Andrei Marmor, 'The Dilemma of Authority' (2011) 2 *Jurisprudence* 121, 125 et seq; Stephen Darwall, *The Second-Person Standpoint: Morality, Respect, and Accountability* (Cambridge (MA), Harvard University Press, 2006) chs 8 and 9.

They exclude considerations outside each individual agent and evaluate instrumental benefits for each agent individually. Whereas the agent in question seems a good starting point for approaching the autonomy-authority relationship, it is ultimately too narrow. Indeed, there is something odd about this *quid-pro-quo*, rather transactional architecture. I provide binding solutions, you obey. Vice versa (in an EU example): I pay a share of the EU budget, so what do I get out of this? The upshot would be that EU law's moral authority varies among Germans, Italians and Latvians, depending on how they benefit, let's say, economically from the EU. As Cruz put it:

> The temptation is that of conceiving the Union as a game in which all the states should win all the time and in all sub-games, never losing or conceding anything, engaging in cooperation only when there is something to win, and trying to reduce costs and maintain or recover as much autonomy as possible for the rest, rolling back the policies which entail any sort of solidarity. This conception would deeply transform and undermine the Union.[42]

The intrinsic value of institutional processes that allow us to cooperate and regulate our affairs together is irrelevant for instrumental theories. They are inherently inept to evaluate the legitimacy of institutions.[43] Since law is the key and not rarely the only instrument to administer political authority, however, it seems counterintuitive to ignore its moral features. That would mean to neglect why we set up political communities on the communal, regional, or state level and beyond in the first place. Various authority theorists have rightly emphasised that, in relation to political authority, there are intrinsic and instrumental reasons to conclude that the value of an institutional procedure is conceptually prior to the 'right' outcome. In Hershovitz' words, 'making decisions together can be more important than getting them right'.[44] In short, it matters for law's authority how laws are made and enforced.

Thirdly, the 'institutional blindness' of instrumental accounts is exacerbated by a questionable assumption in the very architecture of instrumental authority. Instrumental models must assume that there is a specific outcome that is desirable for every participant. But that is surely disputable. To let Christiano speak, the 'trouble with instrumental justifications, however, is that there is serious disagreement on what the best outcomes are supposed to be'.[45] Voting and institutional deliberation are there to decide on the ends the community should pursue, as

[42] Julio Baquero Cruz, *What's Left of the Law of Integration?: Decay and Resistance in European Union Law* (Oxford, OUP, 2018) 128.

[43] Marmor (n 41) 133. Allen Buchanan, 'Institutional Legitimacy' in David Sobel, Peter Vallentyne and Steven Wall (eds), *Oxford Studies in Political Philosophy* (Oxford, OUP, 2018) vol 4, 70–73.

[44] Hershovitz (n 21) 218. Similarly Pavlos Eleftheriadis, 'Citizenship and Obligation' in Julie Dickson and Pavlos Eleftheriadis (eds), *Philosophical Foundations of European Union law* (Oxford, OUP, 2012) 177.

[45] Thomas Christiano, 'A Democratic Theory of Territory and Some Puzzles about Global Democracy' (2006) 37 *Journal of Social Philosophy* 81, 102.

well as on the prioritisation of various ends and on the means to achieve them.[46] I believe, for example, it is fair to assume that there is no consensus about the right outcome in any of the areas of the EU's competence. To name a few, how should EU citizenship be reconciled with national welfare states? To what extent should EU subsidies be tied to keeping with Art 2 TEU values? How should the EU asylum system be redesigned? In fact, there is not even agreement on which competences the EU ought to have in the first place (think only of a competence to raise direct taxes).

A view of the EU as an instrument for Member States to produce outputs even undermines the legitimate authority of EU law in three distinct ways. First, making the authority of law contingent on achieving outputs constitutes shaky ground.[47] The benefits of the promised economic union appear straightforward, but it has been clear for quite some time that they do not materialise equally in all Member States.[48] Second, instrumental authority downplays the political and contested nature of the EU's actions. Of course, one could turn the openness to various outputs into a virtue and emphasise the attractiveness of instrumentalism because it encompasses a wide range of considerations. As we have seen in chapter three, the institutions which emphasise instrumental considerations cover aspects from effectiveness (ECJ), peace and stability (European Council), and economic prosperity (Commission). Each of these benefits, however, presupposes unanimity on their desirability, and entails that failure to produce these outcomes would damage the authority of EU law. Third, the prioritisation of instrumentalist output legitimacy downgrades intrinsic goods of a constitutional system with self-government and fundamental rights chiefly among them. The European Council's instrumentalist mindset during the Euro-crisis led – as we saw – to a normatively questionable precedence of economic gains over input legitimacy and accountability.

For these reasons, I do not think instrumental accounts ought to serve as appropriate standard to evaluate the EU's authority. Their prudential focus clouds the underlying moral problem of political authority. Their exclusive emphasis on the individual subject can't account for the value of political institutions as fora for millions of subjects. And their inherent assumption that there is an uncontested outcome or benefit appear hugely problematic, especially in a multilevel polity like the EU.

Outcomes are of course important in a governance framework. They are important in relation to de facto authority, where it always matters whether a polity/institution actually delivers results on issues of importance for

[46] Jeremy Waldron, *Law and Disagreement* (Oxford, Clarendon, 1999) 243.

[47] See only Joseph Weiler, 'The Authority of European Law: Do We Still Believe in It?' in Wolfgang Heusel and Jean-Philippe Rageade (eds), *The Authority of EU Law: Do We Still Believe In It?* (New York, Springer, 2019) 6 on material promises as precarious basis.

[48] Stephen Weatherill, *Cases and Materials on EU Law*, 12th edn (Oxford, OUP, 2016) 361.

the populace.[49] Additionally, instrumental theories can explain why the EU might be *justified*, ie why it makes sense to have it, especially from the perspectives of the involved states. The factual interdependence of European states makes it the case that if we didn't have the EU, we would have to invent a similar entity sooner or later.[50] But that merely justifies the EU's existence. It doesn't give its laws moral authority.[51] Outcomes, in other words, cannot serve as successful standards for the EU's legitimate authority, ie its capacity to legally and morally bind those who disagree with the outcome. Every outcome is contested and its legitimate pursuit dependent on a prior choice of the constituent units.

C. Political Obligation and Democratic Institutions

Let us, next, look at accounts of the EU's authority which prioritise institutional input and procedures over the quality of any output. When analysing the value of institutions for the EU's authority, it is thereby essential to draw an important distinction between EU institutions (where non-primary EU law is made), and national institutions (which overwhelmingly enforce EU law). I want to discuss them in turn.

i. Democratic Authority

Proponents of democratic authority argue that legitimate political authority stems from the qualities of the law-making procedure in democratic states: from how democracies reach decisions. A democracy respects individual citizens – despite fundamental and reasonable disagreement among them – by giving them an equal voice in deciding about the issues that affect the entire political community.[52] This view admits that the result of the legislative process may not be the *best* one, since there may not even be an on-balance better solution. The moral duty to obey arises instead from the unique capacity of law-making procedures to process the subjects' disparate views and thereby honour their autonomy and dignity.[53] The equal opportunity to influence democratic procedures and institutions justifies requiring the *acceptance* of the outcome of the legislative machinery.

[49] See recently Nadja König and Ludger Schuknecht, 'The Role of Government and Trust in the Market Economy' in Heusel and Rageade (n 47).

[50] Similarly Weatherill (n 1) 415.

[51] A must read on the distinction between justification and legitimacy is A John Simmons, 'Justification and Legitimacy' (1999) 109 *Ethics* 739.

[52] Waldron (n 46) 99 et seq; Christiano (n 22) ch 7. Similarly Christopher Wellman, 'Toward a Liberal Theory of Political Obligation' (2001) 111 *Ethics* 735; David Lefkowitz, 'A Contractualist Defense of Democratic Authority' (2005) 18 *Ratio Juris* 346. Hershovitz (n 21).

[53] Hershovitz (n 21) 213 et seq.

Estlund and Landemore focus on the qualities of legislative processes as well. They don't focus on their moral achievement in light of widespread reasonable disagreement, however. Instead, they argue (setting important differences among them aside) that the legislative procedures in liberal democracies have distinct *epistemic qualities*, ie the means to come up with a 'good' solution, especially due to the diversity of views that they bring together.[54] Estlund's 'epistemic proceduralism' and Landemore's 'democratic reason' in one way or the other base the authority of democratic laws on their propensity to come up with a good decision.

Various scholars have recently attempted to base the legitimate authority of international law on its democratic credentials. Brunnée and Toope support the legitimacy of international law and the political obligation it creates for states based on the value of interactional law-making on the international plane.[55] In their view, the law-making process itself grounds compliance since it clearly expresses the commitment of the individual stakeholders to the common project. Other accounts focus on democratic elements even more directly. For example, Peters (though for the most part as an aspirational project) argues for democratic legitimacy as an appropriate benchmark for international law. She sees neither institutional (a global assembly is possible), nor social (preconditions for deliberation can be created), nor cultural (a demos is not needed) obstacles for global democracy and urges the relevant actors to facilitate it.[56]

Democratic authority grounds the respect for law in the moral achievement of political institutions to give individual citizens equal influence and voice in the production of laws despite pervasive and reasonable disagreement among them on how to govern their society. It implies that people *ought to* consent based on the normative virtues of the institutions and procedures.[57] The focus is not on the individual's isolated relationship to the authority ('I bind myself'), but on the collective enterprise and its institutions ('We bind ourselves to each other').

ii. Democratic Authority at the EU Level?

Can we translate these ideas to the institutional set-up of the EU level? The widespread obsession with the 'democratic deficit' – though it implicitly acknowledges the importance of democracy as a standard to evaluate the EU's rightful rule – invites scepticism. As we saw in chapter three, however, the EP focusses on the input legitimacy provided by a directly elected Parliament in the supranational

[54] Estlund (n 15); Hélène Landemore, *Democratic Reason: Politics, Collective Intelligence, and the Rule of the Many* (Princeton, Princeton University Press, 2013).

[55] Jutta Brunnée and Stephen J Toope, *Legitimacy and Legality in International Law: An Interactional Account* (Cambridge, CUP, 2010) ch 3.

[56] Anne Peters, 'Dual Democracy' in Jan Klabbers, Anne Peters and Geir Ulfstein (eds), *The Constitutionalization of International Law* (Oxford, OUP, 2009).

[57] Simmons (n 51) 261.

architecture. In the literature, Eriksen argues that the normativity of EU law should be assessed based on its compliance with democratic standards. For him, the EU realises democratic ideals as a 'regional cosmopolitan polity'. He lists the 'milestones of EU democratisation, among them the direct election of the EP, EU citizenship, the Charter of Fundamental Rights or the citizens' initiative.[58] Eriksen explicitly distinguishes EU democracy from democracy's manifestation at the state level, and argues that the fusion of constitutional orders (constitutional pluralism), state-less government (no monopoly of force; instead, the normative ideal of constitutional democracy under separation of powers), parliamentary interweaving (the combination of EP and national parliaments) and a layered public sphere (deliberation and contestation within and outside of EU institutions) justify evaluating the EU on the basis of democracy.[59]

I think this is a mistake. For a start, any viable version of democratic authority can certainly not be translated into international society and international organisations. The international order lacks the institutional means to deal equally with deep disagreement, as well as the relevance for people's lives and the societal preconditions to establish democratic arrangements.[60] But to the extent that democracy ought to manifest the values championed by democratic authority theorists, it also fails as a basis for the EU's legitimate authority. The key reasons for democratic authority theories on the national level simply don't apply to the EU.

For one, democratic authority focusses on the democratic essence of national parliamentary procedures, which treat every individual *equally*. They secure individual autonomy by giving everyone an equal chance to influence how the polity in question is governed. The EU is not a democracy in this essential sense. The EP doesn't represent a single *demos* of equal citizens, nor are EU citizens given an equal voice and voting opportunity in EP elections (instead, degressive representation according to Art 14(2) TEU). Eriksen interprets the principle of autonomy as constitutive element of democracy too widely when he defines it as 'those affected by laws should also be authorized to make them'.[61] This definition lacks the crucial element that underpins democracy as a moral standard for rightful rule on the national level: the *equal* respect of citizens through formal decision-making procedures. Equal influence and representation alone secure their individual autonomy. Eriksen may be right about the presence of some other elements of democracy in the EU's architecture. But those, such as 'transparency,

[58] Eriksen (n 24) 48.

[59] ibid 90 et seq.

[60] See Thomas Christiano, 'Democratic Legitimacy and International Institutions' in Samantha Besson and John Tasioulas (eds), *The Philosophy of International Law* (Oxford, OUP, 2010) s 9; Collins (n 10) 221. But cf. Mattias Kumm, 'Democratic Constitutionalism Encounters International Law: Terms of Engagement' in Sujit Choudhry (ed), *The Migration of Constitutional Ideas* (Cambridge, CUP, 2007) 262.

[61] Eriksen (n 24) 17, 62.

participation, representativeness, and accountability'[62] can't compensate for the absence of equal respect, which makes democratic laws authoritative. The latter is intrinsically connected to the moral relationship among the citizens in a democracy.

For another, the EP neither occupies the crucial position its national equivalents enjoy (note only that it has no right of legislative initiative) nor are its policy choices substantively unconstrained (due to the EU's limited competences and the broader economic vision entrenched in primary law).[63] In particular, the epistemic value of the EU's institutional procedures is qualitatively different from what the defenders of the epistemic value of democratic procedures on the national level have in mind.

Democratic authority in its various manifestations thus relies on the specific properties of democratic nation states. It presupposes the existence of a demoscracy which the EU is not. As I will show in chapter five, the idea of 'demoicracy' provides a more promising conceptual framework for translating democratic ideals beyond the state. But what if we focus on national institutions?

iii. Is the Sum Greater than its Parts?

National institutions are crucial for EU-law making and enforcement. The Council of the EU is composed of national ministers and, as a result, profits indirectly from their democratic credentials. National parliaments play a role as EU law-administering institutions when transposing directives or as main actors of the Early-Warning Mechanism to ensure compliance with subsidiarity. Chapter two alluded to the pivotal role national courts and administrative authorities play in the enforcement of EU law. But we can't upscale the strong input-related arguments made above to legitimise EU law. The role of national institutions in making and enforcing EU law is just too different from their respective roles in relation to national law. In short, EU law-making does not profit from the democratic authority of national institutions. But what does Weatherill mean in the passage quoted above, according to which the Member States supply 'the EU … with the political legitimacy to act which on its own it lacks'?

Recently, Eleftheriadis has put forward an argument that puts flesh on the bones of this idea. He argues that international obligations are part and parcel of the state's authority, thereby endowing them with the same moral force. In that framework, the concept of authority has no independent meaning beyond the state, because international legal obligations are internalised in the

[62] Mattias Kumm, 'The Cosmopolitan Turn in Constitutionalism: On the Relationship between Constitutionalism in and beyond the State' in Jeffrey L Dunoff and Joel P Trachtman (eds), *Ruling the World? Constitutionalism, International Law and Global Governance* (Cambridge, CUP, 2009) 273. The presence of these values in EU governance is disputed in Weiler (n 47) 13 et seq.

[63] See also Paul Craig, 'The EU, Democracy and Institutional Structure: Past, Present and Future' in Heusel and Rageade (n 47) 321.

statist framework.[64] They are incorporated in the state's authority. For our purposes, the moral duty to obey EU law is just the same in kind and force as the duty to obey national law, since both emanate from the moral imperative to realise a set of just institutions to facilitate how we relate to each other as individuals on different political levels. That obviates the need to search for distinct legitimation strategies.[65] EU law is, so to speak, cloaked with national law's legitimacy credentials since national institutions call the shots when incorporating and enforcing EU law. National institutions apply EU law in the same way as national law, so the distinct origin in supranational institutions does not matter. Eleftheriadis writes: 'In a way, all EU obligations are now equally domestic obligations'.[66]

In his view, we do not owe political obligation to the EU or its institutions. Instead, we owe the 'duty of jurisdiction' to our home state or to any state of residence (host state), that is the respect for their moral achievement in setting up just institutions.[67] Indeed, we cannot owe political obligation to the EU directly, because it does not constitute such a moral achievement.[68] Our status as EU citizens does not change our moral position towards the EU in the sense that third country nationals owe the same duties to the respective host states. Eleftheriadis' view is that the sum is not greater than its parts. The EU doesn't create its own forum for legitimate authority, but docks onto and enriches the national notions of authority and political obligation. This original and sophisticated model squares the circle by enabling EU law to profit from the legitimate authority of national law in a constitutional state of public right.

Nonetheless, I take issue with both the theoretical structure underpinning Eleftheriadis' argument and with its normative implications. To begin with, sources of law matter for an appraisal of its legitimacy. This is no place to fully defend this claim. Let me just say this: chapter one distinguished between authority claims on different regulatory levels. In my view, such a distinction is conducive to analytical clarity and normatively desirable. One of the dangers I noted, for example, in relation to the contemporary sovereignty discourse is the lack of differentiation between the underlying institutional structures on different regulatory levels, which leads to the unwarranted application of state-bound concepts to supranational institutions. Besides, attention to sources reflects social reality. Judges and other law-administering officials differentiate between the moral value and effect of national law on the one hand, and supra- or international law on the other. There is then a moral intuition that sources matter. Eleftheriadis implicitly

[64] Pavlos Eleftheriadis, 'Federalism and Jurisdiction' in Elke Cloots, Geert De Baere and Stefan Sottiaux (eds), *Federalism in the European Union* (Oxford, Hart Publishing, 2012) 62; Pavlos Eleftheriadis, *A Union of Peoples* (Oxford, OUP, 2020) 193.

[65] Eleftheriadis (n 44) 169, 182 et seq.

[66] Eleftheriadis, 'Federalism and Jurisdiction' (n 64) 62.

[67] Eleftheriadis (n 44) 169, 178, 186 et seq.

[68] ibid 181.

acknowledges that, since his dualism is built on a distinction between national law and international law, their respective institutions, and the different moral achievements they embody.

Moreover, Eleftheriadis' 'progressive internationalism' is unable to accommodate the EU's authority claim as outlined in chapter two. For him, EU citizenship for example is not citizenship at all.[69] More importantly, his dualism turns the institutional aspect of the EU's authority claim upside down. For it rejects the idea that EU law, when compared to international law, marks a qualitative difference by using national institutions to give effect to EU law in the way described in chapter two.[70] Eleftheriadis' model must deny what the EU actually does in terms of political authority. Perhaps not altogether surprising considering the previous chapters, I take issue with the qualification of the EU as an international organisation that belongs to the domain of international law. Under his progressive internationalism, there can only be two types of public institutional arrangements: the constitutional state, where we owe duties of citizenship to each other; and the worldwide moral community, which owes natural duties of justice/civility to each other.[71] *Tertium non datur*. Yet, I insist (quite apart from the breadth and salience of the EU's competences) that EU law seeks to bind the European peoples in a qualitatively distinct way (chapter two). In plain speak, consider the difference between the US' (temporary) withdrawal from the WHO in 2020, and the UK's withdrawal from the EU. The effect of these decisions on the autonomy and self-determination of a constitutional people differ significantly.

I doubt, moreover, that the duty to obey EU law has the same content and moral force as the duty to obey national law. I have argued that the moral obligations EU law claims to impose on us are of a different kind compared to national law. In particular, EU law in the standard case obligates us as collectives and constrains our ability to self-determine our affairs as constitutional peoples. Eleftheriadis, for example, discusses the Dublin III Regulation, which puts the responsibility for migrants on the Member State of first entry.[72] For him, the moral position of a Third Country National is comparable to the one of EU citizens in host Member States, since both are bound by the 'duty of jurisdiction' to any just state other than their home state. In other words, the moral duties imposed by the EU are none other than those stemming from the entire international system. But EU law does not bind us as individual autonomous agents. It addresses the constitutional peoples as collectives. I understand the core moral duty involved in this

[69] Eleftheriadis, *A Union of Peoples* (n 64) 192.

[70] See the discussion ibid 158 et seq.

[71] See, for example, Eleftheriadis, 'Federalism and Jurisdiction' (n 64) 63.

[72] Eleftheriadis (n 44) 160. Regulation (EU) No 604/2013 of the European Parliament and of the Council of 26 June 2013 establishing the criteria and mechanisms for determining the Member State responsible for examining an application for international protection lodged in one of the Member States by a third-country national or a stateless person (recast) (Dublin III Regulation) [2013] OJ L180/31.

element of the Dublin Regime to affect the peoples of the state of first entry. The challenges arising from this system for the Greek and Italian peoples constitute the appropriate moral lens to judge the legitimacy of the Dublin III Regulation, as public discourse confirms. As a result, EU political obligation, viz. the ground and nature of the moral duty to obey EU law, is conceptually different from national political obligation.

Equating EU and national political obligation also faces practical problems. It fails to grasp the reality of conflicts between the authority of national law and that of EU law. Eleftheriadis' framework provides us with no tool to compare and evaluate each legal obligation's legitimacy foundation, nor does it offer an argument how to solve any conflicts in practice. If the moral obligation to obey EU law and national law have the same moral force, the citizen or institution lacks any guidance on how to deal with such conflicts.

Consequently, we can neither apply democratic authority arguments to the EU institutions themselves, nor can we rely on the legitimacy of democratic national institutions to ground EU law's authority.

D. The Recent Popularity of Values

Perhaps substantive constitutional values can help. As explained in chapter three, the Treaties and most of the EU institutions have integrated the values of Art 2 TEU when reflecting on the legitimate authority of the EU.

i. Cosmopolitan Constitutionalism: On the Basis of Values

Substantive standards never occupied a central role in theories of state authority. By contrast, international constitutionalism holds that the authority of international law is grounded on its conformity with and fostering of constitutional values, chiefly fundamental rights and the rule of law.[73] International constitutionalism is a wider field, conventionally subdivided in normative, functional and pluralist approaches. We will focus on the normative limb alone.[74]

The most prominent account of normative international constitutionalism is Kumm's cosmopolitan constitutionalism. It grounds the authority of any public law (national, European, international) on 'universal principles central to liberal democratic constitutionalism' so that the order takes moral precedence

[73] For an overview of manifestations, aims and critique of international constitutionalism, see Klabbers, Peters and Ulfstein (n 56).

[74] By contrast, functional approaches to international constitutionalism analyse to what extent the allocation of (vertical and horizontal) authority is achieved by an international constitution, see Jeffrey L Dunoff and Joel P Trachtman, 'A Functional Approach to International Constitutionalization' in Dunoff and Trachtman (n 62).

which best adheres to these values.[75] For example, he portrays the ECJ's seminal *Kadi* case and its defence of fundamental rights protection against non-reviewable international acts as an instance of this idea. Kumm subsequently restated the idea of constitutionalism as foundation for the legitimate authority of law with particular attention to the *rule of law*, which he then connects with *democracy* and *fundamental rights* protection to form the 'trinitarian formula of constitutionalist faith'.[76] In his view, a

> legal and political system that effectively institutionalises the rule of law is one that fulfils the conditions that need to be fulfilled for law to actually have the authority it claims to have. The content of the rule of law thus becomes a function of the normative grounds that justify its claim to authority.[77]

Buchanan, after refuting state consent-based accounts, advocates for a similar yet more concrete route to justify the legitimate authority of international law. For him, democratic procedures in a loose sense of 'broad accountability' in combination with adhering to substantive fundamental rights protection grounds international authority and constitutes the criteria to evaluate its legitimacy.[78]

ii. Values and the EU's Authority

In 2009, the Lisbon Treaty introduced Art 2 TEU. It made the discourse on values that had commenced with the Charter of Fundamental Rights official:

> The Union is founded on the values of respect for human dignity, freedom, democracy, equality, the rule of law and respect for human rights, including the rights of persons belonging to minorities. These values are common to the Member States in a society in which pluralism, non-discrimination, tolerance, justice, solidarity and equality between women and men prevail.

This is a substantive commitment at the symbolically important outset of the TEU. Waluchow calls these values the 'positive morality' of the EU and thereby underlines their suitability as moral standard to evaluate the legitimate authority of EU law.[79] Whereas this codification is a significant step, it was impossible

[75] Mattias Kumm, 'Rethinking Constitutional Authority: On the Structure and Limits of Constitutional Pluralism' in Matej Avbelj and Jan Komárek (eds), *Constitutional Pluralism in the European Union and Beyond* (Oxford, Hart Publishing, 2012); Kumm (n 62) 605. For a specific focus on fundamental rights in adjudicating the weight of legitimate international authority, see André Nollkaemper, 'Rethinking the Supremacy of International Law' (2010) 65 *Zeitschrift für öffentliches Recht* 65.

[76] Mattias Kumm, 'The Cosmopolitan Turn in Constitutionalism: An Integrated Conception of Public Law' (2013) 20 *Indiana Journal of Global Legal Studies* 605, 609.

[77] Mattias Kumm, 'The Rule of Law, Legitimate Authority and Constitutionalism' in Christoph Bezemek, Michael Portacs and Alexander Somek (eds), *Legal Positivism, Institutionalism and Globalisation: Vienna Lectures on Legal Philosophy* (Oxford, Hart Publishing, 2018) vol 1,117.

[78] Buchanan (n 10). See also Allen Buchanan and Robert O Keohane, 'The Legitimacy of Global Governance Institutions' (2006) 20 *Ethics & International Affairs* 405.

[79] Wil Waluchow, 'Constitutionalism in the European Union: Pipe Dream or Possibility?' in Julie Dickson and Pavlos Eleftheriadis (eds), *Philosophical Foundations of European Union Law* (Oxford, OUP, 2012) 204 et seq.

to anticipate the important role values would play in the practice of EU law. That applies not only to the EU institutions' extensive recourse to them (chapter three). In addition, the rule of law problems in various Member States triggered the first use of the Art 7 TEU procedure, as well as the ECJ's complementing jurisprudence (based on Arts 19 TEU, 267 TFEU (see chapter three)). What is more, the Commission recently for the first time used a violation of the values in Art 2 TEU as self-standing plea in infringement proceeding against Hungary.[80]

This development suggests that the values of Art 2 TEU constitute an appealing basis for the legitimate authority of EU law. I am nonetheless reluctant to accord a primary role to these values in grounding EU law's authority.

iii. Evasive Values

I think the widespread use and popularity of the values listed in Art 2 TEU should raise suspicion. The reason for that suspicion is that the popularity points to their inherent ambiguity. Values like democracy or the rule of law are broad churches. They can be institutionalised and put into action in multiple ways.[81] The question how the values relate to each other only adds complexity to the issue.[82] There will always be reasonable disagreements about what it entails to comply with these values – often a crucial part of judicial review. Making these values *operational*, in other words, constitutes a choice. A choice that highlights the importance of who makes the choice. Critics understandably fear that recourse to values could become an ideological tool rather than an evaluative standard; an 'exercise in legitimation of the EU's own policy preferences, which merely helps advance the institutional agenda'.[83] In short, abstract recourse to those values constitutes precarious ground for underwriting the EU's authority.

Even if one could settle the interpretive question, there is a more fundamental problem in relation to the EU's composite/multilevel/polycentric polity. National constitutional orders are not only a competing forum for implementing these values. They constitute their natural habitat. Most of the values mentioned in Art 2 TEU were developed in the context of the post-Westphalian nation state (notable exception: democracy), as the second sentence implicitly confirms.[84] Admittedly, there is a lot to be said for the view that the EU is based on a *conception*

[80] Case C-769/22 *Commission v Hungary*.

[81] Christoph Möllers, 'Constitutional State of the European Union' in Robert Schütze (ed), *Globalisation and Governance: International Problems, European Solutions* (Cambridge, CUP, 2018) 263; Loïc Azoulai, 'The Madness of Europe, Being Attached to It' (2020) 21 *German Law Journal* 100, 101; Waluchow (n 79) 196.

[82] Ernst-Wolfgang Böckenförde, 'Critique of the Value-Based Grounding of Law [1990]' in Mirjam Künkler and Tine Stein (eds), *Constitutional and Political Theory: Selected Writings* (Oxford, OUP, 2017) 229.

[83] Azoulai (n 81) 101.

[84] For this reason Christian Volk, 'Why Global Constitutionalism Does Not Live up to Its Promises' (2012) 4 *Goettingen Journal of International Law* 551, 564 et seq criticises global constitutionalism's use of concepts which were designed for the nation state.

of the rule of law within the realm of the broader *concept* of the rule of law. As Bolleyer/Reh put it: 'In contrast to its member states, the EU therefore not only needs to balance values; it first needs to decide who should carry which value at what level'.[85]

Think about the primacy debate. If the authority of EU law hinges on the respect for the EU's conception of values, how could it ever take precedence over national law that complies with national conceptions of, let's say, the rule of law? Kumm himself seems to encounter that problem when discussing democracy as one of the three core elements of the 'constitutionalist rule of law'. By requiring a democratic process based on, inter alia, the *equal* right to vote for law to be legitimate,[86] he implicitly rules out that the EU has legitimate authority, simply because the EP is not elected by an equal vote of each EU citizen (see above). Perju powerfully outlined this predicament when discussing the legacy of Böckenförde:

> the inevitability of conflicting interpretations of values between states and the EU creates difficult challenges. How a political community chooses to interpret abstract values … is an indispensable dimension of its self-government. While abstract values might seem common, the specifics of their meaning are so central that the process of interpretation must itself remain within the realm of political self-determination.[87]

I agree. The competing fora for value-protection are the real challenge for cases like *Melloni* or *IHG*. The real issue in *Melloni* is not whether the Council Framework Decision for the European Arrest Warrant (EAW)[88] complies with the fundamental right to effective legal protection. It is whether the Spanish or European interpretation of the fundamental right to effective legal protection informs the case. The normative core is thus related to the character of the underlying political community. Whereas the abstract values on both levels are not at odds with each other, their interpretation and institutional manifestation in each political community trigger the potential for conflict.[89] If Spanish fundamental rights are an expression of Spanish self-determination, however, what stands behind Art 2 TEU and the Charter? In my view (which I explain in detail in chapter five) their demoicratic pedigree, namely the moral force of the joint commitment of all European peoples to protect these values, is key.

Abstract reliance on Art 2 TEU to ground the legitimate authority of EU law hence fails when applied to the interaction with national constitutional systems.

[85] Bolleyer and Reh (n 4) 473.

[86] Kumm (n 77) 124.

[87] Vlad Perju, 'On the (De-)Fragmentation of Statehood in Europe: Reflections on Ernst-Wolfgang Böckenförde's Work on European Integration' (2018) 19 *German Law Journal* 403, 425.

[88] Council Framework Decision of 13 June 2002 on the European arrest warrant and the surrender procedures between Member States [2002] OJ L190/1.

[89] See in relation to human rights Samantha Besson, 'European Human Rights Pluralism' in Miguel Poiares Maduro, Kaarlo Tuori and Suvi Sankari (eds), *Transnational law: Rethinking European Law and Legal Thinking* (Cambridge, CUP, 2014) 187.

Either there is no normative guidance for dealing with conflicts, given that both legal orders are judged against the same 'republican principles' and each manifestation is most likely compatible with the master value.[90] Or we are bound to conclude that national constitutional law always trumps EU law, because national constitutions embody the – one could say – 'original' normatively richer version of these values. What is more, the EU's current handling of the rule of law challenges in Eastern Europe illustrates that the Treaty (especially Art 7 TEU) is by design ill-equipped to enforce these values in practice. There is a sizeable gap between the normative claims and the institutional reservoir to make good on these claims. The Treaty-makers seem to have guarded themselves against 'normative backtalk' from the EU about the fundamental values of their constitutional systems.[91]

Simultaneously, grounding the authority of EU law in keeping with the values of Art 2 TEU encounters problems at the opposite end. Not only is there a palpable danger that EU law would have no viable authority compared to national laws and their 'thick' value background. Quite paradoxically, a value basis could simultaneously make the authority of EU law formally limitless. Why? Because there would be no test for the limits of said authority independent of compliance with these values. A central feature of value-based accounts is their exclusive reliance on substance rather than procedure. Recall only the *Associaçao* jurisprudence as a salient example of a broad value-based reach of EU law in tension with the principle of conferral.[92] The ECJ held that the EU's conception of the rule of law, combined with the obligation on Member States to 'provide remedies sufficient to ensure effective legal protection in the fields covered by Union law' (Art 19 TEU) shapes the very design of national courts and requires them to be independent. Requiring courts to be independent is admittedly part of any plausible conception of the rule of law. But the formal point remains: since the very design of national courts is at stake, this requirement necessarily applies to cases outside the scope of EU law.[93] It is wholly unsurprising that claimants in the wake of this development exploit alleged violations of Art 2 TEU to bring a case under the scope of EU law. Slovenia, for example, brought a territorial dispute with Croatia to the ECJ, arguing that Croatia violated the terms of its accession to the EU and thus violated the rule of law. Slovenia submitted (unsuccessfully) that this sufficed to bring the border dispute within the scope of EU law.[94]

[90] Waluchow (n 79) 210–12.

[91] Isiksel (n 35) 223; Turkuler Isiksel, 'Democracy-Eroding Multilateralism' in Michele Battini and Nadia Urbinati (eds), *The Future of Democracy* (Milan, Feltrinelli forthcoming) 224; Jan Wouters, 'Revisiting Art. 2 TEU: A True Union of Values?' (2020) 5 *European Papers* 255.

[92] Case C-64/16 *Associação* EU:C:2018:117. Similarly, Frank Schorkopf, 'Europäischer Konstitutionalismus Oder Die Normative Behauptung Des „European Way of Life" Potenziale Der Neueren Werterechtsprechung Des EuGH' [2019] *Neue Juristische Wochenschrift* 3418, 3422.

[93] Armin Von Bogdandy and Luke Dimitrios Spieker, 'Countering the Judicial Silencing of Critics: Article 2 TEU Values, Reverse Solange, and the Responsibilities of National Judges' (2019) 15 *European Constitutional Law Review* 391, 395.

[94] See Case C-457/18 *Slovenia v Croatia* EU:C:2020:65.

I don't necessarily disagree with the outcome of *Assoçiaçao*. Once again, who could object to keeping with the values enshrined in Art 2 TEU? There are nonetheless good philosophical arguments against the teleological idea of values as merely 'things to be promoted'. We often have intrinsically good reasons to promote values (like friendship and democracy) that are quite independent of the benefit the realisation of these values brings to the participants.[95] That is why I don't understand accounts based on constitutional values as instrumental accounts. What is more, the unqualified promotion of values in judicial and legal practice can raise its own questions of legitimacy, particularly in relation to the proper delimitation of competence. The preceding discussion of *Assoçiaçao* illustrates that. Members of the Court, who defend such lines of jurisprudence,[96] seem to underestimate that the opposite of a good action is often a well-meant action. Bold judicial attempts to safeguard a certain value 'for the greater good' could damage the broader legitimacy of the political community by impacting on other important safeguards, such as the principle of conferral.[97]

To sum up, I caution against the idea of grounding the authority of the EU and its laws exclusively in values such as those articulated in Art 2 TEU. First, their interpretive openness provides a rather shaky evaluation basis for authority in general. Second, relying on values seems a particularly unhelpful way to position the authority of the EU in relation to the authority of the Member States. Third, the lack of procedures and formal background conditions makes it hard to draw any limits to the reach of EU law, once compliance with these values is established. A value basis thus lacks an essential element of legitimacy: namely, to properly limit the exercise of authority.

None of this is to argue that values should play no role in assessing the authority of EU law. The key, however, is that they can only hold a secondary, supportive function in the architecture of political authority. An account which supports the authority of the EU based on state consent might refer to the values because the Masters of the Treaties in the Lisbon revision incorporated them explicitly in Art 2 TEU. Similarly, constitutional values can be part of instrumental theories of authority, to the extent they help the constituent entities to realise attractive moral goods.[98]

[95] See, at length, Thomas Scanlon, *What We Owe to Each Other* (Cambridge (MA), Harvard University Press, 1998) ch 2.

[96] In relation to the present example see only Koen Lenaerts, 'New Horizons for the Rule of Law Within the EU' (2020) 21 *German Law Journal* 29, 32 et seq. In relation to the Zambrano case law, see Marek Safjan and Dominik Düsterhaus, 'The EU Citizens' Right to Have Rights and the Courts' Duty to Protect It' in Koen Lenaerts and others (eds), *An Ever-Changing Union?: Perspectives on the Future of EU Law in Honour of Allan Rosas* (London, Bloomsbury Publishing, 2019) 203.

[97] Von Bogdandy and Spieker (n 93) 421 et seq are aware of these problems and try to build in internal limits.

[98] For a description of conceptions of justice as instrumental value, see Martijn van den Brink, 'Justice, Legitimacy and the Authority of Legislation within the European Union' (2019) 82 *MLR* 293.

E. Benefits and Burdens: Fair Play Beyond the State

We already encountered fair play theories in chapter three, when we saw that the ECJ included aspects of fairness in its appraisal of EU law's authority. Let me put such arguments in their theoretical context.

i. Fair Play Theories

It's only fair to obey the rules of the game (such as the laws of the political community) if you benefit from the advantages they confer. The intrinsic connection between benefits and burdens as an integral part of a cooperative enterprise describes the essence of fair play accounts of political authority.[99] It would be unfair towards the other stakeholders if some only enjoyed the benefits a political community provides without sharing the burdens, such as committing to obeying the laws of the community. According to Hart,

> when a number of persons conduct any joint enterprise according to rules and thus restrict their liberty, those who have submitted to these restrictions when required have a right to a similar submission from those who have benefited by their submission.[100]

The moral problem these theorists identify is cherry-picking and the harm this causes to the other members of the political community.

Franck uses fairness as an overarching idea to assess, critique and improve the legitimacy of the international system.[101] Lefkovitz also proposes a fair play model of international authority. In his view, states have a moral obligation to obey international law as the flip side of accepting the benefits of the international order. That duty, however, is subject to two quite demanding conditions. The duty grounded in fairness obtains only (i) if they accepted the relevant legal regime (since that voluntariness condition respects their self-determination) and (ii) if they enjoy domestic legitimate authority in relation to their citizens (since without domestic legitimacy, states cannot bind their subjects at all).[102]

The underlying moral issue is free-riding and, ultimately, unfair behaviour towards the other participants of the cooperative scheme. In a political community, abiding by the law affects everyone and is thus not only related to free-riding,

[99] Richard Dagger, *Playing Fair: Political Obligation and the Problems of Punishment* (Oxford, OUP, 2018); George Klosko, *The Principle of Fairness and Political Obligation* (Lanham, Rowman & Littlefield Publishers, 2004); HLA Hart, 'Are There Any Natural Rights?' (1955) 64 The *Philosophical Review* 175.

[100] Hart (n 98) 185. For a concise summary of potential objections see, eg, Dimitry Kochenov, 'EU Citizenship without Duties' (2014) 20 *European Law Journal* 482, 495. For a response to objections try Richard Dagger, 'Authority, Legitimacy, and the Obligation to Obey the Law' (2018) 24 *Legal Theory* 77, 99 et seq.

[101] Thomas Franck, *Fairness in International Law and Institutions* (Oxford, Clarendon, 1995).

[102] David Lefkowitz, 'The Principle of Fairness and States' Duty to Obey International Law' (2011) 24 *Canadian Journal of Law & Jurisprudence* 327.

but also a primary candidate for an obligation we have to each other. The last three words are important. Benefits here do not relate to 'what do I get out of this'? Benefits relate to ordering the interdependence of all the members of a political community. Fair play theories highlight why the individual participants set up the scheme in the first place, namely, due to the need for millions of individuals to organise their interdependent lives on the same territory.

ii. Fair Play Theories in the EU

The potential benefits of the EU are easily identifiable. A regulatory level-playing field, cross-border mobility, economic prosperity, a stronger voice in the world, etc. But has anyone translated this into a fair play theory of the EU's legitimate authority? After all, the strongest objection to fair play accounts on the national level does not apply to the EU. There, Nozick argues that bestowing (unasked) benefits on someone and demanding subsequent payment is objectionable.[103] This argument rests on the assumption that there was no prior voluntary act of submission to the authority. However, as we saw in theory (chapter two) and in practice (Brexit), the EU is formally a voluntary organisation for the addressees of its authority claim, the European peoples. Hence, there is a prior agreement. The benefits of the cooperative scheme EU are not imposed upon them.[104]

There are both academic and judicial traces of fair play accounts in the EU. They rely on two possible bases of fair play theories for EU law's authority, equality and solidarity. In fact, the ECJ gave early credibility to both models when arguing:

> In permitting Member States to profit from the advantages of the Community, the Treaty imposes on them also the obligation to respect its rules. For a State unilaterally to break, according to its own conception of national interest, the equilibrium between advantages and obligations flowing from its adherence to the Community *brings into question the equality of Member States before Community law* and creates discriminations at the expense of their nationals.
>
> *This failure in the duty of solidarity* accepted by Member States by the fact of their adherence to the Community strikes at the fundamental basis of the Community legal order (emphasis added).[105]

As explained in chapter three, the ECJ never employed a single 'clean' account of the EU's authority, which allows it to borrow from fair play theories in this case. Let me address both variations of fair play accounts in turn.

[103] Nozick (n 6) 93 et seq.

[104] But *cf* Kochenov (n 100) 495. For a discussion and rebuttal of various less sweeping objections see Dagger (n 99) ch 5.

[105] Case C-39/72 *Commission v Italy* EU:C:1973:13, paras 24, 25. For a renewed emphasis on equality see also Case C-357/19 *Euro Box Promotion* EU:C:2021:1034, para 249.

iii. The Demanding Argument of Fairness Grounded in Equality

Fabbrini's argument for the unconditional primacy of EU law contains an implicit fair play account of EU law's authority. His argument that national constitutional courts ought to give up their review mechanisms is based on equality (see Art 4(2) TEU).[106] Fabbrini's claim that ultra vires and other review mechanisms constitute cherry-picking is, in essence, an accusation of free-riding on the common scheme set up in the EU. The simple idea – which echoes the ECJ's arguments in *Costa*[107] – is that the equality of the participants in a cooperative scheme can only be secured by a common authority. As soon as the addressees of binding directives decide themselves when to comply, the cooperative scheme – especially the careful balance between benefits and burdens – is jeopardised, and with it the equal dignity of its participants.

While I welcome the change in perspective from a bilateral lens (EU Member State) to the multilateral effects of supremacy in relation to 27 Member States, Fabbrini's conclusions seem too strong to hold. In substance, Fabbrini argues for equality of outcome.[108] By definition, there is then no internal or external limit to EU law's legitimate authority. For one, any rule of EU law is authoritative simply by virtue of its existence as EU law. Lawful EU law is legitimate EU law. For another, there is no space for countervailing national constitutional reservations ever, because the original sin would be to disregard common rules in favour of unilateral rules. Any deviation is prohibited as *unfair*. In essence, such a standard of legitimate authority provides no real test for the moral right to bind the authority's subjects. Instead, it rubber-stamps whatever is decided at the EU level and keeps with EU primary law.

Fabbrini's exclusive focus on equality furthermore loses sight of the fact that Member States themselves are political communities that secure the equality of their citizens, that they guarantee the citizens' democratic self-determination. A fundamental element of fair play theories requires a moral assessment of the character of the polity, however, ie whether it is indeed a cooperative scheme worthy of respect.[109] Fabbrini overlooks that this is necessarily a comparative

[106] Federico Fabbrini, 'After the OMT Case: The Supremacy of EU Law as the Guarantee of the Equality of the Member States' (2015) 16 *German Law Journal* 1003. Similarly Ingolf Pernice, 'Costa v ENEL and Simmenthal: Primacy of European Law' in Miguel Poiares Maduro and Loïc Azoulai (eds), *The Past and Future of EU Law* (Oxford, Hart Publishing, 2010) 49.

[107] See only Case C-6/64 *Costa v ENEL* EU:C:1964:66: '(…) make it impossible for the States (…) to accord precedence to a unilateral and subsequent measure over a legal system accepted by them on a basis of reciprocity. (…) The executive force of Community law cannot vary from one State to another (…) without (…) giving rise to the discrimination prohibited by Article 7'. Therefore, pace Justin Lindeboom, 'Is the Primacy of EU Law Based on the Equality of the Member States? A Comment on the CJEU's Press Release Following the PSPP Judgment' (2020) 21 *German Law Journal* 1032, equality as a rationale for EU law's primacy and authority has noticeable roots in the case law.

[108] Similarly Koen Lenaerts, 'No Member State Is More Equal than Others: The Primacy of EU Law and the Principle of the Equality of the Member States before the Treaties' (*Verfassungsblog*, 8 October 2020), https://verfassungsblog.de/no-member-state-is-more-equal-than-others/.

[109] Dagger (n 99) 102.

exercise in the EU: both the EU and the Member State polities are such cooperative schemes worthy of respect.

Consider then AG Sharpston's recent version of a fair play account that shifts the underlying value from equality to solidarity.

iv. Fairness and Solidarity: A Promising Start

AG Sharpston writes with her characteristic passion:

> Solidarity is the lifeblood of the European project. Through their participation in that project and their citizenship of European Union, *Member States and their nationals have obligations as well as benefits*, duties as well as rights. Sharing in the European 'demos' is not a matter of looking through the Treaties and the secondary legislation to see what one can claim. *It also requires one to shoulder collective responsibilities and (yes) burdens to further the common good.*
>
> Respecting the 'rules of the club' and playing one's proper part in solidarity with fellow Europeans cannot be based on a penny-pinching cost-benefit analysis along the lines (familiar, alas, from Brexiteer rhetoric) of 'what precisely does the EU cost me per week and what exactly do I personally get out of it?' Such self-centredness is a betrayal of the founding fathers' vision for a peaceful and prosperous continent. *It is the antithesis of being a loyal Member State and being worthy, as an individual, of shared European citizenship.* If the European project is to prosper and go forward, we must all do better than that (emphasis added).[110]

Notice how the underlying value of fairness here is not equality, but solidarity. An obvious advantage of grounding a fair play account in solidarity is that solidarity has various firm roots in EU law. It is not only enshrined in important provisions of primary law.[111] You can also trace it throughout the history of EU jurisprudence.[112]

And yet, I take issue with the fact that this solidarity-based fair play model swaps the underlying value. Instead of the autonomy of the individual (in statist authority discussion) or of a collective (in supra- and international discussions), the underlying moral issue suddenly becomes a notion deeply connected to

[110] Case C-715/17 *Commission v Poland*, Opinion of AG Sharpston, EU:C:2019:917, paras 253 et seq. For a similar view, see Baquero Cruz (n 42) 92, 128.

[111] The most important ones are Preamble TEU: 'Desiring to deepen the solidarity between their peoples'; Art 2 TEU 'These values are common to the Member States in a society in which (…) solidarity (…) prevail'; Art 3 TEU: '… shall promote solidarity between generations; (…) shall promote (…) solidarity among Member States; (…) contribute to (…) solidarity and mutual respect among peoples'; Preamble TFEU: 'Intending to confirm the solidarity which binds Europe and the overseas countries'; Art 67 (2) TFEU: '… shall frame a common policy on asylum, immigration and external border control, based on solidarity between Member States'. For a summary and analysis see Lucia Serena Rossi, 'The Principle of Equality Among Member States of the European Union' in Lucia Serena Rossi and Federico Casolari (eds), *The Principle of Equality in EU Law* (New York, Springer, 2017) 37.

[112] Case C-6 and 11/69 *Commission v France* EU:C:1969:68, paras 14–17. Case C-44/14 *Spain v Parliament and Council* EU:C:2015:320, Opinion of AG Wahl, para 35.

justice: fairness.[113] Nozick's intriguing counterexample of the radio station set up voluntarily by your neighbours who then assign you to run it one day a year proves the point. It illustrates that considerations of autonomy are superseded by conceptions of justice.[114] In fair play accounts, obeying the law is based on 'giving everyone what is due to them', rather than securing the very agency and autonomy of the participating stakeholders.

I doubt that considerations of justice should inform accounts of the EU's authority.[115] This is not only due to the observation that justice is not even mentioned in the founding values of Art 2 TEU (though solidarity is). Since theories of authority are based on the tension between autonomy and binding authoritative directives, justice seems to deflect from the fundamental tension between authority and autonomy that we are trying to reconcile. More importantly, there will always be reasonable disagreement about what constitutes a just outcome or what fairness requires in each case. In this important sense legitimacy is prior to justice.[116] I thus find it problematic how fair play theories shift the underlying moral value from autonomy to justice. I noted in chapter one that the problem of authority is intertwined with many of the big questions of political philosophy. Discussions of fairness and solidarity in the EU should be kept distinct from questions of authority and political obligation, however, lest we lose sight of the quite separate underlying moral issues.[117] An unfair and thus unjust outcome is often the *effect* of someone flouting the law, but justice should not serve as the *moral basis* of political obligation.

The way EU law employs the concept of solidarity supports this hesitation. Most of the solidarity jurisprudence Sharpston discusses does not use solidarity as a basis for the legitimate authority of EU law, but as the emanation of distributive justice. And so does the Treaty. In fact, solidarity is often invoked where binding EU law is weak or absent. Take only Art 222 TFEU, according to which 'The Union and its Member States shall act jointly in a spirit of solidarity if a Member State is the object of a terrorist attack or the victim of a natural or man-made disaster'. Similarly, Arts 67 and 80 TFEU mandate that the policies in the Area of Freedom, Security and Justice (especially asylum, immigration, and external border control) 'shall be governed by the principle of solidarity'. The Court has also suggested that the Solidarity Chapter of the Charter is not directly applicable horizontally, ie not enforceable among individuals.[118] This leads me to conclude that

[113] See only Dagger (n 99) 105.

[114] For only one attempt to separate fairness as legitimacy from fairness as justice, see Thomas Franck, *Fairness in International Law and Institutions* (Oxford, Clarendon, 1995) 7 et seq.

[115] Similarly Danny Nicol, 'Can Justice Dethrone Democracy in the European Union? A Reply to Jürgen Neyer' (2012) 50 *Journal of Common Market Studies* 508.

[116] Richard Bellamy, *A Republican Europe of States: Cosmopolitanism, Intergovernmentalism and Democracy in the EU* (Cambridge, CUP, 2019) ch 2; van den Brink (n 98) 295 et seq; Nicol (n 115) 515 et seq.

[117] Similarly Eleftheriadis, *A Union of Peoples* (n 64) chs 8 and 9.

[118] Case C-176/12 *Association de médiation sociale* EU:C:2014:2, para 49.

the repeated invocation of solidarity in EU law does not envision it as a legitimate basis for EU law, but as a principle which ought to govern the broader relations between the participants – especially in areas where binding legal obligations are scarce.[119]

Overall, I think it is mistaken to argue that democracy (broadly understood) is inept to ground the EU's legitimacy and that we must move to justice as a replacement.[120] In chapter five, I attempt to modify the promising moral background of fair play theories to accommodate the above deficiencies.

IV. Conclusion: Anarchy?

In this chapter, I analysed various standards used to evaluate the moral basis of EU law's authority. In doing so, I argued that none is entirely convincing. The straightforward conclusion would be to join the ranks of philosophical anarchists, such as Kochenov,[121] and argue that the EU's exercise of authority is illegitimate. It would follow that EU law does not bind us morally but that it violates our (individual and/or collective) autonomy.

This is not the road I want to go down, however. Instead, I aim to show in the remainder of the book how the most promising moral standards for legitimate authority on the domestic level – those that focus on the value of institutions for a political community and the moral relationship of the individuals living in it – can be adjusted to a supranational political community. We saw in chapter three how the Treaties themselves emphasise the importance of law-administering institutions for creating and supporting a political community that respects the value and rights of its participants. This emphasis constitutes the starting point for my account of 'demoicratic authority'.

[119] Recently, the ECJ operationalised the principle of solidarity in Case C-156/21 *Hungary v Parliament and Council* EU:C:2022:97 para 129, where it held that solidarity is a fundamental principle of EU law to which the budget gives effect. For an analysis of the role of solidarity among the members of the EU, see Andrea Sangiovanni, 'Solidarity in the European Union' (2013) 33 *OJLS* 213.

[120] But *cf* Jürgen Neyer, *The Justification of Europe: A Political Theory of Supranational Integration* (Oxford, OUP, 2012).

[121] Kochenov (n 99). For different reasons, see also Loughlin (n 11) ch 6.

5

Democratic Authority I: The Theory

I. Introduction

In what follows, I defend an account of how to evaluate EU law's moral authority: 'demoicratic authority'. In section II, I start by outlining the idea of demoicracy before extracting the values that ought to underpin law in a demoicracy in section III. The chapter then studies the relationship between demoicratic authority and political obligation in section IV, before section V looks at the limits of demoicratic authority.

II. What is Demoicracy and Why Do We Need it?

Understanding demoicratic authority as a framework to evaluate the EU's authority presupposes an understanding of demoicracy. The following overview is not a fully-fledged defence of the idea of demoicracy, but an introduction that highlights why I endorse it. It is not part of my argument, but the basis of it.

Demo*i*cracy is not a typo. The idea of demoicracy is an attempt to capture the EU as 'democracy beyond the state' without giving the fatal impression that it mimics the features of a nation state democracy. Take demoicracy literally: it specifies the relevant agent(s) underlying the political community – the *demoi* in the plural. And it informs about the 'cracy' (from the Greek verb *kratein*: to govern, to rule) – to allow the peoples to 'govern together but not as one'.[1] Although demoicracy is a relatively recent concept, individual 'demoicrats' have already offered various competing visions.[2] To depart from a common understanding of the idea, let me borrow from Nicolaïdis:

> European demoicracy is a Union of peoples, understood both as states and as citizens, who govern together but not as one. It represents a third way against two alternatives

[1] Kalypso Nicolaïdis, 'European Demoicracy and Its Crisis' (2013) 51 *Journal of Common Market Studies* 351, 351 et seq.

[2] For an overview see Miriam Ronzoni, 'The European Union as a Demoicracy: Really a Third Way?' (2017) 16 *European Journal of Political Theory* 210, 217.

> which both equate democracy with a single demos: ... the EU is neither a Union of democratic states as 'sovereigntists' would have it, nor a Union-as-a democratic state to be as 'federalists' would have it.[3]

Endorsing the no-*demos* thesis distinguishes demoicracy from other attempts at democracy beyond the state. Some of these attempts suggest that a European *demos* already exists.[4] But that would strip the very idea of a constitutional *demos* of any theoretical weight. Clearly, 'the exercise of power by the Union can hardly be interpreted as the will or self-governance of a democratic sovereign'.[5] If living on the territory of the EU sufficed to form a *demos*, it would have no more meaning than calling the inhabitants of Paris or Cornwall a *demos*. Of course, it is disputed just how much social and cultural convergence a *demos* requires (as in a common language, culture or media landscape).[6] We can leave that to the side, however, since one decisive argument against an existing constitutional *demos* in the EU is that currently Europeans neither would nor should accept the decisions of a simple majority.[7] Furthermore, the Treaties (i) avoid the term 'people', (ii) refer to the European 'peoples' an impressive nine times in their two Preambles, and (iii) acknowledge the peoples' separate histories and cultures (Art 167(2) TFEU). In the EU we have today, these features make it impossible to base the existence of a European *demos* on either political reality or constitutional design.

But what is the source of the EU's authority if not a *demos*? For demoicrats, the constitutional peoples of the EU Member States ground the EU's theoretical architecture. As Lenaerts put it in relation to Arts 9 et seq TEU, the 'idea of demoicracy is incorporated into the constitutional fabric of the EU'.[8] Through the EU, the European peoples exercise their self-determination jointly to address issues transcending statist boundaries in an elaborate institutional framework. In that sense, demoicracy expresses the theoretical link between each peoples' independence and their reciprocal interdependence.

[3] Kalypso Nicolaïdis, 'The Idea of European Demoicracy' in Julie Dickson and Pavlos Eleftheriadis (eds), *Philosophical Foundations of European Union Law* (Oxford, OUP, 2012) 254.

[4] *cf* Stefan Oeter, 'Federalism and Democracy' in Armin von Bogdandy and Jürgen Bast (eds), *Principles of European Constitutional Law*, 2nd edn (Oxford, Hart/Beck, 2009) 67; Samantha Besson, 'Deliberative Demoi-Cracy in the European Union: Towards the Deterritorialization of Democracy' in Samantha Besson, José Luis Martí and Verena Seiler (eds), *Deliberative Democracy and its Discontents* (Farnham, Ashgate, 2006).

[5] Armin von Bogdandy, 'Founding Principles' in von Bogdandy and Bast (n 4) 25.

[6] For a detailed discussion, see Eva-Maria Tieke, *Das Subjekt Demokratischer Legitimation in Der Europäischen Union* (Baden-Baden, Tectum, 2016) 270 et seq.

[7] Nicolaïdis (n 1) 356.

[8] Koen Lenaerts, 'Demoicracy, Constitutional Pluralism and The Court of Justice of the European Union' in Luuk van Middelaar, Philippe van Parijs and Herman van Rompuy (eds), *After the Storm: How to Save Democracy in Europe* (Tielt, Lannoo, 2015) 129.

This has a profound effect on self-determination and the role of states in the EU. Due to the participation of each people in the EU's decision-making and enforcement, popular self-determination increases beyond the states' borders. Thus understood, both the EU and the Member States derive their authority from the citizens they serve. They realise the self-determination of these peoples in separate ways: a state facilitates the self-determination of one independent people, whereas the EU helps these distinct peoples to exercise their self-determination jointly in affairs that affect all of them. The EU constitutes a political community without a *demos*, an '"us" made up of others'.[9] Demoicracy, in a nutshell, breaks up the exclusive relationship between people and state, and adds another layer of political community.

Both national and supranational institutions exist to allow a constitutional people to govern itself. While national institutions primarily serve an *independent demos*, they at the same time serve the *interdependent demoi*, together with supranational institutions and under their direction.

That is where the version of demoicracy I endorse contrasts with state-focused accounts of the EU's authority.[10] I don't think it goes far enough to claim that the EU manages the interdependence of states. Not that it doesn't do that – it does. But the UN does that as well. The EU as a political community, by contrast, affects the constitutional peoples on a deeper level. As I tried to show in chapter two, it is not only individual citizens that matter in the EU's governance architecture, aside from state institutions. The voluntary participation of a people in the EU also transforms the political *Gestalt* of the relationship of each *demos* to 'their' state by adding another political community on top. The 'democratic interdependence' of its member-peoples characterises the EU in the sense that their capacity to affect each other's national democracy creates mutual obligations.[11] These institutionalised obligations manifest a moral *commitment* to one another – ultimately based on their factual and normative interdependence – that is legally enforceable in their institutions and on their territories.[12]

Fig 10 shows how authority relationships can be illustrated in a demoicratic framework:

[9] Daniel Innerarity, *Democracy in Europe: A Political Philosophy of the EU* (London, Palgrave Macmillan, 2018) 165, 246 wfr.

[10] Such as Stephen Weatherill, *Law and Values in the European Union* (Oxford, OUP, 2016); Pavlos Eleftheriadis, *A Union of Peoples* (Oxford, OUP, 2020).

[11] Ronzoni (n 2) 217.

[12] Turkuler Isiksel, 'Constitutionalism as Limitation and Licence' in Tom Ginsburg, Mark D Rosen and Georg Vanberg (eds), *Constitutions in Times of Financial Crisis* (Cambridge, CUP, 2019) 191.

Fig 10 Authority Relations in a Demoicratic Framework

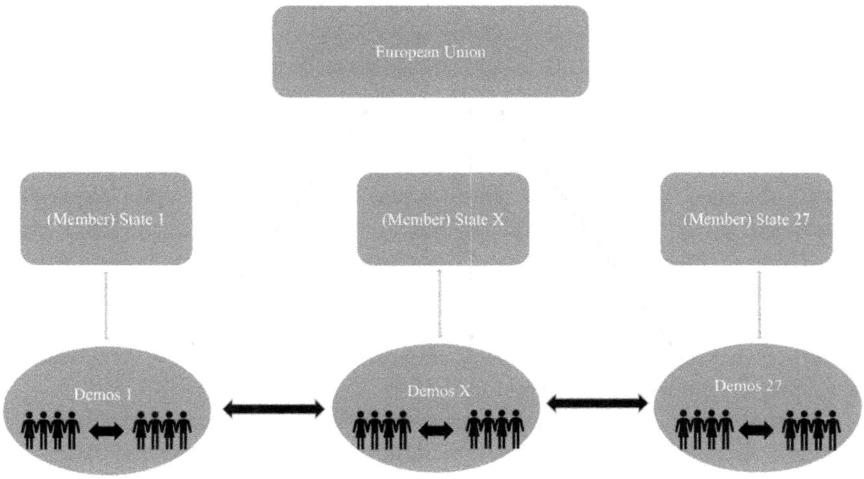

The vertical and diagonal arrows illustrate the nexus between authorisation and authority. Their varying thickness indicates the thicker bond on the national level. The bold horizontal arrows indicate the core moral bonds of the respective political community, ie among citizens in a state, and among peoples in the EU.

The focus on peoples – who act themselves (amending domestic constitutions, referenda, elections), as well as through state officials and as EU citizens – thus listens to the voice of national minorities and viewpoints outside national institutions. Look at the ongoing dismantling of the rule of law in Poland and Hungary. In my view, international and state-centred theories of the EU lack the tools to conceptualise the threat this poses to the legitimate authority of the EU. They can only view it as a problem internally to that Member State, either because the state institutions do not fulfil the duties of justice they owe to their people, or because the Member State consented to the EU Treaties including Art 2 TEU. If we construct the EU as a political community of peoples, however, the citizens in Poland in Hungary have moral claims against the other Europeans based on the duty to uphold the institutional machinery and substantive values set up at the European level.

Conversely, the (institutionalised) interdependence of the Member States implies that violations of the EU's core values by one Member State affect the other EU Member States and peoples in a way they should not be forced to tolerate.[13] The mutual trust between the Member States points to a deeper

[13] Pauliine Koskelo, 'Current Threats to the Rule of Law in the EU: The Foundation on Which the Authority of EU Law Rests' in Wolfgang Heusel and Jean-Philippe Rageade (eds), *The Authority of EU Law: Do We Still Believe In It?* (New York, Springer, 2019) 302.

political community that comes to light when national institutions collaborate transnationally to give effect to EU law, eg by handling claims of EU citizens from other Member States or by enforcing EAWs. Fumbling with the integrity of these national law-administering institutions strikes at the very heart of these mechanisms and thus becomes a concern for the entire EU. It jeopardises the reciprocity underlying the transnational institutional collaboration.

To sum up, demoicracy is a democratic theory for political communities beyond the state. It answers the question how constitutional peoples can realise democratic ideals jointly in areas beyond the reach and capacity of their individual states. Note that the notion of demoicracy is open to various institutional variations, something it has in common with state democracy. On the one hand, one may thus criticise the EU demoicracy for not being democratic enough.[14] On the other, making the EU more democratic in the conventional – ie national – sense may do more harm than good.[15]

For that reason, grounding the legitimate authority of EU law on demoicracy presupposes a clear understanding of the authority-relevant features and values of a demoicratic law-administering system. The next and indeed crucial argumentative step thus is to spell out which features of the EU's demoicratic law-administering system, if brought to bear, could provide normative reasons for the authority of EU law. From 'What is demoicracy and why do we need it?' we now move to 'What gives demoicratic law moral authority?'

III. Demoicratic Authority Explained

The demoicratic authority of EU law should be evaluated based on the manifestation of three values that ought to characterise law-making and law-enforcement among the EU peoples: deliberation, non-domination and equality (see subsection A). Their interplay creates the essence of demoicratic authority (see subsection B).

A. The Values Rooting Demoicratic Authority

The extent to which EU law realises the values of deliberation, non-domination and equality makes up the binding force of EU law. Each of those values contributes a valuable part, but ultimately only their interaction provides the normative reasons for demoicratic authority.

[14] Thorsten Hüller, 'Out of Time? The Democratic Limits of EU Demoicracy' (2016) 23 Journal of European Public Policy 1407.

[15] See only Richard Bellamy, *A Republican Europe of States: Cosmopolitanism, Intergovernmentalism and Democracy in the EU* (Cambridge, CUP, 2019) ch 4; Dieter Grimm, *The Constitution of European Democracy* (Oxford, OUP, 2017).

i. The Right Result where there is no Best Result: Deliberation

One of the most welcome achievements of institution-centred and especially democracy-based theories of national authority is that they highlight the 'circumstances of politics'.[16] This felicitous phrase refers to translating policy choices into binding law in a society of millions of individuals with widespread reasonable disagreement on, well, everything.[17] Add the democratic axiom that you, the reader, like everyone else around you ought to have a say over the laws that subsequently affect you, and you see the problem: why should those who disagree with the policy and thus the law's substance still accept it as authoritative and legitimate? Democratic procedures, which give every citizen an equal vote and thereby the opportunity to influence and be represented, are the single most successful solution to this problem. Pointedly, '(l)aw in a democracy does not merely tell us what we may and may not do – though it does that; law is how we decide what we may and may not do'.[18]

That might be true for state democracies. However, I concluded earlier that we cannot use this observation for the EU's law-making procedures because they lack the democratic pedigree of nation states (chapter four). It is possible, however, to translate the reasoning behind this democratic idea to the EU understood as a demoicracy. After all, the EU provides procedural means to solve collective action problems and to govern a large political community despite widespread disagreement among the peoples of Europe. The EU handles the relations

> between prosperous and less prosperous countries, north and south, centre and periphery, old countries and newcomers, big and small states, conservative and progressive political forces, and different views about the future of integration.[19]

The EU's institutions have the capacity to allow these peoples to determine their joint fate for themselves and thus in a way that respects the democratic axiom. The EU provides an institutional framework where the participating peoples can come together and agree on binding solutions for any issue that transcends the legitimate jurisdiction of the democratic processes in their states. The EU is about the choices of the peoples per se.[20] Their institutional participation and deliberation is vital for grasping the authority of EU law as it secures the peoples' autonomy in the first place. It is hard to argue, for example, that EU law unduly constrains the scope of action for Member States in the many areas that escape the legitimate

[16] Jeremy Waldron, *Law and Disagreement* (Oxford, Clarendon, 1999) 101.

[17] I understand 'reasonable' here in the same way as Laura Valentini does in 'Justice, Disagreement and Democracy' (2013) 43 *British Journal of Political Science* 177, 184.

[18] Scott Hershovitz, 'Legitimacy, Democracy, and Razian Authority' (2003) 9 *Legal Theory* 201, 210.

[19] Julio Baquero Cruz, *What's Left of the Law of Integration?: Decay and Resistance in European Union Law* (Oxford, OUP, 2018) 93.

[20] Francis Cheneval, 'Demoicratic Self-Government in the European Union's Polycentric System: Theoretical Remarks' in Josephine van Zeben and Ana Bobić (eds), *Polycentricity in the European Union* (Cambridge, CUP, 2019) 68. Wolfgang Heusel, 'Legitimität Und Finalität Des Europäischen Projekts' in Heusel and Rageade (n 13) 343 et seq.

reach of unilateral state action because they affect outsiders who, as a consequence, wouldn't have a say in the laws that affect them.[21] Since one people neither ought to impose its own rules on others, nor should it be forced to accept the rules of another, it would be wrong to think that EU law on this matter constitutes an illegitimate intrusion into (collective) autonomy. By giving them a say in how to govern together, the EU respects their autonomy as self-governing peoples.

But how can the value of deliberation give moral force to law, especially in the EU? Law-making institutions and procedures in a demo(i)cratic polity enable the members of a political community to come up with binding law while respecting the equal dignity of each participant. The real magic happens when deliberation translates diverse preferences and reasonable disagreement into binding law for the entire community. Rather than merely aggregating preferences through counting votes, deliberation transforms preferences into binding rules via collective and informed decision-making.[22] As Cheneval puts it:

> (j)ustification and deliberation have to be appropriated by the peoples in binding decisions … Since deliberation remains vague and of uncertain consequence without its subjective appropriation in democratic decision-making procedures, the benefits of deliberation will remain very limited without a formal institutional framework linking the dêmoi as distinct dêmoi.[23]

This captures the moral value of deliberation in law-making procedures. Now to the EU. The fact that deliberation in the EU's legislative proceedings, especially within and among the Council and EP, leads to binding law that both individuals and state institutions can enforce judicially is very important. It marks the qualitative difference to international arrangements. EU law thereby becomes the institutional expression of the EU peoples' mutual commitment to each other. In essence, through their representative officials in these EU institutions the peoples deliberate, make law, and jointly exercise public authority in each other's territory: an astonishing anomaly in an international world of sovereign equals.[24]

To realise its full moral potential, deliberation requires the participation of the appropriate agents.[25] This is tied to the idea that everyone should have an equal say in authoring the legal system which then claims authority over them

[21] Franz Mayer, 'Verfassung Im Nationalstaat: Von Der Gesamtordnung Zur Europäischen Teilordnung?' (2016) 75 *Veröffentlichungen der Vereinigung der Deutschen Staatsrechtslehrer* 7, 39. Similarly in relation to international authority, see Başak Cali, *The Authority of International Law: Obedience, Respect, and Rebuttal* (Oxford, OUP, 2015) 102.

[22] Besson (n 4) 186.

[23] Francis Cheneval, *The Government of The Peoples: On the Idea and Principles of Multilateral Democracy* (London, Palgrave Macmillan, 2011) 85.

[24] Similarly, Claus Dieter Classen, 'Die Gleichheit Der Mitgliedstaaten Und Ihre Ausformungen Im Unionsrecht' [2020] *Europarecht* 255, 262 et seq.

[25] I am not referring to non-governmental actors. But *cf* Francis Cheneval and Frank Schimmelfennig, 'The Case for Demoicracy in the European Union' (2013) 51 *Journal of Common Market Studies* 334, 339 et seq.

and affects them in their daily lives, labelled 'congruence-principle', 'all-affected-principle' or 'autonomy-principle'.[26] Deliberation unfolds its authority-generating value only if the deliberative process includes those affected by the subsequent decision. Regarding issues that transcend state borders, that's where the EU comes in. In the face of actual interdependence, it is clear that '(s)ociety is not sufficiently self-determined when it is only nationally self-determined'.[27] The EU is designed to remedy a true democratic deficit on the national level, which results from one people 'conditioning' another without the latter's input.[28]

This shows that the EU has the capacity to realise the authority-generating force of deliberation in its demoicratic institutions and law-making processes. Chapter six will discuss elements that illustrate the potential and limits of deliberation in the EU's current legislative machinery. Next, we look at the value of non-domination and its potential role in legitimising the exercise of public authority.

ii. Republican Non-Domination Beyond the State

Non-domination is a prominent value of demoicratic thought and can be harnessed to evaluate the demoicratic authority of EU law. Indeed, van den Brink calls it the 'paramount demoicratic value'.[29] For example, Bellamy's recent defence of demoicracy understands the EU as a republican association of states that secures mutual non-domination among the EU peoples. Within this framework, power imbalance (instead of balance), dependency (instead of reciprocity), and/or personal rule (instead of interdependence) create 'circumstances of domination'. These elements need to be erased so that 'laws are under the equal influence and control of those subject to them'.[30]

Domination threatens autonomy – the underlying value of theories of authority – because someone else can arbitrarily interfere in my life or impose duties arbitrarily, ie without taking into account my interests.[31] In the language

[26] Robert Dahl, *After the Revolution?: Authority in a Good Society* (New Haven, Yale University Press, 1990) 49; David Held, *Democracy and the Global Order: From the Modern State to Cosmopolitan Governance* (Cambridge, Polity, 1995) 145 et seq (using it as basis to advocate global democracy). Floris De Witte, 'Interdependence and Contestation in European Integration' (2018) 3 *European Papers* 475, 478. However, de Witte mostly focusses on the subject's capacity to change, rather than author these decisions, hence on *pouvoir constitué* rather than *constituant*. For an overview of the literature, see Sarah Song, 'The Boundary Problem in Democratic Theory: Why the Demos Should Be Bounded by the State' (2012) 4 *International Theory* 39, 48 et seq.

[27] Innerarity (n 9) 251.

[28] ibid.

[29] Martijn van den Brink, 'The European Union's Demoicratic Legislature' (2021) 19 *International Journal of Constitutional Law* 914, 926.

[30] Bellamy (n 15) 61 et seq.

[31] Philip Pettit, *Republicanism: A Theory of Freedom and Government* (Oxford, Clarendon, 1997) 52; James Bohman, 'Nondomination and Transnational Democracy' in Cécile Laborde and John Maynor (eds), *Republicanism and Political Theory* (Hoboken, Wiley, 2008) 197 et seq.

of chapter one, they can make an illegitimate claim on how I lead my life. On a collective level, a national people may take unilateral decisions with tremendous effects on outsiders and especially their popular self-determination. The EU's institutional architecture, if used properly, has an inherent capacity to guard against such domination among its peoples.[32] This applies to both EU law-making and its enforcement.

Let's start with EU law-making. The antidote to domination in law-making is to give each member the capacity to influence the decisions that claim authority over you. This removes any risk of arbitrariness because the deliberative process itself consists of channelling the interests of those affected into binding decisions.[33]

Naturally, there will be disagreement about the means to achieve non-domination, ie which precise institution should have a say in demoicratic law-making. For Bellamy, demoicracy is basically the sum of the national democracies and, therefore, national parliaments should take centre stage as the main bodies for legitimising the EU and for making EU law.[34] I disagree. In my view the focus on national parliaments stems from his lack of distinction between states and *demoi* as separate entities, which prevents him from fully grasping the normative potential of demoicracy as a legitimation strategy on the supranational level. Bellamy's sophisticated republican intergovernmentalism sees the EU as a union of sovereign states and thus as truly international, so that he focusses too much on state representatives as relevant actors. As I see it, Bellamy underplays the importance of the peoples' input in the legislative machinery on the supranational level and the binding enforcement of EU law for securing the very autonomy of the peoples he seeks to protect.[35]

Moreover, even the current limited involvement of national parliaments in EU law-making which act mainly as guardians of subsidiarity has revealed many problems. More national parliament involvement jeopardises the precarious vertical and horizontal institutional balance in the EU. It would overburden the capacity of national parliaments and thereby even weaken national democratic rule, while national parliaments by definition pursue national rather than European interests.[36] More importantly, an even greater role for national parliaments neglects that we have the EP as directly elected – demoicratic – parliament with extensive legislative and budgetary powers.[37] Why would

[32] Nicolaïdis (n 3) 264 et seq.

[33] Pettit (n 31) 35 et seq; Charles Larmore, 'Liberal and Republican Conceptions of Freedom' (2003) 6 *Critical Review of International Social and Political Philosophy* 96, 114.

[34] See only Bellamy (n 15) 65.

[35] For a similar criticism see Robert Schütze, 'Models of Demoicracy: Some Preliminary Thoughts' (2022) 47 *European Law Review* 24, 38 et seq; Ronzoni (n 2) 224 et seq.

[36] For a good summary of the criticism see European Parliamentary Research Service, 'In-Depth Analysis: Subsidiarity – Mechanisms for Monitoring Compliance' July 2018 – PE 625.124 s 3.1.

[37] See only Cristina Fasone, Daniele Gallo and Jan Wouters, 'Re-Connecting Authority and Democratic Legitimacy in the EU: Introductory Remarks' (2020) 5 *European Papers* 175, 179.

we want the national parliaments to do the EP's job, especially if they don't even want to do it?[38]

In my view, you cannot secure non-domination by harnessing national parliaments for the task.[39] While they contribute to the deliberative value of EU law-making through contestation via the card procedure (see Protocol No 2 on the Application of the Principles of Subsidiarity and Proportionality), they are inept to mitigate domination. The EU can only secure non-domination among the peoples if they use EU institutions as fora to exercise their self-government jointly regarding issues that transcend the legitimate reach of their states. Only then will morally valuable deliberation channel the preferences of the representatives of 27 peoples into binding law, which is impossible in national parliaments.

Enforcement is not merely the other side of the coin of law-making. It occupies a vital role in the EU's conception of non-domination. In general, only equal enforcement of the jointly agreed EU law ensures that these rules apply and thus exclude domination by one people. This is especially important in the EU simply because enforcement of law that originates beyond the state through actual legal remedies and the involvement of national institutions and especially citizens is rare.

The EU hence has the capacity to guarantee non-domination among the EU peoples and to thereby secure their viable self-government. In analogy to the state level, where citizens can only secure their autonomy in a state of right, the EU peoples can remain autonomous in a meaningful sense despite their EU membership. Their full autonomy as individual peoples can be secured precisely because they bind themselves to the supranational authority and thereby create the conditions to mitigate the risk of domination. Considering externalities and actual interdependence, this institutional cooperation alone allows them to realise the 'republican ideal of not living at the mercy of another's will'.[40]

iii. The Equality of Peoples

Equality completes the trio of values that underpin demoicratic authority. Through their participation in and commitment to the EU, the EU peoples recognise each other as equal partners in a joint political community. The law-administering institutions facilitate this equality through the deliberation and non-domination just described.

[38] Adam Cygan, 'From Deparliamentarisation to a Parliamentary Renaissance? National Parliaments in the EU Polity' in Sacha Garben, Inge Govaere and Paul Nemitz (eds), *Critical Reflections on Constitutional Democracy in the European Union* (Oxford, Hart Publishing, 2019) 293.

[39] Similarly van den Brink (n 29) 930 et seq.

[40] Larmore (n 33) 110.

Let me briefly come back to Bellamy's republican intergovernmentalism. Bellamy gives priority to national democratic processes. The role of EU institutions in his view is merely to mediate between these peoples to protect the national democratic process through shared control of the *demoi*. EU institutions have no intrinsic value to secure fairness and equality among the EU peoples because their actors neither represent nor are accountable to the EU peoples in a significant way.[41] The best way to remedy any democratic deficit is to involve national parliaments and parties in EU law-making.[42] I do not accept this conclusion. EU institutions alone allow these peoples to come together as equals and decide about the legal obligations that apply to them. Domestic institutions, by contrast, are ineffective in guaranteeing equality with outsiders, as they represent the interests of one people alone. The value of a demoicracy mainly feeds from the workings of supranational institutions, without which the deliberation among equals explained above would be impossible.

A pervasive theme of this book is to identify the appropriate entity that serves as both the addressee of the EU's authority claim and as the source of its moral authority. The present discussion shows why this is necessary. The novel element in the EU's authority claim is that it affects the constitutional peoples themselves. It puts national institutions and territories in the service of the supranational community with transformative effect on how the individual *demoi* govern themselves. It changes both levels of government, within and beyond the state. As Ronzoni explains:

> Demoicracy advocates the equality of European peoples at the EU level, as distinct from both the equality of European citizens and the equality of member states. The aim of the EU is not merely to foster the problem-solving capacity of its member states, but the democratic capacity of its peoples.[43]

EU law disrupts the tested ways of national rule in the service of others, of outsiders. This creates the legitimacy challenge at the heart of this book. Demoicracy may offer this legitimation within limits (see below) by focusing on the very same peoples as a source of the EU's authority. Demoicracy shows that equality among the peoples is only achieved if they relate to each other as equals in institutional fora for law-production and enforcement. Only the binding institutionalisation of their reciprocal duties grounds their full equality.

This focus on peoples explains why neither states and their officials nor citizens are treated as full political equals in the EU. There is no doubt that equality of Member States is a bedrock principle of the EU which finds both legal and institutional expression in the EU's 'constitutional compromise'.[44] Nonetheless,

[41] Bellamy (n 15) 113 et seq.
[42] ibid 4, especially 128 et seq.
[43] Ronzoni (n 2) 218.
[44] Federico Fabbrini, 'States' Equality v States' Power: The Euro-Crisis, Inter-State Relations and the Paradox of Domination' (2015) 17 *Cambridge Yearbook of European Legal Studies* 3, 9.

equality among Member States in the EU does not remain a relatively light international notion of equal state sovereignty, the main purpose of which is not to interfere in each other's business. Although this notion of equality does not disappear completely, as Treaty revision and various unanimity requirements show, Art 4(2) TEU is better understood as the equality of subjects of an authority claim. Art 4(2) TEU reads: 'The Union shall respect the equality of Member States before the Treaties ...'. The wording already indicates that this notion is to be understood as equality among the subjects of an authority (*Hoheitsgewalt*).[45] The addressee of the duty to treat equally here is the EU. The clause creates a legal obligation for the EU to treat its Member States equally in both the making and the enforcement of EU law, to ensure their equality before the law.[46] In that regard, the law-making architecture is designed to accommodate and balance the equality of both the Member States and their peoples.[47] On the flipside, when the Member States act jointly and make EU law, they exercise public authority on the territory of other Member States.[48] In that sense, Art 4(2) enshrines the guarantee that they remain equals through the equal making and enforcement of EU law. This 'equality before EU law' was introduced precisely to counter the fears and strengthen the position of smaller Member States which had lost their veto rights to qualified majority voting.[49] In an important sense, the equality of Member States accordingly goes far beyond the international idea of sovereign equality.[50] Member States are not only sovereign actors designing the EU's normative architecture, but also equal subjects of EU law. This also underpins the morally rich notion of mutual trust among Member State officials, which establishes a presumption of compliance as subjects of EU law based on – ultimately – the values carved out in this chapter.

EU citizens are *legal* equals as well. Non-discrimination underpins EU citizenship (Art 18 TFEU) and 'reflects a fundamental moral norm: to treat the other as oneself and, beyond that, to transcend the distinction between oneself and the other'.[51] Similarly, consider the mainly transnational impetus of EU citizenship explained in chapter two. Since each *demos* remains constituted in a state, only transnationally enforceable EU law can guarantee the recognition of other EU

[45] Classen (n 24) 257 et seq.

[46] Koen Lenaerts, 'The Rule of Law and the Constitutional Identity of the European Union' (Sofia, 5 March 2023), https://evropeiskipravenpregled.eu/the-rule-of-law-and-the-constitutional-identity-of-the-european-union/; Classen (n 24) 264 et seq.

[47] Lucia Serena Rossi, 'The Principle of Equality Among Member States of the European Union' in Lucia Serena Rossi and Federico Casolari (eds), *The Principle of Equality in EU Law* (New York, Springer, 2017) 15.

[48] Classen (n 24) 263.

[49] Andreas Haratsch, 'Die Gleichheit der Mitgliedstaaten in den Institutionen und Entscheidungsverfahren der Europäischen Union – der rechtliche Rahmen' (2020) 55 *Europarecht* 471, 472.

[50] Koen Lenaerts, 'La Vie Après l'avis: Exploring the Principle of Mutual (yet Not Blind) Trust' (2017) 54 *CML Rev* 809.

[51] Baquero Cruz (n 19) 89.

citizens as legal co-equals. But in the absence of an EU-wide *demos*, EU citizens are not *political* equals. The degressive proportionality in voting for the EU Parliament serves as powerful reminder. Demoicracy accommodates these features and puts the ultimate focus on the equality of *demoi* as collectives instead of on citizens as individuals. Though counterintuitive, a political community without a *demos* may legitimately resist treating each citizen as political equal.[52]

This demoicratic perspective thus connects to the EU's authority claim on peoples as carved out in chapter two. There, I concluded that the EU's authority claim is ultimately not concerned with the individual citizen and their autonomy qua human being, but with the collective autonomy of the people of which they form a part. Demoicratic authority emphasises that the making and enforcement of EU law has legitimate authority to the extent it guarantees the equality of the EU's constitutional peoples through giving them an equal say in EU law-making, and by enforcing EU law in the national institutions across the EU's territory. The legitimacy basis changes significantly compared to the national level, however, where it is based on a natural duty to treat other human beings with equal dignity qua humans.[53] The EU's object of protection instead is each peoples' moral achievement of realising democratic self-determination within their respective Member States. Demoicratic authority thus always needs to be reconciled with the autonomy of the peoples to self-determine their affairs at the national level.

It follows that the authority of EU law can't be about equality of outcome, which is why I cautioned in chapter four against fair play accounts which suggest just that. Indeed, both fair play and demoicratic authority argue that solidarity among EU peoples is not about charity. It is about reflecting on our self-interest in relation to the 'others' with whom we form the EU as a political community.[54] In other words, the '*demoi*cratic ideal is to treat the *demoi* as equal political subjects'.[55] For demoicratic authority, however, political legitimacy is prior to justice. This is due to widespread disagreement about what justice requires, and the fact that justice determines what system of rules we ought to adopt.[56] Instead of any concrete benefits, demoicratic authority emphasises the moral value of EU institutions and procedures that enable the European peoples to decide jointly how to regulate their interactions.

Demoicratic authority moreover rectifies the problem that equality-centred fair play accounts insufficiently respect the crucial value affected by the EU's authority, because they can't identify limits and prioritise any EU law over any

[52] van den Brink (n 29) 927 et seq.

[53] See only Thomas Christiano, *The Constitution of Equality: Democratic Authority and its Limits* (Oxford, OUP, 2008) chs 1 and 2.

[54] Innerarity (n 9) 201.

[55] van den Brink (n 29) 926.

[56] See only Christiano (n 53) 237 et seq; Eleftheriadis (n 10) 36.

national law. In my view, none of the values rooting EU law's authority demand that. Equal representation in the deliberations about making EU law does not guarantee prevailing on the outcome. It is about procedural equality. Similarly, non-domination can be realised without equality of outcome.

The procedural equality of peoples that contributes to EU law's demoicratic authority is thus a combination of aggregate representation, equal chance of influencing EU law through deliberation, and uniform enforcement throughout the EU's territory.

B. The Essence of EU Law's Authority

The values of deliberation, non-domination and equality of peoples form the essence of demoicratic authority and underpin the moral force of EU law to the extent to which they are realised. Their reflexive relationship is key in evaluating the demoicratic authority of EU law.

Take deliberation and equality, for instance. The way in which EU institutions treat the EU peoples and their state and citizen representatives as equals has a direct bearing on the deliberative quality of the process. The institutional compromise in relation to aggregation and representation in the Council and the EP provides a forum for valuable deliberation because the preferences and (legal) traditions get a seat at the table that reflects the equal standing of the EU peoples. The moral force of deliberation stems from the capacity of the law-making process to treat the members as equals without guaranteeing that their views ultimately prevail.

Equality and non-domination also stand in a reflexive relationship.[57] For one, enforcing EU law ideally supports a fair scheme of cooperation that guarantees equality in the first place.[58] The non-domination that the EU's particular law-enforcement architecture brings about helps to make the equality of the peoples a legal reality. For another, the equality of the peoples in the EU's institutional architecture is a precondition for securing non-domination among them. Only if we face each other as equal peoples can EU law guarantee our respective autonomy. The reason is that the horizontal moral relationship among the peoples led to the creation of the EU in the first place. It is only possible to remove the risk of domination in the sense of a capacity for arbitrary interference if the constituent units, the EU peoples, can be assured that they enjoy equal status in administering EU law.

[57] For a compelling account of the compatibility of republican non-domination and equality as embodied in democratic ideals, see Nadia Urbinati, 'Competing for Liberty: The Republican Critique of Democracy' (2012) 106 *American Political Science Review* 607.

[58] Neil Walker, 'The Place of European Law' in Gráinne De Búrca and Joseph Weiler (eds), *The Worlds of European Constitutionalism* (Cambridge, CUP, 2012) 89.

The values of deliberation and non-domination add yet another reflexive dimension. On the one hand, non-domination creates the conditions for unconstrained deliberation in the first place.[59] Only if each people can formulate their freely chosen vision of how to govern Europe without being dominated by others, will the exchange of reasons and force of rational argument that grounds the value of deliberation and allows to contest arbitrary interference effectively unfold its greatest moral value.[60] On the other hand, deliberation is a crucial component of non-domination. Deliberation among those affected by subsequent laws removes the risk of arbitrariness and thus the risk of domination. For deliberation is the best way to consider the interests of those affected and be guided by them.[61]

In a nutshell, EU law has legitimate authority to the extent to which its law-making and enforcement institutions treat the EU peoples as equals and secure non-domination among them by allowing them to act together and to translate their disagreements about issues that transcend the legitimate jurisdiction of their states into binding law through deliberation. As a result, participation in the EU can protect the autonomous self-determination of the EU peoples in the first place because EU law that has demoicratic authority does not violate the collective autonomy of the EU peoples. It secures it. In that sense, demoicracy is about freedom.[62] The EU gives its peoples a say in the issues that affect them jointly and prevents illegitimate interference by neighbouring peoples. Figure 11 illustrates what I have said in the last few paragraphs:

Fig 11 The Values of Demoicratic Authority

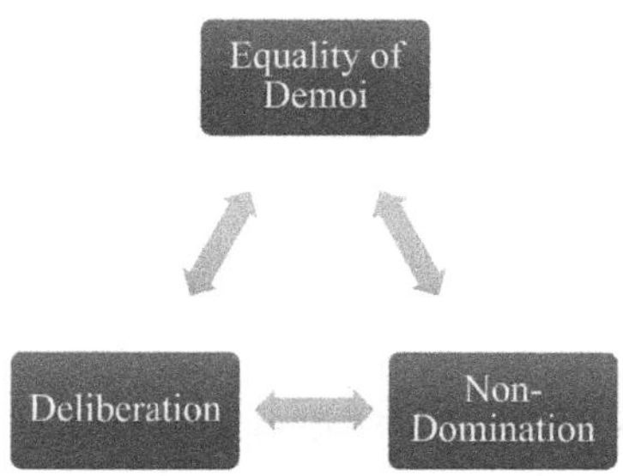

There is no apparent hierarchy among these values. Deliberation will be a more dominant component of some pieces of EU law (especially secondary law made through the ordinary legislative procedure), non-domination of others (for

[59] Bellamy (n 15) 62.

[60] See generally Pettit (n 31) 185 et seq.

[61] Larmore (n 33) 114; Deirdre Curtin, *Postnational Democracy: The European Union in Search of a Political Philosophy* (Alphen aan den Rijn, Kluwer Law International, 1997) 53–55.

[62] Adapted from Urbinati (n 57) 609.

example, ECJ judgments on fundamental freedoms), and equality of others again (laws that require unanimity). The moral authority of EU law is gradual, depending on the extent of its compliance with these values. These values constitute the appropriate benchmark to evaluate the legitimate authority of EU law. That is the essence of demoicratic authority.

Note that I am not pulling anything new out of the hat. Support comes from the Treaties and the Court. As I showed in chapter three, both the ECJ and the Treaties seem to support the idea that the peoples' input into EU law-making constitutes a primary reason for the authority of EU law. Specifically, the Rome Treaty of 1957 has emphasised the value of cooperation among the peoples from the beginning, which is also present in the 1992 TEU. The Court has put flesh on the bones by emphasising the value of EU institutions and the binding law they produce and enforce in facilitating the cooperation of the EU peoples from the outset.

IV. Political Obligation in the EU

Political obligation describes the enquiry as to whether subjects of the law have a moral duty to obey the law. Political obligation thus illustrates the significant impact of theories of authority on social practice because it identifies whether (dis-)obeying the law is prima facie morally right or wrong. In chapter one, I sided with those who argue that legitimate authority triggers a prima facie duty to obey the law. When dealing with political authority beyond the state, the question of political obligation has several layers. We must ask who has a duty to obey EU law (subsection A), what that duty requires (subsection B) and to whom we owe it (subsection C).

A. Who Has a Duty to Obey EU Law?

Membership is usually a good indicator of whom a political community obligates or, at least, claims to obligate. In nation states, individual citizens as members of the political community are the addressees of political obligation. On the international level, by contrast, states are the primary members of the international community and, as a result, addressees of the main international legal and moral duties.

In my constructive interpretation of the EU's authority claim in chapter two, I argued that EU law ultimately addresses and seeks to bind the constitutional peoples of the EU, which – in political and social reality – mainly act in their dual manifestation as citizens and state officials (only rarely do they act directly as peoples). It follows from the argument of demoicratic authority that EU law imposes political obligation on the constitutional peoples. In other words, EU citizens do not have a duty to obey EU law qua individual EU citizens, but as members of a *demos* which participates in the EU as a collective jointly with other collectives. Similarly, any ensuing duty to obey EU law for Member State officials flows from their representing a self-determined people which is committed to EU integration and remains its ultimate legitimacy source. But how exactly does political obligation materialise in the EU?

B. Different Agents – Different Duties

In chapter one, I portrayed the individual manifestations of duties to obey *international* law (especially Çali's obedience, respect and rebuttal) and voiced my suspicion about a single nature of duty for *national* political obligation (where the main disagreement is between compliance and conformity). Independent of the viability of one single account for the nature of political obligation there, the fact that both citizens and state institutions play a role in the EU's daily governance makes it very unlikely that the same can be argued in the EU. We must be open to the idea that EU law imposes different kinds of duties on different agents. Whereas ground and reference point remain the same (demoicratic authority), the duties vary in nature and consequence.

Barber suggests, nonetheless, that the EU only has authority if the addressees of EU duties do what the EU wants because the EU says so.[63] Obeying EU law based on the incorporation of EU law in one's home constitutional framework cannot do the trick, since that would mean that, ultimately, the addressees obey their home state rather than the EU. Barber thus requires strong compliance. I am reluctant to accept this, however. Why should we require compliance instead of conformity for law beyond the state, if it is already dubious as a standard for national legal duties, not least because of the problem of just laws? The comparatively weaker authority claims of legal regimes beyond the state (no coercion, individual autonomy less affected) make it unlikely that they require compliance in the strong sense entertained nationally. Moreover, since political authority is an instance of practical authority, it is counterintuitive to rely on internal psychological differences among agents rather than actual manifestation in practice. Practical authority tells you what to do, and what matters most, accordingly, is what you do. Finally, the present argument is still a moral rather than empirical one. Empirical evidence of officials and individuals who obey EU law because the EU says so (which one would undoubtedly find) is thus not very important. Instead, my aim is to uncover moral reasons why they ought to obey EU law. My point is that the nature of political obligation, ie the precise moral

[63] Nicholas Barber, *The Constitutional State* (Oxford, OUP, 2010) 180.

character and weight of the duty to obey EU law, will vary among different kinds of agents and does not require compliance (acting on it *because* the EU says so).

EU law imposes quantitatively and qualitatively more demanding duties on Member State institutions than on individual EU citizens. Mirroring that, Member State representation is more pronounced in the EU's institutional framework compared to citizen representation.[64] In terms of enforcement, duties on Member State officials even correspond to rights of EU citizens. Direct effect, for example, allows EU citizens to enforce the duties incumbent on Member State institutions; they act as 'custodians of the obligations member states owe to one another'.[65]

This normative architecture shouldn't prompt us to throw out the baby with the bathwater and declare that EU citizenship is without duties.[66] Instead, the core duty of EU citizens flowing from EU law's demoicratic authority is *respect*. They ought to respect EU law because they are not affected in their individual autonomy, but as part of a people committed to EU membership. EU citizens ought to respect EU law and take it as prima facie reason to rightly determine how this specific issue is to be regulated. This duty of respect ultimately flows from the idea that EU law itself expresses the respect among the citizens of the peoples that come together in the EU.[67] In a nutshell, EU citizens ought to respect EU law because they thereby uphold the respect EU law embodies towards all EU citizens. EU citizens thus may not try to dodge EU law if their collective people is constrained by it, since their individual autonomy is not affected as ultimate value. For example, if an employer seeks to circumvent EU anti-discrimination rules by not hiring other EU citizens despite their valid credentials, they fail to respect EU law.

What is the implication for any moral duty to obey EU law for Member State officials? EU law doesn't affect Member State institutions in the same way as national constitutional law or international law do. While the former creates the legal relationship between states and citizens, ie relates states to their home people, the latter affects states more lightly and rarely imposes duties enforceable outside the international level. EU law imposes enforceable legal duties on Member State institutions and officials, that morally require *conformity*, ie acting on them. Demoicratic authority underpins this duty of conformity. Demoicratic authority requires any state official to consider the value of EU law as giving effect to a valuable scheme of cooperation among the EU peoples and to conform to it. In most cases, this duty – of which sincere cooperation in Art 4(3) TEU is the

[64] Paul Craig, 'The EU, Democracy and Institutional Structure: Past, Present and Future' in Heusel and Rageade (n 13) 321.

[65] Turkuler Isiksel, *Europe's Functional Constitution: A Theory of Constitutionalism Beyond the State* (Oxford, OUP, 2016) 61.

[66] But *cf* Dimitry Kochenov, 'EU Citizenship without Duties' (2014) 20 *European Law Journal* 482.

[67] For Larmore (n 33) 115 et seq, this idea of respect underlies republican non-domination as a whole. See also Valentini (n 17) 193.

most prominent codification – requires national officials to apply and enforce EU law as well as they can. In those rare cases, when weighing up whether to obey EU or national law in case of a conflict, it will be a decision between effectuating the national law an autonomous people has given itself, or the supranational law of the joint peoples (more in chapter six). This framework balances the collective autonomy of a people with the authority exercised in the EU jointly with other peoples.

Beyond these rare conflict cases, the representatives' duty to conform with EU law implies a duty to justify and explain decisions at the EU level to their people to gain and maintain support.[68] This is a clear case in which reflecting on the EU's authority and the ensuing obligations helps to evaluate and pin down the moral wrongness of national leaders' frequent attempts to 'blame Brussels' and divert responsibility.

C. To Whom Do We Owe the Duty to Obey EU Law?

Theories of state authority assume that we owe political obligation to the state and not to our fellow citizens.[69] Although literature on extending political obligation beyond the state is rare, when the issue has been addressed it is stated as obvious that one owes the duty to obey EU law to one's own fellow citizens or 'polis'.[70] If, however, the authority of EU law is best evaluated based on the moral value of the EU's demoicratic institutional architecture, as I argue it is, then Europeans and their representatives owe the duty to obey EU law to each other as members of distinct but interrelated peoples. In other words, those wronged by the failure to comply with EU law are the other European peoples who have committed to the EU as a political community beyond the state.

This duty is part of the broader moral 'responsibilities that peoples owe one another'[71] in a demoicracy. In other words, EU political obligation expresses the EU law-related element of the otherwise under-determined moral obligations among the EU peoples (others are, eg, solidarity and transnational justice).[72] Demoicratic institutions facilitate the interaction of EU peoples and, as a result, gain their moral value directly from how these peoples relate to each other through these institutions.[73] By not respecting or not conforming to EU law

[68] On this dual duty of Member State leaders, see Albert Weale, 'Citizenship in Europe and the Logic of Two-Level Political Contracts' (2014) 15 *German Law Journal* 867, 871 et seq.

[69] See only Stephen Perry, 'Associative Obligations and the Obligation to Obey the Law' in Scott Hershovitz (ed), *Exploring Law's Empire: The Jurisprudence of Ronald Dworkin* (Oxford, OUP, 2008) 191.

[70] Pavlos Eleftheriadis, 'Citizenship and Obligation' in Dickson and Eleftheriadis (n 3) 163.

[71] Nicolaïdis (n 1) 356.

[72] See only Andrea Sangiovanni, 'Solidarity in the European Union' (2013) 33 *OJLS* 213, 229.

[73] Joseph Weiler, 'A Constitution for Europe? Some Hard Choices' (2002) 40 *Journal of Common Market Studies* 563, 548; Innerarity (n 9) 249.

endowed with demoicratic authority, I disrespect the moral worth of the community as a whole and ultimately harm the other participating peoples. Remember one of the main findings of chapter one, namely that peoples make claims on each other in a political community. Depending on the nature of the political community in question, this involves different claims by different individuals/ collectives. In the EU, constitutional peoples make claims on each other. As one moral consequence of this, they are reciprocally bound by the institutional regime they choose to manage these claims in (to the extent to which those institutions act legitimately).

So far, I have outlined the idea of demoicracy and how its underlying values give moral force to EU law. Demoicratic authority thus understood gives rise to a prima facie duty to obey the law, although in different manifestations for different actors in the EU. If demoicratic authority wants to be an evaluative standard to distinguish rightful rule from illegitimate power – rather than a tool to rubber-stamp EU law, and thereby turn legitimacy into mere legality – it needs to incorporate limits. Demoicratic authority provides a conceptual framework to identify such internal and external limits. Let me turn to those next.

V. The Limits of Demoicratic Authority

Authority ought to acknowledge limits. Not only because it ought to respect the intrinsic good of autonomy it interferes with, but because limits are a necessary element of legitimate rule. It follows that theoretical accounts of authority should have operable limits as well. It is thus an asset of demoicratic authority as an evaluative standard that the democratic authority of national law imposes *external* limits (subsection A), while demoicratic authority shares the *internal* limits of institution-centred, procedural accounts (subsection B).

A. Democratic Self-Government as External Limit

Defining the boundaries of a political community's authority is ever more important in today's interdependent world, both horizontally among the states and vertically in relation to other regulatory levels.[74] In the EU, the most important boundary 'dispute' occurs between the legitimate reach of EU law versus the legitimate reach of national law. In other words, the democratic authority of Member State law serves as external limit to the demoicratic authority of EU law. That is of course overly simplistic. And yet, this idea redirects our attention to the tension

[74] For the former, see A John Simmons, *Boundaries of Authority* (Oxford, OUP, 2016). For the latter see Nicole Roughan, *Authorities: Conflicts, Cooperation, and Transnational Legal Theory* (Oxford, OUP, 2014).

between the EU's authority claim and the self-determination/autonomy of the EU peoples. This is fundamentally about:

> the idea that, when peoples are constituted as demoi, i.e., when they give themselves democratic institutions, then they are owed respect as collectives by other actors ... and, in particular, its democratic decisions are ... respecting it also means respecting the individuals which form it – hence respecting it does not mean making a choice between the freedom of collective agents and that of individuals.[75]

Ronzoni highlights that EU citizens constitute the agents that deserve respect as members of a constitutional *demos* of a Member State. Respecting their self-determination qua *demos* in their respective state and, consequently, their right to regulate their own affairs, implies respecting each one of them individually. Bellamy deserves much credit for fleshing out this perspective in demoicratic theory: reflecting on the appropriate relationship between the two regulatory levels in a demoicracy (EU level – national level).[76]

In this framework, locks/review mechanisms of national constitutional courts act as external control. These locks constitute external limits to the authority of EU law that are ultimately based on the democratic authority of national law. The national constitutional courts act as guardians of national self-determination as spelled out in the respective national constitutions. Recall that the obligation to obey (EU) law is a prima facie obligation that can be overridden by other moral obligations. In some cases, national democratic self-determination may turn out to produce such an overriding consideration. That not only applies to refusing to apply EU law in their own state vis-à-vis the EU (vertically). The case law according to which the far-reaching idea of mutual trust has limits implies that the conception of national self-determination embodied in a Member State constitution can lead to a refusal to apply an EAW because of deficiencies in another Member State, ie horizontally.[77]

Yet, neither national governments nor constitutional courts can make generous use of popular sovereignty (and democracy-based) arguments against the other EU peoples. The fact that each Member State is a democracy limits the objections one of them can make against the others. As van Middelaar recalls from the negotiations in the Eurozone during the euro crisis, 'Greece was not a single democracy fighting the world of high finance and international organisations ..., but a single democracy that found itself opposed by eighteen other democracies'.[78]

Hence, the democratic authority of national law does not give EU citizens and state officials a blank check to overturn EU law. That would go against the

[75] Ronzoni (n 2) 218.
[76] Bellamy (n 15) especially ch 3.
[77] Case C-404/15 *Aranyosi und Căldăraru* EU:C:2016:198.
[78] Luuk van Middelaar, 'Europe and the Return of Politics' in van Middelaar, van Parijs and van Rompuy (n 8) 213 et seq.

moral weight of the EU law that all the EU peoples committed to. The conceptual point remains, however, that national democratic self-determination sets an external jurisdictional limit to the EU's authority. In other words, the respect for national constitutional identity and diversity not only figures as a legal limit on the EU's action (Art 4(2) TEU), but also as an outer moral limit to the legitimacy of its rule.[79] This rather crude framework by no means entails that EU law cannot legitimately touch, shape, or harness national legal systems for its purposes. The function as an external limit does not ring-fence national law from EU law influence. Instead, democratic self-determination at the national level needs to be balanced with its jurisdictional limits that provide the legitimate scope of action for EU law.

B. The Internal Limits of (Mainly) Procedural Authority

The emphasis on procedural legitimacy through deliberation in my account of demoicratic authority entails that limits of procedural accounts also apply to demoicratic authority. According to Christiano, 'the limits to democratic authority are internal limits in the sense that the limits are grounded in the very same principles as democracy is grounded in'.[80] The values which give law authority simultaneously constitute boundaries of its legitimate authority. The same applies, by analogy, to demoicratic authority and its emphasis on procedural deliberation.

But what are those limits? For one, the violation of the values identified above renders EU law illegitimate from the outset. The standards that make EU law legitimate would simply not be met if EU law itself would foster domination, for example. The next chapter will show in greater detail that the assessment of EU law's authority through demoicratic authority identifies various legitimacy problems.

For another, an important limit of demoicratic authority is the absence of substantial safeguards. Various scholars have pointed out how democratic decision-making procedures can be used to produce vile results. In Weiler's words: 'A democracy of evil people will be evil, even if democratic'.[81] The same

[79] See only Myrto Tsakatika, 'Claims to Legitimacy: The European Commission between Continuity and Change' (2005) 43 *Journal of Common Market Studies* 193, 205; Joseph Raz, 'The Future of State Sovereignty' in Wojciech Sadurski, Michael Sevel and Kevin Walton (eds), *Legitimacy: the State and Beyond* (Oxford, OUP, 2019) 80 et seq.

[80] Thomas Christiano, 'A Democratic Theory of Territory and Some Puzzles about Global Democracy' (2006) 37 *Journal of Social Philosophy* 81, 90.

[81] Joseph Weiler, 'The European Circumstance and the Politics of Meaning: Not on Bread Alone Doth Man Liveth (Deut. 8:3; Mat 4:4)' (2020) 21 *German Law Journal* 96, 96. See earlier Joseph Weiler, 'Federalism without Constitutionalism: Europe's Sonderweg' in Kalypso Nicolaïdis and Robert Howse (eds), *The Federal Vision: Legitimacy and Levels of Governance in the United States and the European Union* (Oxford, OUP, 2001) 66.

is true for the EU's demoicracy. Although that sounds harsh, I have no intention to downplay the risks associated with conceiving of the EU as a demoicracy. To the contrary, chapter two illustrated just how transformational the EU's authority claim is, which makes a discussion of its potential dangers even more urgent. Demoicratic authority thus presents an open flank based on the lack of substantive protection against 'vile' results. The election of authoritarian populists to EU institutions and Member State governments could at some point mean that they oversee a demoicracy whose institutions and laws have considerable influence on the everyday life of the European peoples. In an important sense, the authority of EU law depends on the continued existence of its Member States as democratic states. Only then will the governments and parliamentarians truly represent their citizens.[82] The *demos* needs to continue to govern on the national level for the *demoi* to be able to govern on the supranational level, so to speak.

This unappealing result can somehow be mitigated by the interaction of internal and external limits. As discussed above, the external limit of demoicratic authority is the democratic authority of national law. This in turn leads to a limited window of review mechanisms by national constitutional courts, which thereby may legitimately avoid domination by EU law, as we will see in more detail in the next chapter. Simultaneously, they can and often have put external pressure on EU law to make good on its claim to legitimate authority.

VI. Conclusion

Three pillars underpin the demoicratic authority of EU law: deliberation, non-domination and equality of peoples. These values explain why the law-making and law-enforcement machinery itself has the potential to equip EU law with moral force. EU law allows the peoples to exercise joint self-determination over the issues that affect them in relation to each other.

The question 'Does the EU have the authority it claims for itself?' thus received two answers in this chapter. First, the EU has the authority it claims to the extent that the nature and scope of its claim match with demoicratic authority and the values underpinning it. This can be evaluated for each piece of EU law separately. Second, EU law's authority is not based on the various moral values many EU institutions claim it is. For the reasons given, the mostly implicit perspectives on the moral baseline underlying the authority of EU law as offered by EU institutions and academics alike did not convince me. But that does not mean – pace philosophical anarchists – that EU law has no authority. Here, I attempted to outline a more convincing view of the EU's authority, which helps to evaluate EU law's moral force: demoicratic authority.

[82] van den Brink (n 29) 930 et seq. See also R Daniel Kelemen, 'The "Democratic Deficits" of the US and the EU Compared' in Garben, Govaere and Nemitz (n 38).

EU law within the limits of demoicratic authority protects the self-determination of the EU peoples. We come back full circle to the basics discussed in chapter one in two important ways. First, as I recalled there, authority derives from *auctoritas*: from authorship. The account I have provided here is simple in that it builds on this etymological and conceptual connection: the law of the European Union gains its moral force from allowing the European peoples to decide about their joint fate together: to author their coexistence as a political community beyond the state. Second, I emphasised the importance of claims for moral and political relationships more broadly. Demoicratic authority expresses that EU law is one important way in which the EU peoples make and concretise otherwise under-determined claims they have on each other.

In a final step, let me illustrate the fresh perspective and practical value of demoicratic authority as a conceptual framework by putting it into practice.

6

Demoicratic Authority II: The Practice

I. Introduction

The primary perspective of this book is theoretical. It intends to raise awareness of serious moral questions in relation to the legitimate exercise of the EU's authority. I can nonetheless best illustrate the value of demoicratic authority as an evaluative tool by shedding light on its practical implications. After all, discussions of political authority are necessarily practical. They intend to inform the practical reasoning of both officials of law-administering institutions, and of affected citizens.

Each of the following debates illustrates how demoicratic authority provides a novel framework to conceptualise pressing issues of EU constitutional law. Perhaps even more importantly, this analysis allows us to identify various threats to the authority of EU law.

II. The Potential and Limits for Deliberation

The deliberative value of EU law-making – how it translates the preferences of 27 diverse peoples into binding legal rules – makes up one of the constitutive values of demoicratic authority. The following discussions illustrate the practical effect of the value of deliberation on the authority of EU law. They also highlight the dangers of restricting the realisation of its full potential.

A. Disagreement and Deliberation

Nothing is left of the 'permissive consensus' of the early days of the Community. Today, Member States, EU citizens, transnational organisations, academics and even national constitutional courts question the policy choices of Brussels. While some might say 'Blessed be the good old times!', demoicratic authority suggests that the continued politicisation of EU law- and policy-making has the potential to increase the authority of EU law. In a nutshell, the more controversial the underlying policy debate, the more authority the resulting EU law has. Sternberg is right: 'If there is one key lesson, it is that any claims about the EU's legitimacy, in order to be plausible, have to openly acknowledge the essentially controversial nature of EU politics'.[1]

Calls for the EU to embrace differences not only among its local roots and diverse legal cultures, but also in respect to the substance of political decisions on the supranational level are always welcome.[2] Those differences corroborate the authority of EU law: they help to realise that 'making decisions together can be more important than getting them right'.[3] For two recent examples, remember only the cumbersome negotiations of the appropriate economic response to the COVID 19 crisis in combination with the new Multinational Financial Framework or the intense public scrutiny of the EU's reaction to Russia's war on Ukraine and the ensuing energy crisis. These are not only powerful instances of a European public where the EU peoples are engaged with each other in joint deliberation, both via media outlets and in EU institutional fora, and where they held their leaders and representatives accountable for their decisions. These negotiations and debates also laid bare that the interests of various peoples align ideologically rather than nationally, which enabled institutional and societal deliberations about the appropriate European response to the crises. We witnessed a similarly intense politicisation and deliberation when the EU adopted contentious secondary law that affects EU citizens in their daily lives, such as the General Data Protection Regulation or the Copyright Directive.[4] Those could only be a foretaste considering the far-reaching measures necessary to implement the EU's Fit For 55 Agenda to Combat the Climate Crisis in the coming years. The point I want to make is that EU law in its post-Lisbon form reflects a 'binding dissensus'[5] which – due to that very nature – constitutes a great moral achievement.

The moral force of EU law accordingly increases if the legislative process results in a binding compromise, despite deep yet reasonable disagreements within and among the EU peoples. In short, 'more politics' strengthens law's authority. It seems flawed to portray political differences and conflicting visions among the

[1] Claudia Sternberg, 'Public Opinion in the EU Institutions' Discourses on EU Legitimacy from the Beginnings of Integration to Today' (2016) 54 *Politique Européenne* 24, 46.

[2] See, eg, Michèle Finck and Floris de Witte, 'The Challenge of Challenges' (2020) 21 *German Law Journal* 1.

[3] Scott Hershovitz, 'Legitimacy, Democracy, and Razian Authority' (2003) 9 *Legal Theory* 201, 218 in relation to national law-making.

[4] Regulation (EU) 2016/679 of the European Parliament and of the Council of 27 April 2016 on the protection of natural persons with regard to the processing of personal data and on the free movement of such data, and repealing Directive 95/46/EC (General Data Protection Regulation) [2016] OJ L119/1. Directive (EU) 2019/790 of the European Parliament and of the Council of 17 April 2019 on copyright and related rights in the Digital Single Market and amending Directives 96/9/EC and 2001/29/EC (Copyright Directive) [2019] OJ L130/92.

[5] Luuk van Middelaar, 'Europe and the Return of Politics' in Luuk van Middelaar, Philippe van Parijs and Herman van Rompuy (eds), *After the Storm: How to Save Democracy in Europe* (Tielt, Lannoo, 2015) 244.

Member States and their citizens as a threat to the very existence of the EU. Quite the contrary. Instead of lamenting that this leads to an 'unprecedented climate of decay' in which 'the very idea of integration is shattered to its bones',[6] we should acknowledge that the nature, level and future of EU integration has indeed always been controversial. The argument of demoicratic authority suggests that embracing the contestation among the EU peoples in the production of binding EU law makes that very law more legitimate.

B. Judicial Review

The effect of the politicisation described above on EU law's demoicratic authority has direct consequences for judicial review. Arnull scrutinises EU law against the democratic features of a majoritarian national democracy and – hardly surprising – finds no counter-majoritarian difficulty that would prevent intense judicial review of EU law. The simple reason is that the EU does not constitute a majoritarian state-like democracy that warrants protection of the democratically adopted laws.[7] He thus accepts a greater role for judicial review against 'non-democratic' EU law. Demoicratic authority tells a different story. The moral value of EU law lies in channelling the reasonable disagreements of 27 peoples into binding and enforceable law through institutional deliberation. Judicial review at the EU level ought to respect this moral achievement as part of a supranational conception of separation of powers called institutional balance (Art 13(2) TEU).[8]

What position does the Court take in this debate? On the one hand, the ECJ seems ever more reluctant to interfere with the policy choices and assessments of the EU legislator.[9] The Court recognises the greater authority of intensely debated secondary law, such as the Framework Decision on the EAW or the Citizenship Directive.[10] With regard to the EAW, the ECJ in *Melloni* held that the Framework

[6] Julio Baquero Cruz, *What's Left of the Law of Integration?: Decay and Resistance in European Union Law* (Oxford, OUP, 2018) 170. Similarly Giorgio Maganza, 'Can the Authority of EU Law Be Taken for Granted? A Tale of Principles and Realities' in Wolfgang Heusel and Jean-Philippe Rageade (eds), *The Authority of EU Law: Do We Still Believe In It?* (New York, Springer, 2019) 46.

[7] Anthony Arnull, 'Judicial Review in the European Union' in Anthony Arnull and Damian Chalmers (eds), *The Oxford Handbook of European Union Law* (Oxford, OUP, 2015).

[8] See, in far more detail, Martijn van den Brink, 'The European Union's Demoicratic Legislature' (2021) 19 *International Journal of Constitutional Law* 914.

[9] See only Jacob Öberg, 'The Rise of the Procedural Paradigm: Judicial Review of EU Legislation in Vertical Competence Disputes' (2017) 13 *European Constitutional Law Review* 248, especially at 254.

[10] Directive 2004/38/EC of the European Parliament and of the Council of 29 April 2004 on the right of citizens of the Union and their family members to move and reside freely within the territory of the Member States amending Regulation (EEC) No 1612/68 and repealing Directives 64/221/EEC, 68/360/EEC, 72/194/EEC, 73/148/EEC, 75/34/EEC, 75/35/EEC, 90/364/EEC, 90/365/EEC and 93/96/EEC (Citizenship Directive) [2004] OJ L158/77.

Decision 'reflects the consensus reached by all the Member States' and, as a result, should not be compromised by unilateral national alterations.[11] With regard to the Citizenship Directive, the Court refrains from using primary law to deviate from secondary law, holding that the 'principle of non-discrimination, laid down generally in Article 18 TFEU, is given more specific expression' in the Directive.[12] In contrast, the ECJ is willing to grant more leeway in areas that 'had not been harmonised by the EU legislature'.[13]

On the other hand, van den Brink gathered powerful evidence from a range of policy sectors (eg citizenship, social security coordination, flight compensation) where the Court undermines the choices of the EU legislature.[14] The Court does that: (i) by constitutionalising primary law and thus obliging legislative choices to conform with the Court's interpretation of primary law;[15] (ii) by interpreting legislation contrary to the drafters' intention;[16] or (iii) by purposive reasoning in light of the Treaties more generally.[17]

I agree with van den Brink that the demoicratic authority of EU law militates against these judicial intrusions into the EU legislator's policy choices. While we can't identify a counter-majoritarian difficulty in the sense employed in nation state democracies, the making of EU secondary law constitutes a moral achievement worthy of respect in its own right. Let's look at the role of the EU legislator in this debate more closely in the following subsection.

C. Deliberation in EU Secondary Law-Making

The go-to mechanism to involve those affected in the EU is the making of primary and secondary law. Both mechanisms allow for a variety of representation channels for the peoples of Europe, secondary law-making more robustly so than primary law-making. With a view to the theoretical framework of the preceding chapter, these procedures enable EU law to reflect the 'right' solution from the perspective of the deliberating EU peoples, even if it might not constitute the 'best' solution.[18]

I don't want to suggest that EU law has no epistemic value, however. That is, EU law-making is not ill-equipped to produce 'good' solutions, where 'good'

[11] Case C-399/11 *Melloni* EU:C:2013:107, para 62. Recently confirmed in Case C-416/20 PPU *Generalstaatsanwaltschaft Hamburg* EU:C:2020:1042.

[12] Case C-333/13 *Dano* EU:C:2014:2358, para 61.

[13] Case C-42/17 *M.A.S. und M.B.* EU:C:2017:936, para 44.

[14] van den Brink (n 8) 932 et seq.

[15] For a discussion of several examples, see van den Brink ibid.

[16] Joined Cases C-402/07 and C-432/07 *Sturgeon and others* EU:C:2009:716.

[17] van den Brinck mentions the access to benefits cases, such as Case C-209/03 *Bidar* EU:C:2005:169 and Case C-413/99 *Baumbast* EU:C:2002:493.

[18] Diana Wallis, 'A View from Parliament' in Heusel and Rageade (n 6).

refers to empirical accuracy, desirability and moral correctness.[19] Besides representation and diversity in EU law making itself, let's not forget the less formalised elements of these institutional mechanisms, which are as important for grounding the epistemic value of EU law-making. Often, ideas or policies emerge in different Member States which thus act as drivers and role-models for EU legislation. Take only the regulation of automotive emissions in Germany or of antibiotics in animal feed in Sweden and Denmark, all of which set the EU on a path for higher quality regulations, due to the experience in individual Member States.[20]

The peoples channel their diverse regulatory experiences into the EU law-making process and thus increase the epistemic value of EU law. Conversely, this process also enriches national law-making. Legislative proposals on the national level profit from the exchange on the European level as an exercise in hands-on comparative law. Especially in complex and contentious sectors, law-makers and the public often consider the scheme that is in place in other Member States. Both the Covid pandemic and the energy crisis as a result of the Russian war on Ukraine bear ample proof (which measures to protect from the virus work in Member State A? Should we implement a furlough scheme that worked in Member State B? How does Member State C so successfully shield its citizens from the worst effects of inflation and rising energy prices?). National law-making benefits from this exchange among law-makers in Europe. Thus, while we focus on the legitimising function of deliberation for EU law-making, the EU's deliberative demoicracy enables and facilitates deliberation on many levels (national, European, transnational).[21]

Admittedly, the substantial constraints for deliberation stemming from primary law limit the value of deliberation in EU secondary law-making. The EU's limited competences and the hierarchy between primary and secondary law reinforced by the Court's constitutionalising jurisprudence of first and foremost economic law in the Treaties make an open debate among policy options all but impossible. The epistemic value of EU law is thus weaker than in state democracies.[22] In part, that follows from the very architecture of the EU as a political community beyond the state with limited competences. The fact remains that there is distinct epistemic value to the contributions of the

[19] Hélène Landemore and Scott Page, 'Deliberation and Disagreement: Problem Solving, Prediction, and Positive Dissensus' (2015) 14 *Politics Philosophy & Economics* 229, 230.

[20] Anu Bradford, *The Brussels Effect: How the European Union Rules the World* (Oxford, OUP, 2020) 10.

[21] Samantha Besson, 'Deliberative Demoi-Cracy in the European Union: Towards the Deterritorialization of Democracy' in Samantha Besson, José Luis Martí and Verena Seiler (eds), *Deliberative Democracy and its Discontents* (Farnham, Ashgate, 2006) 199 et seq.

[22] Regarding the epistemic value of democratic laws in states, see David Estlund, *Democratic Authority: A Philosophical Framework* (Princeton, Princeton University Press, 2008); Hélène Landemore, *Democratic Reason: Politics, Collective Intelligence, and the Rule of the Many* (Princeton, Princeton University Press, 2013).

representatives of 27 peoples, even if they are substantively constrained. In short, the demoicratically chosen 'right' solution often has epistemic value that makes a 'good' solution more likely. The difference to state democracies 'is one of degree, not of kind'.[23]

But we shouldn't only focus on deliberation among the peoples alone. Interestingly, the nature of the EU's institutional framework enables one single people (the French, the Czech, the Latvians) to voice and deliberate internal struggles between its more domestic-focused and its more European camps. Here we can see a demoicracy of democracies at work. EU institutions allow us to debate contradictory desires that would remain below the surface of institutional deliberation did the EU not exist. Both MEPs and Heads of State/Ministers represent the EU peoples. In fact, a MEP is first and foremost an elected domestic official who runs on an EU programme. This MEP's proposals may conflict with the government of his own state – also elected by the same people. Both derive their authority from a particular people that thereby may voice contradictory demands in relation to how it wants to be governed. The EU institutions allow for these different representation channels and deliberations in a binding institutional framework. Thereby, the EU's architecture mitigates the risk of persistent minorities to a considerable extent.[24]

At this point, I must pour at least some cold water on the matter. While the process of EU secondary law-making has the potential to realise valuable deliberation, there is also evidence of various obstacles to this realisation. For one, consider the comparatively weak political accountability in both the Commission and the Parliament. As Weiler has emphasised many times, there is no sense of political accountability for policy failures for the Commission, nor do European Parliament elections automatically translate into tangible differences of policy and performance.[25] Whereas the increasing politicisation identified above may mitigate some of those concerns, the need for improvement in this area is obvious. For another, the recent scandal involving Qatar's attempt to influence MEPs and to improve their opinion on and public stance towards the gulf state by bribing them with suitcases full of cash is not only film material. It forces us to remember the persistent risk of regulatory capture through lobbyism, which seems to be especially pronounced in Brussels. While lobbyism as a source of expert knowledge and tool for interest representation is not problematic as such, it needs to be regulated in order to prevent harmful effects on the will-formation and deliberation in the legislative process.[26] Instances like the Qatar corruption scandal thwart the

[23] Paul Craig, 'The EU, Democracy and Institutional Structure: Past, Present and Future' in Heusel and Rageade (n 6) 323.

[24] Less optimistic is Richard Bellamy, *A Republican Europe of States: Cosmopolitanism, Intergovernmentalism and Democracy in the EU* (Cambridge, CUP, 2019) 112 et seq.

[25] Joseph Weiler, 'Van Gend En Loos: The Individual as Subject and Object and the Dilemma of European Legitimacy' (2014) 12 *International Journal of Constitutional Law* 94, 98 et seq.

[26] See at length Doris Dialer and Margarethe Richter (eds), *Lobbying in the European Union: Strategies, Dynamics and Trends* (New York, Springer, 2019).

social legitimacy of the EU legislative process, ie the perception of its legitimacy by the peoples, and consequently risks affecting its moral legitimacy.

This illustration reveals a mixed picture of the authority of EU law, but it showcases the rewarding value of deliberation as an analytical tool to assess EU law's authority. Another threat to the value of deliberation in EU law-making and thus to the authority of EU law stems from the Member States' growing use of international legal mechanisms, to which we turn next:

D. Undermining EU Law-Making Through International Arrangements

Demoicratic authority as a normative framework to evaluate the legitimacy of EU law has a clear position on Member States' recourse to international legal mechanisms outside the EU legal order, such as those we witnessed as a reaction to the financial crisis (EFSF, ESM, etc).[27] These mechanisms (especially in the vicinity of the EU's competences) constitute a threat to the authority of EU law. They circumvent the inherent demoicratic and especially deliberative quality of the EU's institutional machinery, as well as EU law's substantive legal safeguards that distinguish the EU as a political community from international law. How so?

For one, the flight to international law leads to executive dominance and de-parliamentarisation. Garben makes a forceful case for the *illegality* of those mechanisms outside the EU legal order based on the commitment to democracy enshrined in Art 10 TEU and the principle of sincere cooperation.[28] In my view, these legal arguments can be translated into political theory. Such mechanisms are *illegitimate*. They lack institutional integrity and bypass the supranational forum, ie the institutional manifestation of the relations of the EU peoples with each other.[29]

For another, outsourcing EU-related matters to international organisations greatly increases the risk for domination by more powerful Member States, which the EU's institutional architecture is designed to prevent.[30] This is due to the lack of legal safeguards for smaller states and the idea that political might plays an

[27] Another example is the concessions agreement with UK Prime Minister Cameron on the free movement of workers. Rightly very critical of both developments, see Joseph Weiler, 'The Authority of European Law: Do We Still Believe in It?' in Heusel and Rageade (n 6) 4.

[28] Sacha Garben, 'The Constitutional (Im)Balance between "the Market" and "the Social" in the European Union' (2017) 13 *European Constitutional Law Review* 23, 55 et seq. The Court usually disagrees. See only Case C-370/12 *Pringle* EU:C:2012:756. Case T-192/16 *NF v European Council* EU:T:2017:128.

[29] Similarly in relation to the EU-Turkey deal, Valsamis Mitsilegas, 'Trust' (2020) 21 *German Law Journal* 69, 71 et seq.

[30] Federico Fabbrini, 'States' Equality v States' Power: The Euro-Crisis, Inter-State Relations and the Paradox of Domination' (2015) 17 *Cambridge Yearbook of European Legal Studies* 3, 25.

important role in international organisations. International outsourcing thereby also jeopardises the equal political standing of the EU's *demoi*.[31]

This lack of respect for the values of demoicratic law and especially the value of deliberation thus jeopardises the authority of EU law. The ECJ admittedly mitigated some of the 'damage' when it held that EU institutions are bound by their EU law duties even when acting outside EU law.[32] Nonetheless, ex post legal accountability cannot replace *ex ante* political legitimacy, since that upsets the intricate interrelation among the values underlying EU law's authority as identified in the preceding chapter.

Some don't share these concerns, however, and emphasise the national democratic legitimacy of institutions like the ESM, ie their accountability to national ministers and parliaments.[33] Nonetheless, this remote accountability cannot alleviate executive dominance and de-parliamentarisation. Moreover, such international bodies might even harm national democracy itself by disrespecting the budgetary autonomy of national parliaments. Budgetary discretion all but vanishes under these post financial crisis mechanisms.[34] Finally, even if we assume domestic democratic legitimacy, such democratic legitimacy in one state is unable to accommodate the risk of domination among democracies.

The threat of *inter se* agreements among Member States to the authority of EU law increases with their substantive proximity to EU competences. However attractive it might be for national governments to escape the constraints of the EU's institutional architecture, they are there for a reason. The EU binds the EU peoples to one another and allows each of them to influence the obligations they intend to impose on each other. In essence, escaping EU procedures replaces 'integration through law' with 'integration through power'.[35]

Only those who perceive the EU as international forum with no *qualitative* difference to other international organisations are thus unable to identify a legitimacy problem here.[36] But if you view the EU as a political community in which the European peoples relate to each other as institutionally guaranteed equals, few developments constitute a bigger threat to the EU's authority than the international outsourcing described above. This practice neglects the deliberative value of EU law-making, creates the potential for domination, and cannot secure the

[31] van den Brink (n 8) 927.

[32] See Case C-8/15-P *Ledra Advertising* EU:C:2016:701.

[33] Christoph Möllers, 'Constitutional State of the European Union' in Robert Schütze (ed), *Globalisation and Governance: International Problems, European Solutions* (Cambridge, CUP, 2018) 256 et seq.

[34] Turkuler Isiksel, *Europe's Functional Constitution: A Theory of Constitutionalism Beyond the State* (Oxford, OUP, 2016) 225; Christian Joerges, 'How Is a Closer Union Conceivable under Conditions of Ever More Socio-economic and Political Diversity? Constitutionalising Europe's Unitas in Pluralitate' (2018) 24 *European Law Journal* 257, 263 et seq.

[35] Stephen Weatherill, *Law and Values in the European Union* (Oxford, OUP, 2016) 411. See also Erik Oddvar Eriksen, *The Normativity of the European Union* (London, Palgrave Macmillan, 2014) 115, 118.

[36] See, eg, Pavlos Eleftheriadis, *A Union of Peoples* (Oxford, OUP, 2020) chs 8 and 9.

peoples' equality. This shows that a discussion of the ground for EU law's moral force is vital to call out and prevent such harmful practices and their functionalist logic.

But let's not put all the blame on the European Council. The Court has sometimes contributed to such international outsourcing by refusing to review the legality of acts in the heart of the EU's political and institutional architecture. It held that the 'common accord' that concludes the selection process of members of the ECJ according to Art 253 TFEU does not constitute an act of EU institutions under Art 263 TFEU and is thus beyond judicial review.[37] Similarly, the Court held that the Eurogroup does not qualify as EU 'institution' for the purposes of Art 340 TFEU. Its decisions thus can't give rise to non-contractual liability.[38] It seems that the efforts involved in deeming such acts legal – despite their neglect for the EU's institutional architecture and accountability regime – have convinced the Court that it is better to deny jurisdiction in the first place. And yet, this non-justiciability jurisprudence showcases a flawed focus on Member State consent as legitimacy basis and breaks up the careful calibration between political and legal accountability.

This discussion illustrates that the lack of legitimate alternatives usually strengthens the case for the legitimacy of the current institutional set up.[39] The finding that international organisations provide no more or an equally legitimate alternative to the EU's institutional arrangement thus corroborates the EU's legitimacy. This section then not only argues for avoiding any future escape to international law. Following the Schengen example, it also creates a normative incentive to push for the integration of international bodies in the orbit of the EU's competences into the EU's governance architecture.

E. Interim Conclusion

These discussions reveal a mixed picture of the state of the legitimate authority of EU law when evaluated from the perspective of mainly deliberation as authority-generating value. On the one hand, the ever-increasing politicisation of EU law-making emphasises the great moral achievement of agreeing on a legally binding solution for 27 peoples and cautions against strong judicial review by the ECJ. On the other, however, the proper functioning of the process of secondary law-making itself may suffer from a lack of accountability of the involved actors and from a risk of regulatory capture. Moreover, the Member States' recourse to international *inter see* agreements threatens the authority of EU law from the outside, for it bypasses the authority-generating value of the institutional deliberation in the EU's institutional architecture.

[37] Case C-424/20 P(R) *Sharpston* EU:C:2020:705.

[38] Case C-597/18 P *Council v Chrysostomides & Co* EU:C:2020:1028.

[39] NP Adams, 'Legitimacy and Institutional Purpose' (2020) 23 *Critical Review of International Social and Political Philosophy* 292, 301.

III. The Struggle for Non-Domination and Equality

Chapter five emphasised that the EU gives its peoples roughly equal normative influence in the EU's governance through a balance of influence of their representatives in various EU institutions, especially the Councils and the EP. The EU peoples bind each other through enforceable EU law and thereby constrain their inherent capacity to arbitrarily interfere with each other's democracies.[40] The capacity to reduce domination is an inherent feature of the EU's institutional architecture but also of its harnessing of national institutions. EU law leaves most of EU law enforcement to national legal orders, and especially courts. It allows individuals and state institutions (transnationally) to invoke and enforce EU law in domestic institutions. This constitutes an important factor for the EU to legitimately claim to secure non-domination among EU peoples in contrast to international law, where enforcement happens on the international stage. This preeminent role for national law-administering institutions in the enforcement of EU law illustrates the horizontal nature of the EU, where the peoples mobilise their own institutions in the administering, not only of their state, but of their joint political community beyond the state. Through that commitment, national institutions become European institutions. This structure moreover allows EU law to permeate a great array of different legal cultures while national institutions remain in charge. This framework enables us to identify facilitators and problems for the realisation of equality and non-domination as underlying values of the authority of EU law.

A. Primacy and Direct Effect as Enabler of Equality

The value of non-domination can legitimise the continuing use of the Court's structural principles of primacy and direct effect. While it is unfortunate that the ECJ, when engaging with the authority of EU law, hardly ever emphasises the production side of EU law, it is right to emphasise the enforcement of the product. The value of non-domination supports an argument for enforcing EU law under the guidance of the ECJ.

Courts balance the short-term interest of election cycles with the long-term interest of the political community, especially as expressed in the constitution or its equivalent.[41] In the EU, the ECJ makes binding legal pronouncements that channel the legal commitments of a political community encompassing approximately 450 million citizens through the constraints of legal reasoning of an independent

[40] Miriam Ronzoni, 'The European Union as a Demoicracy: Really a Third Way?' (2017) 16 *European Journal of Political Theory* 210, 226.

[41] Pierre Rosanvallon, *Democratic Legitimacy: Impartiality, Reflexivity, Proximity* (Princeton, Princeton University Press, 2011) 163.

Court. Its doctrines of direct effect and primacy make the commitment of the peoples and their representatives to each other more credible.[42] Enforcement ensures that the moral achievement which EU law represents is put into practice in the EU territory and thus secures demoicratic authority. Primacy and direct effect facilitate the even and effective enforcement of EU law and by doing that, they can serve as crucial drivers of non-domination among the peoples. Whereas primacy is more relevant for the equality of peoples under EU law, think of direct effect as handing each EU citizen a tool to challenge transnational domination, ie the imposition of unjustified burdens by host states.[43]

The importance of enforcement is directly linked to the problem of non-compliance. It seems self-evident that flouting legal obligations threatens the authority of any given legal system. There are good reasons, however, not to accept this without qualification, as the following subsection will now illustrate.

B. (Systemic) Non-Compliance and the Constitutional Courts' Use of Review Mechanisms

Not every violation of legal duties immediately shakes up the entire legal order and becomes a risk for its authority.[44] Most of them, like jaywalking, are simply too irrelevant to have any impact on the stability of the system. On the domestic level, only systemic threats may undercut the de facto authority of law. Similar arguments are made on the international level. Due to the difficult enforcement of international law, the notion of compliance of course is broader. Many portray the attempts of delinquent states to justify violations of international law as well as the political consequences of such violations as evidence rather than subversion of international law's compliance pull.[45] But what is the situation in relation to EU law?

The BVerfG's *Weiss* judgment of May 2020 provides an illuminating case-study of how national review mechanisms can become sources of domination. The BVerfG held the ECB's bond-buying Public Sector Purchase Programme (PSPP)

[42] Craig (n 23) 328.

[43] Similarly James Bohman, 'Nondomination and Transnational Democracy' in Cécile Laborde and John Maynor (eds), *Republicanism and Political Theory* (Hoboken, Wiley, 2008) 209.

[44] See only MBE Smith, 'Is There a Prima Facie Obligation to Obey the Law?' (1973) 82 *Yale Law Journal* 950, 956 et seq. Liam Murphy, 'The Normative Force of Law: Individuals and States' in Leslie Green, John Gardner and Brian Leiter (eds), *Oxford Studies in Philosophy of Law* (Oxford, OUP, 2018) vol 3, 107 et seq.

[45] For an example of the former, see Erika Leonaite and Dainius Zalimas, 'The Annexation of Crimea and Attempts to Justify It in the Context of International Law' (2016) 14 *Lithuanian Annual Strategic Review* 11. For an example of the latter, remember only the reactions when the British Secretary of State for Northern Ireland told the British Parliament on 8 September 2020 that the Internal Market Bill would 'break the law in a very specific and limited way'.

as well as the ECJ decision affirming it to be ultra vires for lack of attention to the disproportionate effects of the PSPP on the national competence for economic policy.[46] The German Court thereby imposes its own idiosyncratic understanding of proportionality on EU law and assesses the ECB's actions in the name of the German people.[47] The BVerfG, so to speak, takes the law into its own hands. This judgment has various effects on the present discussion on the authority of EU law in practice.

The judgment constitutes a threat to the moral authority of EU law. The reason is not that the ultra vires review exists. Instead, the problem is that the BVerfG seeks to dominate the other EU peoples in the name of the German people. It imposes a unilateral decision by one people on all the others and thereby wants to make the ECB more German. This is especially harmful since – unlike in other ultra vires rulings in the past[48] – the ruling directly affects the running and governance of an EU institution rather than, for example, the effects of a specific EU law in a Member State. By requiring the ECB to safeguard the interests of the German saver, and by asking the ECJ to do proportionality the German way, the BVerfG tells the EU what to do and thereby ultimately threatens the demo-icratic equality of the EU peoples. Hence, the judgment directly harms the values identified as underpinning EU law's moral force and creates a particular risk of domination.

Moreover, the *Weiss* judgment threatens the de facto authority of EU law, its acceptance in practice by representatives and institutions of the other EU peoples. Some Eastern European governments, especially those with a growing track record of dodging their EU law obligations, were overjoyed and took the judgment to imply that they could legitimately ignore ECJ decisions they dislike.[49] Such dynamics gain moral significance for the EU's authority. EU law is mostly enforced de-centrally through national institutions. The almost complete lack of its own enforcement institutions means that EU law fully depends on the capacity and willingness of national institutions to apply EU law. This enforcement architecture highlights the fragility of the legal order since the combination of supranational and transnational cooperation links enforcement in one Member State to all the others. As Lenaerts puts it in relation to judicial independence and attacks on the national judiciary by Member States, these attacks cannot 'be brushed aside

[46] BVerfG, Judgment of 05 May 2020–2 BvR 859/15 (*Weiss*), paras 123 et seq, 167 et seq.

[47] See only Franz Mayer, 'To Boldly Go Where No Court Has Gone Before. The German Federal Constitutional Court's Ultra Vires Decision of May 5, 2020' (2020) 21 *German Law Journal* 1116, 1123 et seq. See also BVerfG, Judgment of 21 June 2016–2 BvR 2728/13 (*Gauweiler*), dissenting opinions of Judges Lübbe-Wolff and Gerhardt, para 18.

[48] Danish Constitutional Court, 15/20146.12.2016, *Dansk Industri (DI)* acting for Ajos. Czech Constitutional Court, Pl. US 5/12 31.1.2012, *Landtova*.

[49] Zosia Wanat and Lili Bayer, 'EU Top Court's Authority Challenged by Poland and Hungary' (*Politico*, 13 May 2020), www.politico.eu/article/ecj-authority-challenged-by-poland-and-hungary/.

as being "no one else's business". On the contrary, due to the essential nature of judicial independence in the EU legal order, they are "everyone's business".[50] This observation can be generalised. It applies to all of EU law enforcement. As explained earlier, the EU is only normatively viable if the individual *demoi* can trust each other with such fundamental decisions like handing over their nationals for criminal prosecution as part of the EAW mechanism. In short, national enforcement itself makes it the case that EU law violations by national law-administering institutions gain systemic relevance.[51]

Apart from the innumerable constitutional, legal, political and economic questions it raises, the *Weiss* judgment illustrates an important institutional point I made in the preceding chapter. It shows that a national parliament is the wrong forum for holding a supranational central bank accountable. In a cheeky twist of events, the German MEP Sven Simon tried to resolve the impasse created by the judgment. He asked the ECB (which is accountable to the EP (Art 284 TFEU)) for clarification and intended to fulfil the BVerfG's order on behalf of the German Parliament.[52] In fact, national parliamentarians seem to accept the division of labour between two directly elected parliaments: one responsible for an independent *demos*, one for the interdependent *demoi*.

None of this is to argue that national courts and authorities should not critically engage with the practice of EU institutions and insist on their own constitutional fundamentals. On a conceptual level, here is a viable role for the review mechanisms of national constitutional courts. When applied properly, they are a vital instrument to protect the collective autonomy of the people the EU's authority claim interferes with.[53] Once those review mechanisms are put into practice, there is no equality of outcome (since that particular piece of EU law is then unenforceable in that Member State). But the EU's authority framework is still respected because its supporting values are not violated. In other words, because the application of EU law in, let's say, *ultra vires* cases would be an exercise of domination and an illegitimate interference with the autonomy of the people, the use of the review mechanism is justified.

But it is imperative to administer these reservations without jeopardising the legitimate authority of EU law and its underlying values. National constitutional

[50] Koen Lenaerts, 'The Rule of Law and the Constitutional Identity of the European Union' (Sofia, 5 March 2023), https://evropeiskipravenpregled.eu/the-rule-of-law-and-the-constitutional-identity-of-the-european-union/.

[51] Similarly Peter-Christian Müller-Graff, 'Die Wirtschafts- Und Währungsunion Als Herausforderung Der Autorität Des Unionsrechts' in Heusel and Rageade (n 6) 209.

[52] To which ECB President Lagarde responded. Christine Lagarde, 'To MEP Sven Simon' (Frankfurt am Main, 29 June 2020), www.ecb.europa.eu/pub/pdf/other/ecb.mepletter200629_Simon~ece6ead766.en.pdf.

[53] An alarming example, which doesn't even try to accord any prima facie authority to the EU legal order, is the decision of the Polish Constitutional Tribunal, K 3/21,*Warsaw*, 07.10.2021. For insightful commentary, see Editorial Comments, 'Clear and Present Danger: Poland, the Rule of Law & Primacy' (2021) 58 *CMLR* 1635.

courts do not have to give up (all of) their review mechanisms, but the present argument urges them to reconsider the normative basis and practical application of these reviews in light of EU law's demoicratic authority. The bottom line is this: a robust understanding of demoicratic authority suggests that external safeguards based on national constitutions are only legitimate to the extent that they do not threaten the values underpinning EU law's authority.

C. Uneven Application of EU Law in Brussels and at Home

Whenever EU institutions enforce EU law unequally, they endanger the authority of EU law. For example, the Commission should not be more lenient with one Member State than with another (remember former Commission President Juncker telling the public that France may dodge the budget rules 'because it is France').[54] EU institutions cannot be seen to favour individual peoples and states.[55] Demoicratic authority means, at its core, that the EU peoples have a guarantee through the EU law-making and law-enforcement architecture that they engage and deliberate with each other as equals. Unjustified uneven application of EU law disregards their equality and their right to non-domination. Uneven application moreover insinuates that big and powerful Member States can get away with law-breaking, thereby cementing the fact that they are already more likely to break EU law.[56] Note that this does not contradict the above argument for embracing diversity and political opposition within EU law-making. For EU law that embraces diversity and gives leeway to Member States (such as directives and other secondary law with margins of appreciation) can and should still be enforced equally. In other words, sometimes varying application of EU law ought to derive from an inbuilt recognition of diversity, not from an uneven application.

An incipient form of systemic and therefore problematic non-compliance has emerged in Poland, where the Government continues to ignore ECJ judgments. Since those judgments often result from infringement proceedings according to Arts 258 and 259 TFEU, there is no national court to hold the Government accountable. For example, refusing to follow an ECJ interim relief order to cease lignite extraction shows that reality always surpasses textbooks when it comes to catchy illustrations.[57] The coal mine is situated on Polish territory, but right at the border to the Czech Republic and Germany. The extraction activity seems to violate

[54] See also Claus Dieter Classen, 'Die Gleichheit Der Mitgliedstaaten Und Ihre Ausformungen Im Unionsrecht' [2020] *Europarecht* 255, 267 et seq.

[55] Similarly Baquero Cruz (n 6) 200; Müller-Graff (n 51) 210.

[56] Tanja Börzel and others, 'Obstinate and Inefficient: Why Member States Do Not Comply With European Law' (2010) 43 *Comparative Political Studies* 1363.

[57] Case C-121/21 *Czech Republic v Poland* EU:C:2021:420, Order of the Vice President. For more detail, see Maximilian Steinbeiß, 'Borders' (*Verfassungsblog*, 28 May 2021), https://verfassungsblog.de/borders/.

EU environmental law and has an especially devastating effect on groundwater in the Czech Republic. In other words, Poland arbitrarily interferes, ie dominates the neighbouring peoples. It harms them without giving them a say in regulating such activities. The refusal of the Polish Government to follow the ECJ order, in short, threatens the moral authority of EU law because it undermines EU law's ability to secure non-domination.

D. Interim Conclusion

Looking at these debates in EU constitutional law from the perspective of safeguarding equality and mitigating domination results in a mixed picture again. While the ECJ's use of primacy and direct effect has the capacity to support demoicratic authority, systemic non-compliance by national governments, the uneven application of EU law by EU institutions, and the potential over-use of review mechanisms by national constitutional courts create significant threats to the authority of EU law. A crucial aspect of this perspective is that it shows how a focus on the behaviour of or towards individual Member States alone is insufficient. Instead, the repercussions of these practices on the other peoples of Europe create a risk for the authority of EU law.

Apart from this scrutiny of the pros and cons of EU law's compliance with the values underpinning its demoicratic authority, the present framework provides a fresh perspective on the pervasive discussion about how the authority of EU law relates to the authority of national law (who would have thought that possible).

IV. A Guide to Navigate Conflicts

Potential conflicts about the interpretation and scope of application of EU law stem from the different perspectives of the ECJ on the one hand, and national constitutional courts on the other, in relation to the ultimate decision-making authority in Europe. Whereas the ECJ claims for itself the authority to decide about the status, validity and applicability of EU law throughout the EU territory ('autonomy of EU law'), national constitutional courts reserve the right to check the compatibility of EU law against fundamental principles of their constitutions.[58]

Many scholars have attempted to conceptualise these opposing claims or proposed a pragmatic solution for when they clash in practice under the headings of monism, dualism or pluralism. The focus of their work is on the

[58] For an insightful summary see Monica Claes, 'The Primacy of EU Law in European and National Law' in Damian Chalmers and Anthony Arnull (eds), *The Oxford Handbook of European Union Law* (Oxford, OUP, 2015).

sovereignty-related question of who decides when push comes to shove (ultimate decision-making, *Kompetenz-Kompetenz*). My angle is different. It compares the moral reasons for the authority of each legal order and seeks to extract a normative guide to solve potential conflicts in each given case. In other words, I intend to propose a standard for evaluating the relative weight of the authority claims of EU law and national law by recourse to the very reasons that make both authoritative.[59]

Member States and the EU, so I argue, serve the EU peoples as complementary fora for different tasks, each with their own genuine moral authority. Such an understanding goes against two intellectually rather lazy trends in opposite camps. While some designate the nation state as a reactionary ethnic escape room and the EU as a promised land of the future, others portray the EU as an unaccountable technocracy and the nation state as a sole repository for normatively acceptable political rule. The key to a more constructive approach for evaluating the authoritative force of laws from both orders in relation to each other, lies in a focus on the collective agents that underpin them.

A good reason for the authority of democratically enacted national law in the Member States stems from the moral achievement of institutionally resolving reasonable disputes among the members of the polity while treating each citizen equally (see chapter four). EU law is consequently illegitimate if it impinges on what is properly left to the national democratic process. From the perspective of the EU's legitimate authority, Weatherill is right: 'An EU which is imposed on the peoples of Europe contains the seeds of its own destruction'.[60] Rephrased to fit the framework of this book, a demoicracy wrongs its *demoi* if it curtails their independent space for self-determination. The inbuilt idea of demoicracy is respect for the continued existence and viability of its members as independent collectives. Only when EU law does not impose illegitimate constraints on national democracies by interfering in areas which are neither part of regulating the interdependence of the peoples, nor necessarily and rightly affected by EU integration, does it rule legitimately. Sure, this leaves great interpretive leeway for individual cases in practice. This theoretical framework nonetheless helps to rationalise EU case law that stays away from how to regulate abortion[61] or non-cross-border insurance contracts for breast implants.[62] Thus understood, demoicratic authority provides a conceptual framework to explain why centralisation as such, which neglects diversity and focuses entirely on uniformity, ultimately harms the authority of EU law.[63]

[59] For a call to develop such perspectives, see Roger Cotterrell, 'Transnational Legal Authority: A Socio-Legal Perspective' in Maksymilian Del Mar and Roger Cotterrell (eds), *Authority in Transnational Legal Theory: Theorising Across Disciplines* (Cheltenham, Elgar, 2016) 256.

[60] Weatherill (n 35) 418.

[61] Case C-159/90 *Grogan* EU:C:1991:378.

[62] Case C-581/18 *TÜV Rheinland* EU:C:2020:453.

[63] Similarly Stephen Tierney, '"We the Peoples": Constituent Power and Constitutionalism in Plurinational States' in Martin Loughlin and Neil Walker (eds), *The Paradox of Constitutionalism* (Oxford, OUP, 2007) 244 et seq.

But that is not a one-way street. The legitimacy of national democratic procedures and the ensuing law, conversely, is jeopardised whenever national law impinges on areas which ought to be dealt with beyond the realm of the nation state. Member State democratic legitimacy has jurisdictional limits. A crucial part of my argument is that the EU can operate complementary to national democratic procedures if it steps in where national democratic authority fails. The EU is well apt to address issues in relation to which unilateral state measures would cause harm to outsiders (by not including them in decision-making processes that result in laws that affect them). In these cases, only the EU institutions can ensure and facilitate meaningful deliberation, non-domination and ultimately the equality of the EU peoples.

Which guidance follows from that for conflicts between EU and national law? So far, Isiksel rightly states that most would frame the comparison of their moral bases as one 'between alternate sources of constitutional authority, namely democratic rule on the one hand, and effective government on the other'.[64] I think that should change.

Think of the scenario underlying *Melloni*. As is well known, the ECJ interpreted Art 53 Charter of Fundamental Rights of the European Union to preclude the application of national fundamental rights to harmonised secondary law. The Court's unfortunate language of 'primacy, unity, and effectiveness',[65] may usefully be re-interpreted as a demoicratic argument. The Court simply holds that the idiosyncratic Spanish understanding of the right to fair trial must not prevail over the exhaustive conditions that result from the EU legislative procedure in the EAW Framework Decision. It is troubling that the Court did not explicitly assess the compliance of the Framework Decision with EU fundamental rights. Assuming such compliance, however, the Court can be understood to say that leaving the Framework Decision to the control of each national constitution gives rise to unilateral dominance of the others by imposing one's own fundamental standard on other peoples. This illustrates how the underlying values of demoicratic authority (deliberation, equality, non-domination) sometimes stand in tension with each other, since the EAW Framework Decision is a Council Decision without EP involvement and thus without the full deliberation that underpins demoicratic authority. As discussed in chapter five and exemplified above, the authority of EU law is gradual, and each piece of EU law reflects a different level of compliance with its underlying values and thus a different level of morally binding force. In the case of *Melloni*, the Court was right to hold that a national fundamental rights scrutiny would jeopardise the integrity of that particular piece of legislation that secures equality and non-domination.

But the Court doesn't always get it right. Recall that we are trying to get normative guidance for potential conflicts from the variants of collective

[64] Isiksel (n 34) 50 et seq.
[65] *Melloni* (n 10) para 60.

self-determination underlying both political communities. In *Rimšēvičs*, the ECJ used the institutional entanglement of the ECB and national central banks not to merely *disapply* a national administrative decision to oust the Latvian central bank governor. No, the ECJ felt it could legitimately *annul* the national decision itself. According to the Court, the 'less marked distinction' between the legal orders in that area and the 'hybrid status of national central bank governors within the European System of Central Banks' allows EU law to interfere in such a drastic way.[66] As I explain elsewhere, the Court thereby illegitimately intruded into the proper sphere of national self-determination. For self-determination entails that a people creates laws through its national law-making institutions and national courts alone have the authority to invalidate those laws.[67] That much was respected by the EU's authority claim, which hitherto usually restricted itself to *disapply* conflicting national law and thereby respected the different chains of validity.[68] From the perspective of demoicratic authority, the failure of the judgment that annuls a national decision consists of encroaching upon the natural prerogative of a people to invalidate its laws according to its own constitutional standards as a crucial expression of how it wants to govern itself. A law a people has given itself in a democratic process (and any decision based on such a law) can only be invalidated by the procedure that this people's constitution provides for.

In both cases (*Melloni* and *Rimšēvičs*), the issue is not only about enforcement and domination. The crucial question becomes whether the democratic solution on the national level or the demoicratic agreement on the EU level should prevail. The comparison of the underlying agents reveals the moral weight of each decision and who should make the decision according to the all-affected principle. The conceptual lens of democratic and demoicratic authority enables at least approximative normative guidance on how to resolve potential conflicts. It simply means that deference to national democratic self-government on the part of the EU is not a one-way street, despite the absence of Democratic (capital D) institutional procedures at the EU level.[69] By contrast, the consent framework that underpins the national constitutional courts' reasoning (see chapter three) unfortunately does not allow these courts to consider the integrity of the EU's institutional framework as a self-standing source of legitimate law among peoples.

The decisive question in case of a conflict becomes whether the binding norms *one people* has given itself should prevail or the European norms generated through the collaboration of the *joint peoples* of Europe.

[66] Case C-202/18 *Rimšēvičs v Latvia* EU:C:2019:139, paras 69, 70.

[67] Josef Weinzierl, 'Der EuGH erklärt erstmalig nationales Recht für ungültig – Anmerkung zum Urteil des EuGH v. 26.2.2019, Rs. C-202/18 (Rimšēvičs)' (2019) 54 *Europarecht* 434.

[68] For recent developments to the contrary, see Michael Dougan, 'The Primacy of Union Law over Incompatible National Measures: Beyond Disapplication and Towards a Remedy of Nullity?' (2022) 59 *CMLR* 1301.

[69] But see Vlad Perju, 'On the (De-)Fragmentation of Statehood in Europe: Reflections on Ernst-Wolfgang Böckenförde's Work on European Integration' (2018) 19 *German Law Journal* 403, 425 et seq.

The discussion of this fruitful framework for conceptualising jurisdictional conflicts brings us back to the central theme of the book, namely under which conditions it is legitimate for EU law to impose duties on the peoples of its Member States. EU law cloaked with legitimate authority enables the European peoples to realise democratic ideals beyond the state by giving them a say in decisions that subsequently affect them. This is not only important because it makes the states more democratic.[70] Indeed, 'acting through the EU the sum of State powers is expanded so it becomes greater than its parts'.[71] The EU then provides a complementary demo(i)cratic forum with intrinsic value for the peoples of Europe. It is complementary to the national processes since both realise democratic ideals (authoring the laws that claim authority over you) in their respective jurisdictions. This complementary nature has a negative and a positive dimension.

The negative dimension implies outlawing, or at least managing negative externalities. Such externalities arise when unilateral state decisions have negative effects and impose costs on neighbouring states and their peoples (classic example: emissions).[72] The positive dimension stems from including all those affected in supranational decision-making procedures. In both dimensions, the EU thus remedies the widespread democratic deficit of imposing decisions on outsiders of the nation state without giving them a say. The problem is that '(d)emocracies barely have instruments to assure that "outside" identities and interests are considered in their decision-making processes'.[73] The EU is theoretically capable of remedying this deficit by providing an institutional set up to make and enforce laws that bind its peoples. This is how demoicracy answers the challenge of safeguarding self-determination as the normative nucleus of democracy in an interdependent Europe and through that provides normative reasons for the authoritative force of EU law.

V. Conclusion

This brief analysis of various practical questions of EU constitutional law illustrates the attractiveness of demoicratic authority as a conceptual lens through which to evaluate EU law's authority. It shows that the values of deliberation, non-domination and equality provide sharp analytical tools to assess the normative force of EU law, especially regarding its place in a multilevel system

[70] See only Athanasios Psygkas, *From the Democratic Deficit to a Democratic Surplus: Constructing Administrative Democracy in Europe* (Oxford, OUP, 2017).

[71] Weatherill (n 35) 396.

[72] Daniel Innerarity, *Democracy in Europe: A Political Philosophy of the EU* (London, Palgrave Macmillan, 2018) 239.

[73] ibid 242.

of government in Europe. This chapter also encourages the reader to use the tools employed in this chapter to make up their own mind about the state of the authority of EU law.

It is however, but one of my aims to make a convincing case for demoicratic authority as a persuasive evaluative tool. My most important aim with this book is to initiate a debate about the grounds for the moral authority of EU law in the first place. For too long, it has been overshadowed by the court-centred focus on sovereignty-related ultimate authority. The narrow focus on rare conflict cases has all too often obscured the broader moral issues the EU's authority claim raises for the autonomy and self-determination of the EU peoples. If I succeed in encouraging that debate about the moral ground of the EU's authority, I will have achieved more than I could have hoped for.

BIBLIOGRAPHY

Adams NP, 'Legitimacy and Institutional Purpose' (2020) 23 *Critical Review of International Social and Political Philosophy* 292

Adler-Nissen R, 'Opting Out of an Ever Closer Union: The Integration Doxa and the Management of Sovereignty' (2011) 34 *West European Politics* 1092

Alter K, *Establishing the Supremacy of European Law: The Making of an International Rule of Law in Europe* (Oxford, OUP, 2003)

Applbaum AI, 'Legitimacy without the Duty to Obey' (2010) 38 *Philosophy & Public Affairs* 215

Arendt H, 'What Is Authority?' in Hannah Arendt (ed), *Between Past and Future* (New York, The Viking Press, 1961)

Arnull A, 'Judicial Review in the European Union' in Anthony Arnull and Damian Chalmers (eds), *The Oxford Handbook of European Union Law* (Oxford, OUP, 2015)

Avbelj M, 'Theorizing Sovereignty and European Integration: Sovereignty and European Integration' (2014) 27 *Ratio Juris* 344

Avbelj M, 'A Sovereign Europe as a Future of Sovereignty' (2020) 2020 5 *European Papers* 299

Azoulai L, 'The Madness of Europe, Being Attached to It' (2020) 21 *German Law Journal* 100

——, 'The (Mis)Construction of the European Individual Two Essays on Union Citizenship Law' *Law* 2014/14

Bailleux A, 'The Two Faces of European Sovereignty' (2020) 2020 5 *European Papers* 303

Baquero Cruz J, *What's Left of the Law of Integration?: Decay and Resistance in European Union Law* (Oxford, OUP, 2018)

Barber N, *The Constitutional State* (Oxford, OUP, 2010)

——, *The Principles of Constitutionalism* (Oxford, OUP, 2018)

Barbou Des Places S, 'Taking the Language of "European Sovereignty" Seriously' (2020) 2020 5 *European Papers* 287

Barnett M and Finnemore M, *Rules for the World: International Organizations in Global Politics* (New York, Cornell University Press, 2004)

Beck G, 'The EU Constitution, Sovereignty and the Problem of Primacy' in Nicholas Barber, Maria Cahill and Richard Ekins (eds), *The Rise and Fall of the European Constitution* (Oxford, Hart Publishing, 2019)

Beetham D, *The Legitimation of Power*, 2nd edn (London, Palgrave Macmillan, 2013)

Bellamy R, *A Republican Europe of States: Cosmopolitanism, Intergovernmentalism and Democracy in the EU* (Cambridge, CUP, 2019)

Benn S, 'The Uses of "Sovereignty"' (1955) 3 *Political Studies* 109

Besson S, 'Deliberative Demoi-Cracy in the European Union: Towards the Deterritorialization of Democracy' in Samantha Besson, José Luis Martí and Verena Seiler (eds), *Deliberative Democracy and its Discontents* (Farnham, Ashgate, 2006)

——, 'The Authority of International Law: Lifting the State Veil' (2009) 31 *Sydney Law Review* 343

——, 'Sovereignty, International Law and Democracy' (2011) 22 *European Journal of International Law* 373

——, 'European Human Rights Pluralism' in Miguel Poiares Maduro, Kaarlo Tuori and Suvi Sankari (eds), *Transnational Law: Rethinking European Law and Legal Thinking* (Cambridge, CUP, 2014)

——, 'State Consent and Disagreement in International Law-Making. Dissolving the Paradox' (2016) 29 *Leiden Journal of International Law* 289

Biegoń D, 'Specifying the Arena of Possibilities: Post-structuralist Narrative Analysis and the European Commission's Legitimation Strategies' (2013) 51 *Journal of Common Market Studies* 194

Böckenförde E-W, 'Critique of the Value-Based Grounding of Law [1990]' in Mirjam Künkler and Tine Stein (eds), *Constitutional and Political Theory: Selected Writings* (Oxford, OUP, 2017)
Bodansky D, 'The Legitimacy of International Governance: A Coming Challenge for International Environmental Law?' (1999) 93 *American Journal of International Law* 596
Bogdandy A von, 'Founding Principles' in Armin von Bogdandy and Jürgen Bast (eds), *Principles of European Constitutional Law*, 2nd edn (Oxford, Hart/Beck, 2010)
Bogdandy A von, Dann P and Goldmann M, 'Developing the Publicness of Public International Law: Towards a Legal Framework for Global Governance Activities' (2008) 9 *German Law Journal* 1375
Bogdandy A von, Goldmann M and Venzke I, 'From Public International to International Public Law: Translating World Public Opinion into International Public Authority' (2017) 28 *European Journal of International Law* 115
Bogdandy A von, and Spieker LD, 'Countering the Judicial Silencing of Critics: Article 2 TEU Values, Reverse Solange, and the Responsibilities of National Judges' (2019) 15 *European Constitutional Law Review* 391
Bohman J, 'Nondomination and Transnational Democracy' in Cécile Laborde and John Maynor (eds), *Republicanism and Political Theory* (Hoboken, Wiley, 2008)
Bolleyer N and Reh C, 'EU Legitimacy Revisited: The Normative Foundations of a Multilevel Polity' (2012) 19 *Journal of European Public Policy* 472
Börzel T and others, 'Obstinate and Inefficient: Why Member States Do Not Comply With European Law' (2010) 43 *Comparative Political Studies* 1363
Börzel T and Sedelmeier U, 'Larger and More Law Abiding? The Impact of Enlargement on Compliance in the European Union' (2017) 24 *Journal of European Public Policy* 197
Bradford A, *The Brussels Effect: How the European Union Rules the World* (Oxford, OUP, 2020)
Brunnée J and Toope SJ, *Legitimacy and Legality in International Law: An Interactional Account* (Cambridge, CUP, 2010)
Buchanan A, 'The Legitimacy of International Law' in Samantha Besson and John Tasioulas (eds), *The Philosophy of International Law* (Oxford, OUP, 2010)
——, 'Institutional Legitimacy' in David Sobel, Peter Vallentyne and Steven Wall (eds), *Oxford Studies in Political Philosophy* (Oxford, OUP, 2018) vol 4
Buchanan A and Keohane RO, 'The Legitimacy of Global Governance Institutions' (2006) 20 *Ethics & International Affairs* 405
Cali B, *The Authority of International Law: Obedience, Respect, and Rebuttal* (Oxford, OUP, 2015)
Chalmers D, Davies G and Monti G, *European Union Law*, 4th edn (Cambridge, CUP, 2019)
Cheneval F, *The Government of the Peoples: On the Idea and Principles of Multilateral Democracy* (London, Palgrave Macmillan, 2011)
——, 'Demoicratic Self-Government in the European Union's Polycentric System: Theoretical Remarks' in Josephine van Zeben and Ana Bobić (eds), *Polycentricity in the European Union* (Cambridge, CUP, 2019)
Cheneval F and Nicolaidis K, 'The Social Construction of Demoicracy in the European Union' (2017) 16 *European Journal of Political Theory* 235
Cheneval F and Schimmelfennig F, 'The Case for Demoicracy in the European Union' (2013) 51 *Journal of Common Market Studies* 334
Christiano T, 'The Authority of Democracy' (2004) 12 *Journal of Political Philosophy* 266
——, 'A Democratic Theory of Territory and Some Puzzles about Global Democracy' (2006) 37 *Journal of Social Philosophy* 81
——, *The Constitution of Equality: Democratic Authority and Its Limits* (Oxford, OUP, 2008)
——, 'Democratic Legitimacy and International Institutions' in Samantha Besson and John Tasioulas (eds), *The Philosophy of International Law* (Oxford, OUP, 2010)
——, 'The Legitimacy of International Institutions' in Andrei Marmor (ed), *The Routledge Companion to Philosophy of Law* (Abingdon, Routledge, 2012)
Christie G, 'On the Moral Obligation to Obey the Law Essay' (1990) 6 *Duke Law Journal* 1311
Claes M, 'The Primacy of EU Law in European and National Law' in Damian Chalmers and Anthony Arnull (eds), *The Oxford Handbook of European Union Law* (Oxford, OUP, 2015)

Clarke DS, 'Exclusionary Reasons' (1977) 86 *Mind* 252
Classen CD, 'Die Gleichheit Der Mitgliedstaaten Und Ihre Ausformungen Im Unionsrecht' [2020] *Europarecht* 255
Collins R, 'Consent, Obligation and the Legitimate Authority of International Law' in Patrick Capps and Henrik Palmer Olsen (eds), *Legal Authority Beyond the State* (Cambridge, CUP, 2018)
Copp D, 'The Idea of a Legitimate State' (1999) 28 *Philosophy & Public Affairs* 3
Cotterrell R, 'Transnational Legal Authority: A Socio-Legal Perspective' in Maksymilian Del Mar and Roger Cotterrell (eds), *Authority in Transnational Legal Theory: Theorising Across Disciplines* (Cheltenham, Elgar, 2016)
Craig P, 'Democracy and Rule-making Within the EC: An Empirical and Normative Assessment' (1997) 3 *European Law Journal* 105
——, 'Integration, Democracy, and Legitimacy' in Paul Craig and G De Búrca (eds), *The Evolution of EU Law*, 2nd edn (Oxford, OUP, 2011)
——, 'The EU, Democracy and Institutional Structure: Past, Present and Future' in Wolfgang Heusel and Jean-Philippe Rageade (eds), *The Authority of EU Law: Do We Still Believe In It?* (New York, Springer, 2019)
——, 'EU Membership: Formal and Substantive Dimensions' (2020) 22 *Cambridge Yearbook of European Legal Studies* 1
Craig P and De Búrca G, *EU Law: Text, Cases, and Materials*, 7th edn (Oxford, OUP, 2020)
Curtin D, *Postnational Democracy: The European Union in Search of a Political Philosophy* (Alphen aan den Rijn, Kluwer Law International, 1997)
Cygan A, 'From Deparliamentarisation to a Parliamentary Renaissance? National Parliaments in the EU Polity' in Sacha Garben, Inge Govaere and Paul Nemitz (eds), *Critical Reflections on Constitutional Democracy in the European Union* (Oxford, Hart Publishing, 2019)
Dagger R, 'Authority, Legitimacy, and the Obligation to Obey the Law' (2018) 24 *Legal Theory* 77
——, *Playing Fair: Political Obligation and the Problems of Punishment* (Oxford, OUP, 2018)
Dahl R, *After the Revolution?: Authority in a Good Society* (New Haven, Yale University Press 1990)
Darwall S, *The Second-Person Standpoint: Morality, Respect, and Accountability* (Cambridge (MA), Harvard University Press 2006)
——, 'Authority, Accountability, and Preemption' (2011) 2 *Jurisprudence* 103
——, *Morality, Authority, and Law: Essays in Second-Personal Ethics I* (Oxford, OUP, 2013)
Davidson A, 'Through Thick and Thin: "European Identification" for a Justified and Legitimate European Union' (2008) 4 *Journal of Contemporary European Research* 32
De Búrca G, 'The Quest for Legitimacy in the European Union' (1996) 59 *MLR* 349
De Witte B, 'Direct Effect, Primacy, And the Nature of the Legal Order' in Paul Craig and Gráinne De Búrca (eds), *The Evolution of EU Law*, 2nd edn (Oxford, OUP, 2011)
De Witte F, 'Interdependence and Contestation in European Integration' (2018) 3 *European Papers* 475
——, 'Here Be Dragons: Legal Geography and EU Law' (2022) I *European Law Open* 113
Dialer D and Richter M (eds), *Lobbying in the European Union: Strategies, Dynamics and Trends* (New York, Springer, 2019)
Dougan M, 'The Primacy of Union Law over Incompatible National Measures: Beyond Disapplication and towards a Remedy of Nullity?' (2022) 59 *CMLR* 1301
Dunoff JL and Trachtman JP, 'A Functional Approach to International Constitutionalization' in Jeffrey L Dunoff and Joel P Trachtman (eds), *Ruling the World?: Constitutionalism, International Law, and Global Governance* (Cambridge, CUP, 2009)
Dworkin R, *Justice for Hedgehogs* (Cambridge (MA), Harvard University Press, 2011)
Eberlein B and Grande E, 'Reconstituting Political Authority in Europe: Transnational Regulatory Networks and the Informalization of Governance in the European Union' in Edgar Grande and Louis Pauly (eds), *Complex Sovereignty: Reconstituting Political Authority in the Twenty-First Century* (Toronto, University of Toronto Press, 2017)
Eckes C, 'EU Autonomy: Jurisdictional Sovereignty by a Different Name?' (2020) 2020 5 *European Papers* 319

Eckes C and Wessel R, 'The European Union from an International Perspective Sovereignty, Statehood, and Special Treatment' in Takis Tridimas and Robert Schütze (eds), *The Oxford Principles of European Union Law – Volume 1: The European Union Legal Order* (Oxford, OUP, 2018)
Editorial Comments, 'Clear and Present Danger: Poland, the Rule of Law & Primacy' (2021) 58 *CMLR* 1635
Eleftheriadis P, 'The Idea of a European Constitution' (2007) 27 *OJLS* 1
——, *Legal Rights* (Oxford, OUP, 2008)
——, 'Federalism and Jurisdiction' in Elke Cloots, Geert De Baere and Stefan Sottiaux (eds), *Federalism in the European Union* (Oxford, Hart Publishing, 2012)
——, 'Citizenship and Obligation' in Julie Dickson and Pavlos Eleftheriadis (eds), *Philosophical Foundations of European Union law* (Oxford, OUP, 2013)
——, *A Union of Peoples* (Oxford, OUP, 2020)
Eriksen EO, *The Normativity of the European Union* (London, Palgrave Macmillan, 2014)
Estlund D, *Democratic Authority: A Philosophical Framework* (Princeton, Princeton University Press, 2008)
Fabbrini F, 'After the OMT Case: The Supremacy of EU Law as the Guarantee of the Equality of the Member States' (2015) 16 *German Law Journal* 1003
——, 'States' Equality v States' Power: The Euro-Crisis, Inter-State Relations and the Paradox of Domination' (2015) 17 *Cambridge Yearbook of European Legal Studies* 3
Fasone C, Gallo D and Wouters J, 'Re-Connecting Authority and Democratic Legitimacy in the EU: Introductory Remarks' (2020) 5 *European Papers* 175
Feinberg J, *Rights, Justice, and the Bounds of Liberty: Essays in Social Philosophy* (Princeton, Princeton University Press, 2014)
Finck M and de Witte F, 'The Challenge of Challenges' (2020) 21 *German Law Journal* 1
Flathman RE, *The Practice of Political Authority: Authority and the Authoritative* (Chicago, University of Chicago Press, 1980)
Follesdal A, 'The Legitimate Authority of International Courts and Its Limits' in Patrick Capps and Henrik Palmer Olsen (eds), *Legal Authority beyond the State* (Cambridge, CUP, 2018)
Franck T, *Fairness in International Law and Institutions* (Oxford, Clarendon Press, 1995)
Friedman RB, 'On the Concept of Authority in Political Philosophy' in Richard E Flathman (ed), *Concepts in Social and Political Philosophy* (New York, Macmillan, 1973)
Ganesh A, *Rightful Relations with Distant Strangers: Kant, the EU, and the Wider World* (Oxford, Hart Publishing, 2021)
Garben S, 'The Constitutional (Im)Balance between "the Market" and "the Social" in the European Union' (2017) *European Constitutional Law Review* 23
Gardner J, 'How Law Claims, What Law Claims' in Matthias Klatt (ed), *Institutionalized Reason: The Jurisprudence of Robert Alexy* (Oxford, OUP, 2012)
Goldsmith JL and Posner EA, *The Limits of International Law* (Oxford, OUP, 2005)
Green L, *The Authority of the State* (Oxford, Clarendon Press, 1988)
——, 'Rights of Exit' (1998) 4 *Legal Theory* 165
Grimm D, 'Sovereignty in the European Union' in Johan Van der Walt and Jeffrey Ellsworth (eds), *Constitutional Sovereignty and Social Solidarity in Europe* (Baden-Baden, Nomos, 2015)
——, *Sovereignty: The Origin and Future of a Political and Legal Concept* (New York, Columbia University Press, 2015)
——, *The Constitution of European Democracy* (Oxford, OUP, 2017)
Haratsch A, 'Die Gleichheit der Mitgliedstaaten in den Institutionen und Entscheidungsverfahren der Europäischen Union – der rechtliche Rahmen' (2020) 55 *Europarecht* 471
Hart HLA, 'Are There Any Natural Rights?' (1955) 64 *The Philosophical Review* 175
Held D, *Democracy and the Global Order: From the Modern State to Cosmopolitan Governance* (Cambridge, Polity, 1995)
Hershovitz S, 'Legitimacy, Democracy, and Razian Authority' (2003) 9 *Legal Theory* 201
——, 'The Authority of Law' in Andrew Marmor (ed), *The Routledge Companion to Philosophy of Law* (Abingdon, Routledge, 2012)

Heusel W, 'Legitimität Und Finalität Des Europäischen Projekts' in Wolfgang Heusel and Jean-Philippe Rageade (eds), *The Authority of EU Law: Do We Still Believe In It?* (New York, Springer, 2019)
Heusel W and Rageade J-P (eds), *The Authority of EU Law: Do We Still Believe In It?* (New York, Springer, 2019)
Hillion C, 'EU Enlargement' in Paul Craig and Graínne De Búrca (eds), *The Evolution of EU Law*, 2nd edn (Oxford, OUP, 2011)
Hobbes T, *Elementa philosophica de cive* (Apud Ludovicum Elzevirium 1647)
——, *Leviathan* (Continuum, 2005)
Hüller T, 'Out of Time? The Democratic Limits of EU Demoicracy' (2016) 23 *Journal of European Public Policy* 1407
Hurrelmann A, 'Legitimacy and European Union Politics' in William Thompson (ed), *Oxford Research Encyclopedias: Politics* (Oxford, OUP, 2014)
Innerarity D, *Democracy in Europe: A Political Philosophy of the EU* (London, Palgrave Macmillan, 2018)
Isiksel T, 'The Dream of a Commercial Peace' in Luuk van Middelaar, Philippe van Parijs and Herman van Rompuy (eds), *After the Storm: How to Save Democracy in Europe* (Tielt, Lannoo, 2015)
——, *Europe's Functional Constitution: A Theory of Constitutionalism Beyond the State* (Oxford, OUP, 2016)
——, 'Constitutionalism as Limitation and Licence' in Tom Ginsburg, Mark D Rosen and Georg Vanberg (eds), *Constitutions in Times of Financial Crisis* (Cambridge, CUP, 2019)
——, 'Cosmopolitanism and International Economic Institutions' (2020) 82 *Journal of Politics* 211
——, 'Democracy-Eroding Multilateralism' in Michele Battini and Nadia Urbinati (eds), *The Future of Democracy* (Feltrinelli forthcoming)
Jaakkola J, 'Enhancing Political Representation Through the European Economic Constitution? Regressive Politics of Democratic Inclusion' (2019) 15 *European Constitutional Law Review* 194
Jan Wouters, 'Revisiting Art. 2 TEU: A True Union of Values?' (2020) 2020 5 *European Papers* 255
Joerges C, 'How Is a Closer Union Conceivable under Conditions of Ever More Socio-economic and Political Diversity? Constitutionalising Europe's Unitas in Pluralitate' (2018) 24 *European Law Journal* 257
Kant I, 'Toward Perpetual Peace' in Pauline Kleingeld (ed), David Colclasure (tr), *Toward Perpetual Peace and other Writings on Politics, Peace, and History* (New Haven, Yale University Press, 2006)
Kelemen RD, 'The "Democratic Deficits" of the US and the EU Compared' in Sacha Garben, Inge Govaere and Paul F Nemitz (eds), *Critical Reflections on Constitutional Democracy in the European Union* (Oxford, Hart Publishing, 2019)
Klabbers J, Peters A and Ulfstein G (eds), *The Constitutionalization of International Law* (Oxford, OUP, 2009)
Klosko G, *The Principle of Fairness and Political Obligation* (Lanham, Rowman & Littlefield Publishers, 2004)
Kochenov D, 'EU Citizenship without Duties' (2014) 20 *European Law Journal* 482
König N and Schuknecht L, 'The Role of Government and Trust in the Market Economy' in Wolfgang Heusel and Jean-Philippe Rageade (eds), *The Authority of EU Law: Do We Still Believe In It?* (New York, Springer, 2019)
Koskelo P, 'Current Threats to the Rule of Law in the EU: The Foundation on Which the Authority of EU Law Rests' in Wolfgang Heusel and Jean-Philippe Rageade (eds), *The Authority of EU Law: Do We Still Believe In It?* (NewYork, Springer, 2019)
Krisch N, 'Authority, Solid and Liquid, in the Postnational Sphere' in Maksyimilian Del Mar and Roger Cotterrell (eds), *Authority in Transnational Legal Theory* (Cheltenham, Elgar, 2016)
Kumm M, 'Democratic Constitutionalism Encounters International Law: Terms of Engagement' in Sujit Choudhry (ed), *The Migration of Constitutional Ideas* (Cambridge, CUP, 2007)
——, 'The Cosmopolitan Turn in Constitutionalism: On the Relationship between Constitutionalism in and beyond the State' in Jeffrey L Dunoff and Joel P Trachtman (eds), *Ruling the World? Constitutionalism, International Law and Global Governance* (Cambridge, CUP, 2009)

——, 'Rethinking Constitutional Authority: On the Structure and Limits of Constitutional Pluralism' in Matej Avbelj and Jan Komárek (eds), *Constitutional Pluralism in the European Union and Beyond* (Oxford, Hart Publishing, 2012)

——, 'The Cosmopolitan Turn in Constitutionalism: An Integrated Conception of Public Law' (2013) 20 *Indiana Journal of Global Legal Studies* 605

——, 'The Rule of Law, Legitimate Authority and Constitutionalism' in Christoph Bezemek, Michael Portacs and Alexander Somek (eds), *Legal Positivism, Institutionalism and Globalisation: Vienna Lectures on Legal Philosophy* (Oxford, Hart Publishing, 2018) vol 1

Lacey J, 'Conceptually Mapping the European Union: A Demoi-Cratic Analysis' (2016) 38 *Journal of European Integration* 61

Lake DA, 'Rightful Rules: Authority, Order, and the Foundations of Global Governance' (2010) 54 *International Studies Quarterly* 587

Landemore H, *Democratic Reason: Politics, Collective Intelligence, and the Rule of the Many* (Princeton, Princeton University Press, 2013)

Landemore H and Page S, 'Deliberation and Disagreement: Problem Solving, Prediction, and Positive Dissensus' (2015) 14 *Politics Philosophy & Economics* 229

Larmore C, 'Liberal and Republican Conceptions of Freedom' (2003) 6 *Critical Review of International Social and Political Philosophy* 96

Larsen S, *The Constitutional Theory of the Federation and the European Union* (Oxford, OUP, 2021)

Lefkowitz D, 'A Contractualist Defense of Democratic Authority' (2005) 18 *Ratio Juris* 346

——, 'The Duty to Obey the Law' (2006) 1 *Philosophy Compass* 571

——, 'On the Foundation of Rights to Political Self-Determination: Secession, Nonintervention, and Democratic Governance' (2008) 39 *Journal of Social Philosophy* 492

——, 'The Principle of Fairness and States' Duty to Obey International Law' (2011) 24 *Canadian Journal of Law & Jurisprudence* 327

Lenaerts K, 'Demoicracy, Constitutional Pluralism and The Court of Justice of the European Union' in Luuk van Middelaar, Philippe van Parijs and Herman van Rompuy (eds), *After the Storm: How to Save Democracy in Europe* (Tielt, Lannoo, 2015)

——, 'La Vie Après l'avis: Exploring the Principle of Mutual (yet Not Blind) Trust' (2017) 54 *CMLR* 805

——, 'New Horizons for the Rule of Law Within the EU' (2020) 21 *German Law Journal* 29

——, 'No Member State Is More Equal than Others: The Primacy of EU Law and the Principle of the Equality of the Member States before the Treaties' (*Verfassungsblog*, 8 October 2020), https://verfassungsblog.de/no-member-state-is-more-equal-than-others

——, 'The Rule of Law and the Constitutional Identity of the European Union' (*Sofia*, 5 March 2023), https://evropeiskipravenpregled.eu/the-rule-of-law-and-the-constitutional-identity-of-the-european-union/

Leonaite E and Zalimas D, 'The Annexation of Crimea and Attempts to Justify It in the Context of International Law' (2016) 14 *Lithuanian Annual Strategic Review* 11

Lindeboom J, 'Is the Primacy of EU Law Based on the Equality of the Member States? A Comment on the CJEU's Press Release Following the PSPP Judgment' (2020) 21 *German Law Journal* 1032

Lindseth P, *Power and Legitimacy: Reconciling Europe and the Nation-State* (Oxford, OUP, 2010)

Locke J, *Two Treatises of Government and A Letter Concerning Toleration* (edited by I Shapiro) (New Haven, Yale University Press, 2003)

Loughlin M, *The Idea of Public Law* (Oxford, OUP, 2004)

——, 'Constitutional Pluralism: An Oxymoron?' (2014) 3 *Global Constitutionalism* 9

——, 'The Erosion of Sovereignty' (2016) 45 *Netherlands Journal of Legal Philosophy* 57

Louis J-V, *The Community Legal Order*, 2nd edn (EC Official Publications, 1993)

MacCormick N, *Questioning Sovereignty: Law, State, and Nation in the European Commonwealth* (Oxford, OUP, 1999)

Madsen M, 'Bolstering Authority by Enhancing Communication : How Checks and Balances and Feedback Loops Can Strengthen the Authority of the European Court of Human Rights' in Joana Mendes and Ingo Venzke (eds), *Who Should do What in European and International Law?* (Oxford, Hart Publishing, 2018)

Maduro MP, 'How Constitutional Can the European Union Be? The Tension Between Intergovernamentalism and Constitutionalism in the European Union' in Joseph Weiler and Christopher Eisgruber (eds), *Altneuland: The EU Constitution in a Contextual Perspective* (Jean Monnet Working Paper 5/04)

Maganza G, 'Can the Authority of EU Law Be Taken for Granted? A Tale of Principles and Realities' in Wolfgang Heusel and Jean-Philippe Rageade (eds), *The Authority of EU Law: Do We Still Believe In It?* (New York, Springer, 2019)

Majone G, 'Europe's "Democratic Deficit": The Question of Standards' (1998) 4 *European Law Journal* 5

——, *Rethinking the Union of Europe Post-Crisis: Has Integration Gone Too Far?* (Cambridge, CUP, 2014)

Malcolm N, *Sense on Sovereignty* (Centre for Policy Studies, 1991)

Marmor A, 'An Institutional Conception of Authority' (2011) 39 *Philosophy & Public Affairs* 238

——, 'The Dilemma of Authority' (2011) 2 *Jurisprudence* 121

Mayer F, 'Van Gend En Loos: The Foundation of a Community of Law' in Miguel Poiares Maduro and Loïc Azoulai (eds), *The Past and Future of EU law* (Oxford, Hart Publishing, 2010)

——, 'Verfassung Im Nationalstaat: Von Der Gesamtordnung Zur Europäischen Teilordnung?' (2016) 75 *Veröffentlichungen der Vereinigung der Deutschen Staatsrechtslehrer* 7

——, 'To Boldly Go Where No Court Has Gone Before. The German Federal Constitutional Court's Ultra Vires Decision of May 5, 2020' (2020) 21 *German Law Journal* 1116

Menon A and Weatherill S, 'Transnational Legitimacy in a Globalising World: How the European Union Rescues Its States' (2008) 31 *West European Politics* 397

Middelaar L van, 'Europe and the Return of Politics' in Luuk van Middelaar, Philippe van Parijs and Herman van Rompuy (eds), *After the Storm: How to Save Democracy in Europe* (Tielt, Lannoo, 2015)

Minsky M, *The Emotion Machine* (New York, Simon & Schuster, 2006)

Mitsilegas V, 'Trust' (2020) 21 *German Law Journal* 69

Möllers C, 'Constitutional State of the European Union' in Robert Schütze (ed), *Globalisation and Governance: International Problems, European Solutions* (Cambridge, CUP, 2018)

Müller-Graff P-C, 'Die Wirtschafts- Und Währungsunion Als Herausforderung Der Autorität Des Unionsrechts' in Wolfgang Heusel and Jean-Philippe Rageade (eds), *The Authority of EU Law: Do We Still Believe In It?* (New York, Springer, 2019)

Murphy L, 'The Normative Force of Law: Individuals and States' in Leslie Green, John Gardner and Brian Leiter (eds), *Oxford Studies in Philosophy of Law* (Oxford, OUP, 2018) vol 3

Neuvonen PJ, *Equal Citizenship and Its Limits in EU Law: We the Burden?* (Oxford, Hart Publishing, 2016)

Neyer J, *The Justification of Europe: A Political Theory of Supranational Integration* (Oxford, OUP, 2012)

Nicol D, 'Can Justice Dethrone Democracy in the European Union? A Reply to Jürgen Neyer' (2012) 50 *Journal of Common Market Studies* 508

Nicolaïdis K, 'The Idea of European Demoicracy' in Julie Dickson and Pavlos Eleftheriadis (eds), *Philosophical Foundations of European Union Law* (Oxford, OUP, 2012)

——, 'European Demoicracy and Its Crisis' (2013) 51 *Journal of Common Market Studies* 351

Nollkaemper A, 'Rethinking the Supremacy of International Law' (2010) 65 *Zeitschrift für öffentliches Recht* 65

Nozick R, *Anarchy, State and Utopia* (Oxford, Blackwell, 1974)

Öberg J, 'The Rise of the Procedural Paradigm: Judicial Review of EU Legislation in Vertical Competence Disputes' (2017) 13 *European Constitutional Law Review* 248

Obradovic D, 'Community Law and the Doctrine of Divisible Sovereignty' (1993) 20 *Legal Issues of Economic Integration* 1

Oeter S, 'Federalism and Democracy' in Armin von Bogdandy and Jürgen Bast (eds), *Principles of European Constitutional Law*, 2nd edn (Oxford, Hart/Beck, 2009)

Papadopoulou L, '"All Good Things Come in Threes": From a Double to a Triple Democratic Legitimacy of the European Union' in Lina Papadopoulou, Ingolf Pernice and Joseph Weiler (eds), *Legitimacy Issues of the European Union in the Face of Crisis* (Oxford, Hart/Nomos, 2017)
Pavel CE, 'The International Rule of Law' (2020) 23 *Critical Review of International Social and Political Philosophy* 332
Perju V, 'On the (De-)Fragmentation of Statehood in Europe: Reflections on Ernst-Wolfgang Böckenförde's Work on European Integration' (2018) 19 *German Law Journal* 403
Pernice I, 'Costa v ENEL and Simmenthal: Primacy of European Law' in Miguel Poiares Maduro and Loïc Azoulai (eds), *The Past and Future of EU Law* (Oxford, Hart Publishing, 2010)
Perry S, 'Associative Obligations and the Obligation to Obey the Law' in Scott Hershovitz (ed), *Exploring Law's Empire: The Jurisprudence of Ronald Dworkin* (Oxford, OUP, 2008)
Pescatore P, *The Law of Integration* (New York, Springer, 1974)
Peters A, 'Dual Democracy' in Jan Klabbers, Anne Peters and Geir Ulfstein (eds), *The Constitutionalization of International Law* (Oxford, OUP, 2009)
——, 'Membership in the Global Constitutional Community' in Jan Klabbers, Anne Peters and Geir Ulfstein (eds), *The Constitutionalization of International Law* (Oxford, OUP, 2009)
Peters RS, 'Authority' in Richard E Flathman (ed), *Concepts in Social & Political Philosophy* (New York, Collier Macmillan, 1973)
Pettit P, *Republicanism: A Theory of Freedom and Government* (Oxford, Clarendon Press, 1997)
Plato, Euthyphro. Apology. Crito. Phaedo. (Christopher Emlyn-Jones and William Preddy trs, Cambridge (MA), Harvard University Press, 2017)
Psygkas A, *From the Democratic Deficit to a Democratic Surplus: Constructing Administrative Democracy in Europe* (Oxford, OUP, 2017)
Puetter U, *The European Council and the Council: New Intergovernmentalism and Institutional Change* (Oxford, OUP, 2014)
Rawls J, *A Theory of Justice* (Cambridge (MA), Harvard University Press, 1999)
Raz J, *The Authority of Law: Essays on Law and Morality*, 2nd edn (Oxford, OUP, 2009)
——, *The Morality of Freedom* (Oxford, Clarendon, 1986)
——, *Authority* (New York, New York University Press, 1990)
——, *Ethics in the Public Domain: Essays in the Morality of Law and Politics*, rev edn (Oxford, Clarendon, 1995)
——, 'Government by Consent', *Ethics in the Public Domain: Essays in the Morality of Law and Politics* (Oxford, Clarendon, 1995)
——, *Practical Reason and Norms* (Oxford, OUP, 1999)
——, 'The Problem of Authority: Revisiting the Service Conception' (2006) 90 *Minnesota Law Review* 1003
——, 'Why the State?' in Nicole Roughan and Andrew Halpin (eds), In Pursuit of Pluralist Jurisprudence (Cambridge, CUP, 2017)
——, 'The Future of State Sovereignty' in Wojciech Sadurski, Michael Sevel and Kevin Walton (eds), *Legitimacy: The State and Beyond* (Oxford, OUP, 2019)
——, 'The Democratic Deficit' (King's College London Dickson Poon School of Law, Legal Studies Research Paper Series) 2018–07
Ronzoni M, 'The European Union as a Demoicracy: Really a Third Way?' (2017) 16 *European Journal of Political Theory* 210
Rosanvallon P, *Democratic Legitimacy: Impartiality, Reflexivity, Proximity* (Princeton, Princeton University Press, 2011)
Rossi LS, 'The Principle of Equality Among Member States of the European Union' in Lucia Serena Rossi and Federico Casolari (eds), *The Principle of Equality in EU Law* (New York, Springer, 2017)
Roughan N, *Authorities: Conflicts, Cooperation, and Transnational Legal Theory* (Oxford, OUP, 2014)
——, 'From Authority to Authorities: Bridging the Social/Normative Divide' in Roger Cotterrell and Maksymilian Del Mar (eds), *Authority in Transnational Legal Theory* (Cheltenham, Elgar, 2016)

Šadl U, 'The Role of Effet Utile in Preserving the Continuity and Authority of European Union Law: Evidence from the Citation Web of the Pre-Accession Case Law of the Court of Justice of the EU' (2015) 8 *European Journal of Legal Studies* 18
Safjan M and Düsterhaus D, 'The EU Citizens' Right to Have Rights and the Courts' Duty to Protect It' in Koen Lenaerts and others (eds), *An Ever-Changing Union?: Perspectives on the Future of EU Law in Honour of Allan Rosas* (London, Bloomsbury Publishing, 2019)
Saint Augustine, *City of God: De Civitate Dei Contra Paganos* (Limovianet, 2013)
Sand I-J, 'Varieties of Authority in International Law' in Patrick Capps and Henrik Palmer Olsen (eds), *Legal Authority Beyond the State* (Cambridge, CUP, 2018)
Sangiovanni A, 'Solidarity in the European Union' (2013) 33 *OJLS* 213
Sartorius R, 'Political Authority and Political Obligation' (1981) 67 *Virginia Law Review* 3
Sassen S, *Territory, Authority, Rights: From Medieval to Global Assemblages* (Princeton, Princeton University Press, 2008)
Scanlon T, *What We Owe to Each Other* (Cambridge (MA), Harvard University Press, 1998)
Scharpf F, *Governing in Europe: Effective and Democratic?* (Oxford, OUP, 1999)
——, 'Legitimacy in the Multilevel European Polity' (2009) 1 *European Political Science Review* 173
Schmidt VA, *Europe's Crisis of Legitimacy: Governing by Rules and Ruling by Numbers in the Eurozone* (Oxford, OUP, 2020)
Schorkopf F, 'Europäischer Konstitutionalismus Oder Die Normative Behauptung Des "European Way of Life" Potenziale Der Neueren Werterechtsprechung Des EuGH' [2019] NJW 3418
Schütze R, *European Constitutional Law*, 2nd edn (Cambridge, CUP, 2016)
——, 'Models of Demoicracy: Some Preliminary Thoughts' (2022) 47 *European Law Review* 24
Searle J, *Speech Acts: An Essay in the Philosophy of Language* (Cambridge, CUP, 1969)
Sheehan J, 'The Problem of Sovereignty in European History' (2006) 111 *The American Historical Review* 1
Simmonds N, 'Why People Obey the Law by Tom R. Tyler' (1991) 50 *Cambridge Law Journal* 174
Simmons AJ, 'Justification and Legitimacy' (1999) 109 *Ethics* 739
——, *Boundaries of Authority* (Oxford, OUP, 2016)
Smith MBE, 'Is There a Prima Facie Obligation to Obey the Law?' (1973) 82 *Yale Law Journal* 950
Somek A, *Individualism: An Essay on the Authority of the European Union* (Oxford, OUP, 2008)
Song E, 'Strong and Weak Legitimacy' (2011) 27 *Southwest Philosophy Review* 167
Song S, 'The Boundary Problem in Democratic Theory: Why the Demos Should Be Bounded by the State' (2012) 4 *International Theory* 39
Sternberg C, 'Political Legitimacy between Democracy and Effectiveness: Trade-Offs, Interdependencies, and Discursive Constructions by the EU Institutions' (2015) 7 *European Political Science Review* 615
——, 'Public Opinion in the EU Institutions' Discourses on EU Legitimacy from the Beginnings of Integration to Today' (2016) 54 *Politique européenne* 24
Straumann B, *Crisis and Constitutionalism: Roman Political Thought from the Fall of the Republic to the Age of Revolution* (Oxford, OUP, 2016)
Tasioulas J, 'The Legitimacy of International Law' in John Tasioulas and Samantha Besson (eds), *The Philosophy of International Law* (Oxford, OUP, 2010)
Temple-Lang J, 'Chapter VII – The Draft Treaty Establishing the European Union and the Member States: Ireland' in Roland Bieber, Jean-Paul Jacqué and Joseph Weiler (eds), *An Ever Closer Union: A Critical Analysis of the Draft Treaty Establishing the European Union* (Office for Official Publications of the European Communities ; European University Institute, 1985)
Tieke E-M, *Das Subjekt Demokratischer Legitimation in Der Europäischen Union* (Baden-Baden, Tectum, 2016)
Tierney S, '"We the Peoples": Constituent Power and Constitutionalism in Plurinational States' in Martin Loughlin and Neil Walker (eds), *The Paradox of Constitutionalism* (Oxford, OUP, 2007)
Troper M, 'The Survival of Sovereignty' in Hent Kalmo and Quentin Skinner (eds), *Sovereignty in Fragments: The Past, Present and Future of a Contested Concept* (Cambridge, CUP, 2010)

——, 'The Modern State and the Concept of Authority' in Roger Cotterrell and Maksymilian Del Mar (eds), *Authority in Transnational Legal Theory* (Cheltenham, Elgar, 2016)
Tsakatika M, 'Claims to Legitimacy: The European Commission between Continuity and Change' (2005) 43 *Journal of Common Market Studies* 193
Tuori K, *European Constitutionalism* (Cambridge, CUP, 2017)
Urbinati N, 'Competing for Liberty: The Republican Critique of Democracy' (2012) 106 *American Political Science Review* 607
Valentini L, 'Justice, Disagreement and Democracy' (2013) 43 *British Journal of Political Science* 177
——, 'The Content-Independence of Political Obligation: What It Is and How to Test It' (2018) 24 *Legal Theory* 135
van den Brink M, 'Justice, Legitimacy and the Authority of Legislation within the European Union' (2019) 82 *MLR* 293
——, 'The European Union's Demoicratic Legislature' (2021) 19 *International Journal of Constitutional Law* 914
van Rossem JW, 'The Autonomy of EU Law: More Is Less?' in Ramses Wessel and Steven Blockmans (eds), *Between Autonomy and Dependence* (The Hague, TMC Asser Press, 2013)
Verellen T, 'European Sovereignty Now? A Reflection on What It Means to Speak of "European Sovereignty"' (2020) 5 *European Papers* 307
Voelsen D and Schettler LV, 'International Political Authority: On the Meaning and Scope of Justified Hierarchy in International Relations' (2019) 33 *International Relations* 540
Volk C, 'Why Global Constitutionalism Does Not Live up to Its Promises' (2012) 4 *Goettingen Journal of International Law* 551
——, 'The Problem of Sovereignty in Globalized Times' [2019] *Law, Culture and the Humanities* 1
Von Achenbach J, 'Verfassungswandel durch Selbstorganisation: Triloge im europäischen Gesetzgebungsverfahren' (2016) 55 *Der Staat* 1
Waitz G, 'Das Wesen Des Bundesstaats', *Grundzüge der Politik* (Nürnberg, Homann, 1862)
Waldron J, 'Theoretical Foundations of Liberalism' (1987) 37 *Philosophical Quarterly* 127
——, *Law and Disagreement* (Oxford, Clarendon Press, 1999)
——, 'The Rule of International Law' (2006) 30 *Harvard Journal of Law and Public Policy* 15
Walker N, 'Late Sovereignty in the European Union' in Neil Walker (ed), *Sovereignty in Transition* (Oxford, Hart Publishing, 2003)
——, 'Sovereignty Frames and Sovereignty Claims' in Richard Rawlings, Peter Leyland and Alison Young (eds), *Sovereignty and the Law* (Oxford, OUP, 2012)
——, 'The Place of European Law' in Graínne De Búrca and Joseph Weiler (eds), *The Worlds of European Constitutionalism* (Cambridge, CUP, 2012)
Wallis D, 'A View from Parliament' in Wolfgang Heusel and Jean-Philippe Rageade (eds), *The Authority of EU Law: Do We Still Believe In It?* (New York, Springer, 2019)
Waluchow W, 'Constitutionalism in the European Union: Pipe Dream or Possibility?' in Julie Dickson and Pavlos Eleftheriadis (eds), *Philosophical Foundations of European Union Law* (Oxford, OUP, 2012)
Weale A, 'Citizenship in Europe and the Logic of Two-Level Political Contracts' (2014) 15 *German Law Journal* 867
Weatherill S, *Cases and Materials on EU Law*, 12th edn (Oxford, OUP, 2016)
——, *Law and Values in the European Union* (Oxford, OUP, 2016)
Weber M, 'Politics as a Vocation', From Max Weber: Essays in Sociology (Abingdon, Routledge, 2009)
Weiler J, *The Constitution of Europe: 'Do the New Clothes Have an Emperor?' And Other Essays on European Integration* (Cambridge, CUP, 1999)
——, 'Federalism without Constitutionalism: Europe's Sonderweg' in Kalypso Nicolaïdis and Robert Howse (eds), *The Federal Vision: Legitimacy and Levels of Governance in the United States and the European Union* (Oxford, OUP, 2001)
——, 'A Constitution for Europe? Some Hard Choices' (2002) 40 *Journal of Common Market Studies* 563

——, 'Van Gend En Loos: The Individual as Subject and Object and the Dilemma of European Legitimacy' (2014) 25 *European Journal Of International Law* 83
——, 'Van Gend En Loos: The Individual as Subject and Object and the Dilemma of European Legitimacy' (2014) 12 *International Journal of Constitutional Law* 94
——, 'The Authority of European Law: Do We Still Believe in It?' in Wolfgang Heusel and Jean-Philippe Rageade (eds), *The Authority of EU Law: Do We Still Believe In It?* (New York, Springer, 2019)
——, 'The European Circumstance and the Politics of Meaning: Not on Bread Alone Doth Man Liveth (Deut. 8:3; Mat 4:4)' (2020) 21 *German Law Journal* 96
Weinzierl J, 'Der EuGH erklärt erstmalig nationales Recht für ungültig – Anmerkung zum Urteil des EuGH v. 26.2.2019, Rs. C-202/18 (Rimšēvičs)' (2019) 54 *Europarecht* 434
——, 'An Army of Peoples? A Demoicratic Perspective on a Future European Army' (2021) 6 *European Papers* 1049
——, 'Territoriality beyond the State: The EU's Territorial Claims and the Search for Their Legitimacy' (2021) 22 *German Law Journal* 650
Wellman C, 'Toward a Liberal Theory of Political Obligation' (2001) 111 *Ethics* 735
Werner WG and De Wilde JH, 'The Endurance of Sovereignty' (2001) 7 *European Journal of International Relations* 283
Wernicke S, 'Au Nom de Qui? The European Court of Justice between Member States, Civil Society and Union Citizens' (2007) 13 *European Law Journal* 380
Wilkinson M, 'The Specter of Authoritarian Liberalism: Reflections on the Constitutional Crisis of the European Union' (2013) 14 *German Law Journal* 527
——, 'Constitutional Pluralism: Chronicle of a Death Foretold?' (2017) 23 *European Law Journal* 213
Wille A, *The Normalization of the European Commission: Politics and Bureaucracy in the EU Executive* (Oxford, OUP, 2013)
Wolff RP, 'The Conflict between Authority and Autonomy' in Joseph Raz (ed), *Authority* (New York, New York University Press, 1990)

INDEX

www.ingramcontent.com/pod-product-compliance
Ingram Content Group UK Ltd.
Pitfield, Milton Keynes, MK11 3LW, UK
UKHW020819290926
15470UKWH00003B/1246

9 781509 965045